FILM
SCRIPTS

SEVEN SAMURAI

a film by

Akira Kurosawa

English translation and introduction
by Donald Richie

Lorrimer Publishing

Published by Lorrimer Publishing Incorporated
First Printing 1970
Revised edition 1984
Publisher and Editor: Andrew Sinclair

ISBN paper 0 85647 086 4

Distributed exclusively in the United States of America, its territories,
possessions, protectorates, mandated territories, the Philippines and the
Dominion of Canada by Frederick Ungar Publishing Company Inc.,
36 Cooper Square, New York, N.Y. 10003

Distributed exclusively in the United Kingdom and Commonwealth by
Lorrimer (Sales) Limited
Inquiries should be addressed to Lorrimer Publishing Limited, 16 Tite
Street, London SW3 4HZ.

Cover design: Fred Price

British Library Cataloguing in Publication Data

Kurosawa, Akira
    Seven samurai.
    I. Title   II. Shichinin no samurai. *English*
    791.43'72   PN1997

    ISBN 0-85647-086-4

CONTENTS

A NOTE ON THIS EDITION

As Donald Richie points out in his introduction, the original 200-minute version of *Seven Samurai* was considerably cut before its general release. There are no prints or reliable script of this original version in existence and so the present publication is based on the Toho script of the 160-minute version, the studio continuity, and movieola viewings of the Japanese, American and British prints of the film. Donald Richie translated and compiled the principal material and checked it with the Japanese and American prints. Additional material was added by Nicola Hayden after viewings of a print obtained from the British distributor, in order to make it as accurate a rendering as possible of the film which the English or American spectator will see on the screen. The version released in the United States was further cut and lacks the following shots: 68-79; 187-193; 308-340; 513-526; 579-591; 603-612; 677-679; 1000-1001; 1006-1017. These omissions considerably weaken the film. We do not know, for example, why Shino had her hair cut, and indeed have no way of knowing, at first, that she is not a boy. We do not realise that Kikuchiyo was emulating Kyuzo in going out and getting a gun, and consequently the delicate parallels in feeling among Katsushiro, Kyuzo and Kikuchiyo are lost.

Acknowledgements and thanks are due to Donald Richie, Kurosawa Productions, Toho Company Ltd. and UniJapan Film for providing stills; also to Connoisseur Films for providing a print of the film. Donald Richie's introduction has been extracted from his book *The Films of Akira Kurosawa*, published by the University of California Press, 1965.

Erratum : The name of the leading samurai, which is spelt Kanbei in the main body of the script, should read Kambei throughout, as elsewhere in the book.

INTRODUCTION

Donald Richie

Kurosawa had long wanted to make a real *jidai-geki,* a real period-film. Though, at this time, fully half of all Japanese films made were *jidai-geki,* the ' real ' ones were very rare. Most of them were (then as now) *chambara,* simple sword-fight films. Japanese critics are fond of comparing the *chambara* with the American Western (the *seibu-geki*) and the comparison is appropriate. But, just as there are meaningful Westerns (*The Covered Wagon, Cimarron,* and *Stagecoach*), so there are meaningful *jidai-geki.* One can, in fact, trace the development of the ' real ' Japanese period-films from the early pictures of Daisuke Ito and Mansaku Itami, through Sadao Yamanaka and Kenji Mizoguchi, to Masaki Kobayashi, and Kurosawa himself. These latter are ' real ' because they do not stop at simple historical reconstruction, inhabited by stock figures (which is true of costume-pictures all over the world), but insist upon the validity of the past, and the continuing meaning of the historical. That the rule should be otherwise in Japan (so famous for its being a museum in which nothing is thrown away, almost notorious for its regard for the past, practically infamous for its historical sense) is surprising, but otherwise it is. The ordinary *jidai-geki* has no more vital connection to the past than does any Steve Reeves epic.

Kurosawa, then, wanted to present the past as meaningful, but do it within the framework of the *jidai-geki* (something he was to do again in *The Hidden Fortress,* in *Yojimbo,* and particularly in *Sanjuro*); at the same time, he says, he wanted to make a picture that was also completely entertaining. (He did not consider *Rashomon* either a *jidai-geki* or entertaining.) This is what he meant when he said : ' Japanese films all tend to be *assari shite iru* [light, plain, simple but wholesome], just like *ochazuke* [green tea over rice, a dish the *assari* connotations of which are so celebrated that Ozu — " the most Japanese of all Japanese directors " — used it as a film title once] but I think we ought to have both richer foods and

5

richer films. And so I thought I would make a film which was entertaining enough to eat, as it were.'

Entertaining it certainly is: convincing, thrilling, meaningful, compelling. It remains (along with *Ikiru*) the director's own favourite. At the same time it is completely serious. Most film-makers believe that to be entertaining you also have to be amusing, just as most musicians believe that to play fast you must also play loud. Kurosawa knows otherwise. He also knows that nothing compels (particularly in a film) more than immaculate realism, and that this is even more true in a historical film where the reality has long vanished, and we are used to seeing only the slipshod reconstructions and interpretations of others — something the director particularly holds against the ordinary period-film. In this regard Kurosawa's remarks on Mizoguchi are interesting.

' His greatness was that he never gave up trying to heighten the reality of each scene. He never made compromises. He never said that something or other " would do." Instead, he pulled — or pushed — everyone along with him until they had created the feeling which matched that of his own inner image. An ordinary director is quite incapable of this. And in this lay his true spirit as a director — for he had the temperament of a true creator. He pushed and bullied and he was often criticised for this but he held out, and he created masterpieces. This attitude towards creation is not at all easy, but a director like him is especially necessary in Japan where this kind of pushing is so resisted. . . . Of all Japanese directors I have the greatest admiration for him but, at the same time, I can't say that everything he did was equally good. If he portrays an old merchant you get marvelously successful scenes, like those in *A Tale from Chikamatsu,* but he was no good at samurai. In *Ugetsu,* when you get to the war scenes it just isn't war. A long time ago he did *Chushingura* and he left out the last scene [the great vendetta with much fighting and swordplay] which isn't surprising at all. Our historical worlds are actually different. His central figures are women and the world he describes is largely either that of women or of merchants. That is not my world. I think I am best at delineating *bushi* [warriors, samurai]. . . . But, in the death of Mizoguchi, Japanese film lost its truest creator.'

Certainly the realism of the Mizoguchi historical film (a realism shared with Yamanaka and Itami) is enormously compelling but of equal importance is Mizoguchi's almost continual insistence that history be regarded as contemporary in that its problems were no less unique, no less personal, than are ours, and further — given the perspective of history — we are more likely to appreciate something of ourselves when it is given us out of our own historical context.

This, to be sure, *does* happen in the ordinary *jidai-geki,* just as it happens in the Kabuki, but the perspective we are offered is all too often that of the single, set view, the ordinary ' historical outlook.' It is acknowledged that the past gives perspective; at the same time it is decided for us just what that perspective is, and it is invariable: the Kabuki, like the ordinary *chambara,* has decided *for* us. All past Japanese problems were about the conflict between love and duty. A lord loves a lady but he, alas, is a lord with a lord's responsibilities, so he gives her up; father loves his son but must also take care of his lord's son, enemy comes demanding the head of the latter youngster, and — after what visible agonies only the Kabuki-goer can imagine — the man lets his own boy be decapitated; and so on.

But, as E. M. Forster, in another context, has wisely remarked: ' The contest lay not between love and duty. Perhaps there never is such a contest. It lay between the real and the pretended.' Indeed, there never is such a contest, and one of Kurosawa's concerns, both as a thinker and as a film-maker is with myriad ways in which he indicates just this. The way of the Kabuki, the way of *chambara* is much too facile for him. At the same time the fact that it exists (and is believed in, even now, by a great number of Japanese), is a continual spur, a continuous thorn in the side, a constant pain in the neck. He resents the pretended — that is, the illusion. And he delights in revealing it as illusion. Reality is much more difficult to deal with, of course, and consequently a major theme in any of his films is just this search for reality. That it often results in failure tells much about us and, perhaps, something about the nature of reality itself.

The important thing, therefore, is that his people concern themselves with this search for meaning and do not allow themselves to be too misled by illusion. Kurosawa knows perfectly well that illusion is necessary and one of his pictures (*The Lower Depths*) is about just that. At the same time, he would invite us — in the

7

very face of apparently certain defeat — to pursue the real in so far as we are able, to face life, and to settle for nothing less.

This is, of course, what *Ikiru* is about, and the interest continues throughout all of his films until now. In *Seven Samurai,* we have a particularly impressive example, however, because, since it is a historical film, we can see more clearly, we can see freshly. We have become so used to our own epoch that we don't even see it any more. We are blind to it. The period of civil wars, the presumably exotic and distant sixteenth-century, however — that is another matter. Things become clear and in a way the problem becomes simpler. Since it becomes simpler, Kurosawa may go further in his explorations than he has done before. He can, as it were, go beyond reality and try to find what is there.

Needless perhaps to add, he has said none of the above nor has he ever himself given me any reason for believing that he would ever say it. He is much less dogmatic than I am here making him seem. Rather, as Kajiro Yamamoto had noticed years before, he would be ' completely engrossed in separating what is real from what is false,' at the same time, never once forgetting that he was making an entertaining film.

The Story

A small village is yearly invaded by bandits and the farmers lose their crops and sometimes their lives. This year the elders decide to do something about it. They have heard of a village which once hired masterless samurai and was saved. They decide to do the same and send some of their number to search for willing samurai. Since there is no pay, merely food, a place to sleep, and the fun of fighting, the farmers are fortunate that they first meet Kambei (Takashi Shimura), a strong and dedicated man who decides to make their cause his own. A young *ronin,* Katsushiro (Ko Kimura) joins him, then he accidentally meets an old friend, Shichiroji (Daisuke Kato). He himself chooses Gorobei (Yoshio Inaba) who in turn chooses Heihachi (Minoru Chiaki). A master swordsman, Kyuzo (Seiji Miyaguchi) joins, and so, eventually, does Kikuchiyo (Toshiro Mifune), a farmer's son himself, who has been following them around for some time, attracted — as all of them are — by Kambei.

Once in the village they prepare for war. Not waiting for the first attack, they storm the bandits' fort, burn it and kill a number of the bandits — though Heihachi is also killed. The bandits attack the village and they repulse them, though Gorobei is killed. Then they hit upon the plan of allowing a few in and spearing them to death. In the final battle both Kyuzo and Kikuchiyo are killed — but the bandits are all dead.

It is spring, once more the rice-planting season has come. Of the original seven samurai, only three are left and they soon will go their separate ways.

As the précis indicates, the picture is about three groups of people: the farmers, the bandits, and the samurai. There are over a hundred farmers, forty bandits and just seven samurai. Kurosawa keeps these three units apart in various ways. The first sequence shows the bandits, and then we do not see any more of them until an hour and ten minutes (in the ' standard ' export version of the film) has elapsed. The second sequence shows the village as a group (gathered together in a closed circle), and it is not until the final battle that they mingle with samurai and bandits. The third sequence is about the selecting of the samurai and they, too, form a unit which is not broken into until the battle. The music also insists upon differentiation. The credit music is low drums and this becomes associated with the bandits; the farmers' music is folk-music, flute and percussion; the samurai music is a low humming (male chorus), the main ' theme ' of the picture, and fanfare-like horn calls. These three kinds of music may be heard in conjunction but are never heard together.

Those who want to see *Seven Samurai* as social epic in the Soviet manner (the ' Soviet manner ' of the 1930's) have excellent reason for doing so. The picture *is* about groups of people and their social actions. But to see it only as a Russian-style social epic is both to ignore the ending (something no Russian in the 1930's would have filmed) and to neglect the fact that the film is not only about people — it is also, and mainly, about persons.

It is about the seven samurai as individuals (though Kurosawa does not so individualise the bandits, and there are only a few of the farmers who are given personal profilès) and, as an adventure-story, is entirely about *their* exploits and how *each* reacts to this great adventure. For these are no ordinary samurai, and no ordinary men.

We first see Takashi Shimura having his head shaved. This usually means either punishment (for a samurai to lose his top-knot means that he is declassé and no longer a samurai) or that he is going to leave the world (to become a priest). As the watching Mifune discovers, however, it is neither. In what seems to be return for two balls of rice, he will save the child of a farmer, kidnapped and held prisoner by a madman. Shimura is given a priest's robe and the rice balls. He approaches the house where the madman is holding the child, impersonates a priest, catches the kidnapper off guard, kills him and saves the child. The parents are happy, the local farmers are full of congratulations. Then they all go away, back to their work.

The farmers searching for samurai to help them, decide that this is one they want. But he is also being followed by young Kimura, who begs to become his disciple, and by Mifune who can make nothing whatever of such apparently unmotivated goodness. Finally one of the farmers kneels in front of him and pleads. Shimura sees that one or two samurai would be useless — seven would be needed. . . . The farmers are so disappointed that they begin to cry. A laborer makes fun of them. . . .

This decides Shimura because he is the kind of man who makes decisions in this way. In the same way he allowed himself to be shaved and to save the child, for no reward at all. It is as though by personal example he will set the world right, and this is what so captivates Kimura and intrigues Mifune.

Just as Shimura knows himself, so he also knows other men. He devises a test for his future fellow-samurai. Kimura is to hide behind the door and bring down a stick on the head of the applicant. If the man senses something amiss and manages not to get hit, he is good enough for the task. He sees Inaba in the street and says to try him. This samurai does not even enter the door, but can see something is wrong even from the outside. He joins them. . . .

Kato, Shimura's old friend, is found by accident. Kimura stands by watching, and the leader asks: ' Are you tired of fighting? '

Kato is not and joins them. Eventually, all seven are gathered and go to the village. . . .

Shimura's intentions are social — that is, he will save the village. At the same time, as leader, he never makes the mistake to which leaders are prone. He continues to view men as individuals and to make allowances for their individuality. In a wry way he even makes allowances for whatever individuality the bandits possess. . . .

At the end of the film when the villagers have forgotten the samurai who saved them, have turned their attention to the rice-planting, Shimura (of the three surviving) is the only one not hurt or disappointed. After the battle he has said to his old friend Kato, said with wonder and awe : ' Again, we've survived.' At the end of the film he turns to his friend and says, philosophically : ' And again we've lost.'

Few things surprise Shimura. He is like the pilgrim-priest in *The Lower Depths* because he knows better than to hope. All a man can do, he seems to say, is to do his best. If he does his best for himself that is one thing; but it is better to do your best for others: even if the task is dangerous and without reward; even if (as here) it is absurd. Still, it is better to have done it. The farmers are saved (whatever that means); the village still stands (whatever that means); and these three are alive (whatever that means). Something has been accomplished, and if it is meaningless then that is small concern of ours.

This is heroism, and of a kind that particularly appeals to Kurosawa. It is stoic, hopeless in the strongest possible sense, and generous. It is for this reason that Shimura has become a leader, and it is why his character so interests his men that they are willing to die for him. He knows that men are individuals; he knows that all social actions are collective; he recognises the gulf that exists between these two — and he still chooses to act.

The other samurai share something of this. Obviously, or they would not have been attracted to the pointless adventure. Inaba most closely resembles Shimura and it is he who becomes second-in-command; and it is he who finds Chiaki. Finds him chopping wood, an occupation unheard of for a samurai. . . .

The swordsman Miyaguchi, is a complete professional; we know this because we have seen him fight. He says very little, is closed, and — like his sword itself — only uses himself when he needs to. We know that he is lethal, though peaceful, and there is one beautiful scene of him alone in the forest where he carefully picks a single flower and looks at it. He incorporates the true spirit of *bushi* — somehing which none of the others do. He is killed, ironically, by a bullet.

11

The youngest samurai, Kimura, has an enormous veneration for the swordsman, even more than for Shimura. When the latter comes back with the gun, strolls into camp, and prepares for sleep, Kimura approaches him, eyes shining, and says: 'You are a wonderful person,' — at which, for the only time in the picture, the swordsman smiles.

He, too, is attracted by the boy and the only time he displays any curiosity is when the boy meets and gives his rice to a girl. Kimura had originally met her in the forest while he lagged behind picking flowers. Since she has had her long hair cut short by her father, he takes her for a boy — which was the father's intention, since he mistrusted the samurai. She is also picking flowers and they accidentally meet. . . . The others treat Kimura as the child they think he is, though there are some indications that he is growing up. . . .

Later, he makes love for the first time, and the very next day, kills his first man. He himself has become a man. Yet, when the swordsman is suddenly killed by a stray shot, he kneels into the mud and weeps as though his heart is breaking. Shimura looks at him. The boy remembers to ask if there are any more bandits. No, there are no more. Then he flings himself to the ground, sobbing, while Shimura looks. The child is not yet quite a man.

It is, indirectly, through the swordsman and the boy that Mifune dies. Like all the rest of the samurai he wants the regard of Shimura, and he also (like the swordsman) enjoys the adulation of the youth. When the latter begins telling him how wonderful the swordsman is, Mifune is sarcastic, but it is just after that that he goes out and gets the gun. And when he sees the boy weeping, it is he who goes after the bandit chief, and kills him — though he himself is killed in the attempt.

And bravery is not at all natural to him. To be sure, it is to no one, it must be acquired, but Mifune has acquired little enough of it. A buffoon, a standard joke to the rest, it is nonetheless he who kills the final and most important bandit — as though, by this action, he will vindicate himself in the eyes of both the leader and the boy.

Unlike the others, he is no warrior. Indeed, if things had happened differently he might just as well have been one of the bandits. But his parents were killed by bandits, and he was orphaned. This is shown in a single scene where, during the burning of the mill, the dying mother gives her living child to him. He holds it in his arms, astonished, up to his thighs in the stream, the burning mill behind him, then suddenly sits down in the water and bursts into tears. . . .

Mifune is also a farmer's son, and though he has come a long way from the soil he has never forgotten the enmity traditional not only between farmer and bandit, but also farmer and samurai. At one point he hopes to please his comrades by bringing them armour which he has found hidden away in the village. The others are solemn because they know that the armour was stolen from samurai whom perhaps the villagers themselves murdered. . . .

He is a farmer's son but he dies as a samurai. And it is perhaps he whom the others will miss the most, precisely because he was so weak, so very human. Shimura appears almost superhuman, but Mifune is completely human. And it is he who therefore sees the dilemma that even Shimura has missed. Aren't, then, samurai and bandits to be equated? — aren't the actions of each equally absurd? — and don't they really do much the same things?

It is a startling question. One which Kurosawa has asked in *Stray Dog* and will ask again in *High and Low*. Good and bad might be identical. The farmers would find it so. They are almost as distrustful of the samurai as they are of the bandits. For them it is plainly a choice between evils. We are thus prepared for the final scene.

The opening sequence with Shimura has shown a gratuitous action, one for which he expects neither reward nor acclaim. The laborer, and now Mifune, have indicated that one need not expect to find generosity, gratitude, or other such civilised luxuries among the peasants. And at the end, therefore, when the three remaining samurai are ignored by the farmers who are, obviously, only waiting for them to leave (and in a scene carefully prepared since it was just these three — Shimura, Kato and Kimura — who were present when the leader asks Kato : ' Tired of fighting? '), Shimura may say : ' We've lost again '. *Kato looks surprised . . .* Shimura : ' No, the farmers are the winners. . . . Not us '.

What did Shimura hope to win? He knew the entire venture was quixotic; he knew it would be without reward; he knew that its only profit was in the ' fun of it.' To be disappointed in the

13

farmers was to have hoped, and this is something which, until now, he has not allowed himself. Yet he had hoped to win, and further had hoped that this winning would somehow change something. He has become human enough to confuse ends and means and forget that everything is means and that there is no end. The true wisdom (cold, comfortless) would have been to enjoy the ' fun ' while he had it, to (put in a way which Kurosawa would never be guilty of saying) realise that *being* is the sole end, and that *becoming* turns into snare and delusion if looked for, hoped for.

This does not mean, of course, that *becoming* is impossible. Indeed, it is impossible *not* to *become*. Nor does this mean that wishes and will have no power — indeed, they have considerable power, as *Ikiru* has indicated. But what disappoints is when one allows the illusion (the unfulfilled wish) to supersede reality (ungrateful peasants, dead comrades).

Kurosawa made *Seven Samurai* because, in part, he deeply resented the facility of the ordinary *chambara* with its specious conflict between inclination and duty. Yet — at the end of this film — he shows us that, beyond illusion (duty), inclination becomes truly lonely, truly frightening. What will they do now, now that the work at hand is finished, proved of no particular value, now that they see themselves perfectly equated with the very enemy against whom they fought? Their only choice is to go on and have another unprofitable adventure and, perhaps, to remember this time that it is the adventure itself that counts, not its hoped-for consequences.

Seven Samurai is an epic all right — it is an epic of the human spirit because very few films indeed have dared to go this far, to show this much, to indicate the astonishing and frightening scope of the struggle, and to dare suggest personal bravery, gratuitous action, and choice in the very face of the chaos that threatens to overwhelm.

Treatment

Like the Russians (Eisenstein, Dovshenko) to whose epics *Seven Samurai* has often been compared, Kurosawa — here perhaps more than in any other single film — insisted that the motion-picture be composed entirely of *motion*. The film opens with fast pans of the bandits riding over hills, and ends with the chaos of the battle itself, motion so swift we can almost not see it at all. There is no shot that does not have motion, either in the object photographed, or in the movement of the camera itself. The motion may be small (the quivering nostrils in the long-held image of the village elder) or it may be great (the huge, sweeping frescoes of the charges) but it is always there.

At the same time, another kind of motion is present. Kurosawa, always an economical film-maker, uses a number of short-cuts which hasten the pace of the story itself. . . .

Sometimes scenes are telescoped and put into one. There is a beautiful example of this during the funeral of Chiaki. All are gathered around the mound and Mifune dashes back to get their banner (which Chiaki had made) and climbs a roof to put it on the ridge-pole — a gesture of defiance. He suddenly looks at the hills and there, as though in answer (a marvelous image), come wave after wave of bandits, riding down on the village, heralding the first of the major battles. As Mifune looks, there is a wide pan which moves from village to hills. At the same time the sounds of weeping turn to cries of alarm from the villagers, to cries of exultation from the samurai — who now want to fight. Within this single scene not only has action been carried forward but — as though the pan had caused it which, in a way it did — the entire mood has been changed, in just two seconds, from abject sorrow to the most fierce joy.

Another means of telescoping is through the interlinking of very short (usually funny) scenes, connected with wipes, that Kurosawa has used from *They Who Step on the Tiger's Tail* onward. It is seen at its funniest both here and in *Sanjuro*. The samurai are being taken to the village, and their journey is seen in a mosaic of tiny scenes the point of which is that they are being followed by Mifune who, taciturn, apparently stupid, wants to join them, and at the same time cannot bring himself to. The entire sequence (covering a seemingly enormous journey) takes just three minutes and at the end Mifune, looking down at the village, utters his ironic and prophetic remark which (in retrospect at any rate) makes him appear much more human, much less of the clown: ' Whew — what a dung pile. I'd certainly hate to die in a place like that.'

All of these short-cuts and telescopings, all of this motion on the screen, means that the picture moves very fast indeed. It is so swift that Kurosawa has availed himself of at least several devices to insure that he does not lose his audience. The first of these is the banner and, at the same time, a list which Shimura draws up in which the number of circles indicates the number of bandits. Like the bullets in *Stray Dog*; like the money in *One Wonderful Sunday*, the viewer keeps score, as it were, by seeing how many down, how many to go. Each scratched circle means one less bandit. . . .

Finally, in the last reel, we are shown *how* a battle occurs. It resembles what we have been prepared for, but at the same time it is entirely different. Shimura speaking in measured tones and pointing to his map is one thing; this inferno of men and horses, rain and mud, is quite another thing. Reality is very different from illusion.

Even on a technical level, quite removed from the context which gives it its final meaning, this last reel is one of the greatest of cinematic accomplishments. It is chaotic but never chaos; disordered but orderly in its disorder. The rain pours down; bandits dash in; horses neigh and rear; Shimura poses, bow ready; Mifune slashes; an arrow thuds home and we glimpse it only for the fraction of a second necessary; riderless horses rear in terror; a samurai slips; Mifune grabs another sword. All of these images and literally hundreds more are crowded into a final reel which galvanises the screen. (Having already given us plenty of excitement in the earlier battles, here Kurosawa does himself one better and uses telephoto lenses — a rarity in 1954 — to bring the action directly into the laps of the audience. The first of these telescopic shots is a horse-fall which seems to occur directly where the camera is and rarely fails to evoke a gasp from the audience.)

At the same time, in the final reel, we again see that what keeps this film (and all of Kurosawa's films) so completely vital is, after all, the cutting, and consequently the tempo. We have had indication of this before in the film. In the hunting-for-the-samurai section, a set piece like the journey-to-the-village which follows, Kurosawa shows us the four farmers in two pairs, each searching through the same town. In between each image of a pair of farmers looking from right to left, or left to right, their eyes following the samurai, sweeping pans of the samurai themselves are intercut. Thus the sweeping pans are answered by sweeping movements of the eyes of the peasants. The delight of this sequence (the delight of

16

the hunt, of the unknown, accompanied on the sound track by music unmistakably of that intent), lies in the very brevity of each shot. Each is no longer than two seconds. Thus, even in a simple sequence such as this, expectation and excitement are generated through the cutting.

Mifune's fine scene with the armour is another example of Kurosawa's editing. It plays so very well and is so powerful that it is only on re-seeing that one notices, first, that Mifune acts directly into the camera (which is one of the reasons for the power — as in the final close-up in *The Lower Depths*) and second, that each shot of Mifune is a bit shorter than the one which went before. The tempo is accelerated by the cutting, and these long scenes become shorter. The next to last (Shimura) and last (Mifune) are the conventional one-two shots, each lasting for a conventional amount of time. . . .

Besides technique, however, there is something else about this film (and about most of Kurosawa's pictures) that defies analysis because there are no words to describe the effect. What I mean might be called the irrational rightness of an apparently gratuitous image in its proper place, and the image that I always think of is that wonderful and mysterious scene in *Zéro de conduite* where it is apparently Sunday. Papa is reading the paper, and the boy's little sister moves the fishbowl (hanging on a chain from its stand) so that when the brother removes his blindfold he can see the sun touching it. The scene moves me to tears and I have no idea why. It was not economical of Vigo to have included it, it ' means ' nothing — and it is beautiful beyond words.

Part of the beauty of such scenes (actually rather common in all sorts of films, good, bad, and indifferent) is just that they are ' thrown away ' as it were, that they have no place, that they do not ostensibly contribute, that they even constitute what has been called bad film-making. It is not the beauty of these unexpected images, however, that captivates (plenty of films, particularly Japanese films, are filled with irrelevant and beautiful scenes which completely fail to move) but their mystery. They *must* remain unexplained. It has been said that after a film is over all that remains are a few scattered images, and if they remain then the film was memorable. That is true so far as it goes but one must add that if the images remain, it means only that the images were

17

for some reason or other memorable. Further, if one remembers carefully one finds that it is only the uneconomical, mysterious images which remain. . . .

What one remembers best from this superbly economical film then are those scenes which seem most uneconomical — that is, those which apparently add nothing to it. There is a short cut during the burning of the bandit's fort where we watch a woman awake, see the fire, and yet refuse to warn the others. (She is the wife of one of the farmers, raped and carried away by the bandits.) The scene is beautiful enough, this hopeless farm woman, clothed in stolen silk, half obscured by the wisps of smoke — but Kurosawa renders it utterly mysterious (and completely right) by inserting beneath it the sound of the Noh flute with unearthly effect — a trick he later repeated, less gratuitously, in *The Throne of Blood* and *The Hidden Fortress*. Again, there is the short scene where a prisoner has been caught, and the oldest woman in the village — she who has lost all of her sons — is called to come and murder him. She marches slowly forward, a hoe in her hand, terribly old, terribly bent, a crone. And though we sympathise, the image is one of horror — it is death itself because we have seen, and will see, men killed and think little of it, but here is death itself with a hoe, mysterious, unwilled. Or, those several shots of the avenue of cryptomerias, and two bonfires, one far and one near. This is where the bandits will come but we do not yet know this. Instead, the trees, the fires, the night — all are mysterious, memorable. Or, that magnificent image which we see after Mifune has rescued the baby and burst into tears. The mill is burning and Mifune is sitting in the stream, looking at the child and crying. The next scene is a simple shot of the water-wheel turning, as it always has. But the wheel is on fire. Or, that curiously long close-up of the dead Mifune. He has stolen some armour but his bottom is unprotected. Now he lies on a narrow bridge, on his face, and the rain is washing away the dirt from his buttocks. He lies there like a child — all men with bare bottoms look like children — yet he is dead, and faintly ridiculous in death, and yet he was our friend for we have come to love him. All of this we must think as we sit through the seconds of this simple, unnecessary, and unforgettable scene.

Or, my favourite among all of these magical images, that following Shimura's saying that the bandits are all dead, and Kimura's sinking, weeping, into the mud. The screen slowly darkens. It is as though the end has come, and one hopes it has not, because this, somehow, is not enough and because, even more strongly, we do not want to leave these men yet. The screen gets darker and darker. They are lost in the gloom. We sit in the darkness and then we hear music. It is the music of the farmers, and the screen lightens to reveal one of the most delightful and heart-breaking of sequences: the rice-planting.

It is seen as dance, which indeed rice-planting is in Japan. A small orchestra (flute, drums, bells, singer) accompanies the girls as they plunge the new shoots into the wet earth, all in unison. Since this is the way rice is actually planted, we accept it as real. At the same time, after the uproar, pain, horror, grief of the final battle, we had not expected a divertissement. Strictly speaking, the entire rice-planting sequence is unnecessary to the film; not speaking strictly at all, it is vital — perhaps because it relaxes, with its very beauty and its anticlimax. Nerves have been played upon and wrought up to an extent completely unusual in an action-picture, and suddenly — childlike beauty. When tears flow in *Seven Samurai,* they flow here.

Then comes the great final scene with its reminiscence of the opening scene, followed by Shimura's profoundly ironic remark, and the picture ends on the splendid image of the high grave-hill with four naked swords stuck into the top, and three mere men standing below. And, under this, the child-like music of the peasants fades and is replaced by the music associated with the samurai.

Kurosawa has given us beauty in the midst of knowledge, a kind of reassurance while questioning all reassurances. At the same time that he questions deeds, hopes, thoughts, he has purposely played upon our emotions and we, too, have become open and child-like. More, in this profoundly subtle and mysterious final sequence (samurai and peasants; fighting and rice-planting; silence and music; darkness and light), he has indicated hope. We are all, after all, human; we all feel the same — we are all peasants at heart.

Production

The production difficulties of *Seven Samurai* have become legend. Long before it was released it had become very widely discussed.

It had taken well over a year to make and already it had become the most expensive film which Toho had ever undertaken. By the time it was finished, it had become the most expensive picture ever made in Japan. The company, afraid, tried to get Kurosawa to come back to Tokyo (most of the picture was made on location which was one of the things which made it so expensive, and he retaliated by threatening to quit. He afterwards spoke of the ' intense labour ' of making a really entertaining film. ' Something always comes up. We didn't have enough horses; it rained all the time. It was just the kind of picture that is impossible to make in this country.'

It was perhaps this film which gave Kurosawa his nickname of *tenno* or ' emperor ' because of his alleged dictatorial mannerisms. It is telling, however, that no one of his staff has ever used the word and that, on the contrary, it is the Japanese press which is so fond of it that it still uses it. However, Kurosawa could indeed be very dictatorial to his company — because this was just the kind of pushing which he so admired in Mizoguchi. At the same time, he deeply resented the bad press that the film was getting before it was even finished. In answer to the charge of wasting time he snapped back : ' And why not. I was only location hunting. The location must be perfect and a director may spend months hunting for just the right one. Why not —-it doesn't cost money.' When told he was spending too much he launched an attack himself. ' You try to give a film a little pictorial scope and the journalists jump on you for spending too much money. That is what I really hate about them — they are only an extended form of advertising. They talk big and make pictures sound important to make themselves seem more important. The more they try the greater they lie. For instance, one of my aims — as it is with every director — is to stay inside the budget. But something always happens and I go over it. How the journalists pounce on me and say I am squandering precious resources. Yet, right now, Olivier and I are both making *Macbeth* [this was in 1957; the reference was to *The Throne of Blood;* Olivier's film was merely projected, never completed] and I bet I could finance my whole film just for the cost of one of his larger scenes. Japanese films are made too cheaply.'

Once released, the film had great box office success but evoked little critical enthusiasm even though Kurosawa had prepared a manifesto which said, in part, '*jidai-geki* faces a dead-end, there are no talented *jidai-geki* producers,' and something must be done about it — the implication being that he had. The critics, while realising that the film was indeed in the line of Yamanaka and Mizoguchi, almost wilfully misunderstood. One of them complained that it was not very democratic of him to condemn the poor farmers; another, that he was saying the farmers were not worth saving. . . . Another critic wondered about the wisdom of such emphasis on what was, in effect, civil war in these present troubled times. (A hint which Kurosawa took full advantage of : *The Throne of Blood, The Hidden Fortress, Yojimbo, Sanjuro* are directly — and *Record of a Living Being* and *The Bad Sleep Well* indirectly — about civil war.) There were, to be sure, some perceptive judgements but it is only now, over a decade later, that the critics speak in measured terms of ' this epoch-making masterpiece.'

Still, as Kurosawa consoled himself ' it was released uncut — in Japan at any rate. [The original version was two hundred minutes in length and was shown, in 1954, only in the key major cities. A shortened version played second and third runs. A second shortened version was made for export and this one-hundred-sixty minute film is the one most people have seen. A third was made for the Venice festival. The American version (called *The Magnificent Seven* until John Sturgis' remake caused all prints to be recalled — in America at any rate) was an RKO-butchered edition of this second version. The German version is also cut from the second Japanese version but less damage has been done. There are no prints of the original in Japan and even negatives of the cut-outs have disappeared.] But we had to shorten it for Venice. Naturally no one understood it. They all complained about the first half's being confused. It certainly was. The second half the Venice people liked well enough because that only had a few minor cuts which, as a matter of fact, helped it.'

Nevertheless, *Seven Samurai* has, outside Japan in 1954, never really been seen. This is one of the major cinematic tragedies — just as lamentable as those better-known ones of *Greed, The Wedding March, The Magnificent Ambersons,* and *Ivan the Terrible.* It is not only Kurosawa's most vital picture, it is also perhaps the best Japanese film ever made.

21

CREDITS:

Script by	Shinobu Hashimoto, Hideo Oguni, and Akira Kurosawa
Directed by	Akira Kurosawa
Produced by	Shojiro Motoki
Production company	A Toho production, 1954
Music composed by	Fumio Hayasaka
Director of photography	Asakazu Nakai
Lighting cameraman	Shigeru Mori
Art direction by	So Matsuyama
Art consultants	Seison Maeda and Kohei Ezaki
Fencing direction by	Yoshio Sugino
Archery direction by	Ienori Kaneko and Shigeru Endo
Assistant director	Hiromichi Horikawa
Sound recordist	Fumio Yanoguchi
Process	Black and white
Length and running time of original version	5,480 metres; 200 minutes
Length and running time of cut version	4,401 metres; 160 minutes
Original negative of cut version in existence; no prints of uncut version in existence; cut version prints in general circulation	
Original version released	April 26th, 1954
Cut version released	May/June, 1954
Distributed in Great Britain by	Connoisseur Films Ltd
Distributed in the United States of America by	Audio Film Center

CAST:

The samurai

Kambei, leader of the samurai	Takashi Shimura
Kikuchiyo	Toshiro Mifune
Gorobei	Yoshio Inaba

Kyuzo	Seiji Miyaguchi
Heihachi	Minoru Chiaki
Shichiroji	Daisuke Kato
Katsushiro	Ko Kimura

The farmers

Gisaku, the village patriarch	Kuninori Kodo
Manzo	Kamatari Fujiwara
Rikichi	Yoshio Tsuchiya
Yohei	Bokuzen Hidari
Mosuke	Yoshio Kosugi
Gosaku	Keiji Sakakida

The villagers

	Jiro Kumagai
	Haruko Toyama
	Tsuneo Katagiri
	Yasuhisa Tsutsumi
Shino, Manzo's daughter	Keiko Tsushima
Grandfather	Toranosuke Ogawa
Husband	Yu Akitsu
Wife	Noriko Sengoku

Masterless samurai	Gen Shimizu
Tall samurai	Jun Tasaki
Other samurai	Isao Yamagata
Labourer	Jun Tatari
Stall keeper	Atsushi Watanabe
Minstrel	Sojin Kamiyama
Rikichi's wife	Yukiko Shimazaki
Thief	Eijiro Higashino

The bandits

	Kichijiro Ueda
	Shimpei Takagi
	Akira Tani
	Haruo Nakajima
	Takashi Narita
	Senkichi Omura
	Shuno Takahara
	Masanobu Okubo

SEVEN SAMURAI

1. Credits fade in and out, white on black, with music associated with the bandits over: drums, gongs and bassoons. After the credits, a title.

TITLE : The Sengoku Period was a time of civil wars; it was a lawless era and in the country the farmers were at the mercy of bands of brigands.

[TITLE : Around the time of the St. Bartholomew Day Massacre in France, Japan was in the throes of Civil Wars.

TITLE : And the farmers everywhere were being crushed under the iron heels of cruel brigands.]*

2. Dissolve into long shot, looking across a grassy, rolling plain to the horizon with the dawn sky above. Bandits appear on horseback on the horizon, (Still on page 33) and ride across towards camera, which pans as they pass.

3. Medium shot of one of the bandits galloping past, camera panning left with him; hold as the others gallop past after him.

4. Long shot of the bandits galloping across frame, silhouetted against the sky. Pan left, then hold as they pass.

5. Very long shot of the bandits galloping up a slope against the sky.

6. Quick dissolve to a medium shot looking along a path; the bandits ride up in the foreground, and turn, going away up the path.

7. Medium shot of another part of the countryside with grass and trees in the foreground. The bandits gallop past in the background. Pan left with them as they gallop up an incline.

8. Dissolve to a high angle medium shot of the bandits, seen from behind, who stop their horses at the top of a hill, looking down into a valley where the roofs of houses can be seen. They move forward slightly, to get a better look.

9. Medium close-up of the BANDIT CHIEF and his CAPTAIN.

---

* This is the sub-title superimposed on versions released in the U.K.

CAPTAIN : We'll take this place next.

10. High angle long shot looking down onto the village. It is peaceful and quiet. Smoke drifts up from one or two chimneys. The bandits agree noisily, off.

11. Low angle medium close-up of the CHIEF *on his horse, with the horse's head nearest camera.*

CHIEF : We took it last autumn. They haven't got anything worth taking yet. Let's wait.

As he speaks he has difficulty in controlling his horse, which swings round and round.

12. Low angle medium close-up of the CAPTAIN *on his horse.*

CAPTAIN : All right. We'll come back after the barley harvest. *He turns his horse.*

13. Medium shot of three bandits wheeling their horses round and galloping past camera.

14. Medium shot, looking up the slope. The bandits gallop from the foreground up to the top of the hill. The CHIEF *follows. Loud sound of galloping hoofs.*

15. High angle long shot from the ridge of the village below, with a rough hedge of brushwood in the foreground. The hoofbeats gradually fade away in the distance. Silence. Suddenly part of the hedge begins to rise. It is the load of faggots carried by a FARMER *as he waited, hidden behind the hedge and listened to the bandits. His face appears from behind the hedge below the load of faggots, pale and scared. A bird sings, off. The* FARMER *turns and runs down the hill.*

16. Wipe to a very long high angle shot of the village. The villagers are gathered in a circle in the open space in the centre of the village. (Still on page 33)

17. High angle long shot of the villagers crouched in a circle. The bird continues its song, off.

18. High angle medium long shot of the villagers, crouched in a circle, motionless.

19. Medium shot of some of the farmers right in the centre of the circle, with women and children crouched down behind them. Someone is moaning and wailing, off.

20. Medium shot of another group of villagers.

21. Medium shot of another group, all crouched forward in despair.

WOMAN *off* : There are no gods here any more . . .

22. High angle medium shot of other villagers, all crouched down, back to camera.

23. High angle medium shot of four villagers, backs to camera, with the sun shining down on them.

24. Medium close-up of a WOMAN, *back to camera, crouched down so that only her backside and the soles of her feet can be seen, with a young* GIRL, *also back to camera, leaning over her to comfort her.*

WOMAN *sobbing* : . . . Taxes, forced labour, war, drought — and now the bandits!

Camera tilts up slightly to medium close-up of two of the farmers who look at the WOMAN *with anxiety.*

25. Medium shot of the farmers in the centre of the circle. The WOMAN *can just be seen near them, weeping in despair. The bird sings again, off. Tilt up as one of the farmers on the left finally stands up. It is* RIKICHI. *(Still on page 33)*

26. Big close-up of RIKICHI.

RIKICHI : Let's kill them — kill them all. *Passionately* : . . . so they'll never, never come here again!

27. Close-up of YOHEI, *another, older farmer, partly obscured by* RIKICHI's *hand which is visible in the foreground. Three other farmers can be seen in the background.*

YOHEI *frightened* : You can't do that!

28. Big close-up of RIKICHI.

29. Medium close-up of YOHEI, *with others behind.* RIKICHI's *hand is in the foreground, his fist tightly clenched.*

30. Medium close-up of another farmer, MANZO, *with other villagers behind him.*

MANZO : It's impossible.

31. Big close-up of RIKICHI, *looking down at the villagers, out of shot.*

32. Medium shot of RIKICHI *standing, surrounded by the seated villagers, only their heads in shot. Pan slightly right as he makes a threatening movement towards* MANZO, *who sits back to camera. Another man,* MOSUKE, *restrains him. Pan left as* MANZO *gets up and walks up to* RIKICHI *who is being held back by* MOSUKE.

RIKICHI : You manage to kill all the samurai you catch, all right, but you can't kill the bandits!

MOSUKE : Stop it! This is no time for quarrelling.

33. Close-up of MANZO *as he sits down.* RIKICHI, *held by* MOSUKE, *is visible in the background.*

MANZO : But we haven't a chance. What if we lost? They'd kill us all! They'd kill the pregnant women, even. And the babies!

RIKICHI *trying to free himself* : I've had enough. I'd rather take that chance than go on like this. Let's either kill them or be killed by them.

MOSUKE : Rikichi! RIKICHI *breaks away from him.*

MANZO : We were born to suffer. It's our lot in life.

34. Close-up of RIKICHI *as he sits down beside* MANZO *and buries his head in his arms.* RIKICHI *does not look at* MANZO.

MANZO : If they come, let's not fight. Let's give them the harvest . . . *a* WOMAN *next to him sinks down at these words and some villagers begin to weep quietly, off* . . . but ask for just enough so we don't starve. We'll beg, we'll go down on our knees.

He begins to sob as well. RIKICHI *turns towards him.*

35. High angle medium long shot of the circle of villagers, all bowed down, some of their backs heaving with sobs. Continuing his movement, RIKICHI *stands up in the centre.* MOSUKE *rushes up and holds him back as he begins to harangue* MANZO.

RIKICHI : And you think they'll listen? Have you forgotten what we had to go through to keep the little rice that we have now? *Many of the villagers look up at these words.*

Tilt up slightly as RIKICHI *strides out of the circle and stands alone, his shoulders bowed, back to camera.*

36. Medium shot of RIKICHI *facing camera in the foreground, with the villagers sitting crouched behind him,* MOSUKE *standing in their midst.* RIKICHI *drops down onto his haunches and buries his head in his arms.* MOSUKE *comes to the edge of the circle, looks worriedly towards* RIKICHI *(Still on page 33) and then turns back to the motionless villagers.*

MOSUKE : Let's go and see Gisaku and let him decide.

MOSUKE *comes up to* RIKICHI *and sympathetically lays a hand on his shoulder as some of the villagers stand up slowly and turn to follow him. Gradually all the villagers stand up as the shot dissolves.*

37. Dissolve to medium long shot of a water mill, the wheel turning.

*38. Medium shot of the great mill wheel turning, with the
sound of rushing water. The stream runs past it into the
foreground.*

*39. A closer medium shot of the mill wheel turning in the
boulder strewn stream.*

40. Close-up of the face of GISAKU, *a very old man, who is the
village patriarch. His eyes are shut, his mouth tightly closed:
the regular sound of the turning mill wheel can be heard off.
Behind* GISAKU, *in soft focus, are a young* GIRL *and a* MAN.

RIKICHI *off* : Bargain with them? You give the wolf your leg and
he'll take your arms too. You can't bargain with them. You reason
with them now, give them something, and they'll be here in the
autumn just the same.

MANZO *off* : If they do come, and we lose, what then?

RIKICHI *furiously off* : So we lose. Without the barley we'll die
anyway.

The OLD MAN *suddenly opens his eyes and looks straight into
camera. A pause.*

GISAKU *deliberately* : We'll fight.

41. Close-up of RIKICHI, *his eyes shining with surprise and joy.*

42. Close-up of GISAKU, *nearest camera in profile, with* MANZO
in the background, looking terrified.

MANZO : We can't. We're farmers, not soldiers.

GISAKU : Then we'll hire samurai.

43. Medium shot of GISAKU *surrounded by the group of
farmers. (Still on page 33)*

MANZO : What? Hire samurai? Who ever heard of such a thing?

GISAKU : I did.

44. Big close-up of GISAKU, *facing camera.*

GISAKU : Years ago, when all of you were still babies, our village
was burned out by the bandits. When I was running away I saw
something. There was one village left unburned. It had hired
samurai.

45. Medium close-up of MANZO *and* GISAKU.

MANZO : There are all kinds of villages, all kinds of farmers. We're
too poor. We can only afford to eat barley.

46. Medium close-up of RIKICHI *standing up, over* MANZO,

who is back to camera in the foreground, only his head in shot.

RIKICHI : We could eat millet.

47. Reverse angle medium close-up of MANZO *standing up, facing* RIKICHI, *whose head is visible in the foreground.* GISAKU's *head is between them.*

MANZO : But would they fight for us — only for food?

Tilt down as MANZO *sits down, holding on medium close-up with* GISAKU *and* RIKICHI *in the foreground.*

MANZO : Samurai are very proud.

48. Close-up of GISAKU.

GISAKU : You must find hungry samurai . . . even bears come out of the forest when they are hungry.

49. Wipe to medium close-up of a SAMURAI *in profile, walking along a street in a town. Music in. Camera pans slightly left as he walks; hold as he walks off, revealing another* SAMURAI, *in medium shot, walking in the opposite direction. Pan right with him as he comes into the foreground and hold as he passes in front of* RIKICHI, MOSUKE, YOHEI *and* MANZO. *They watch him go.*

50. Close-up of RIKICHI *nearest camera and* MOSUKE *just behind him, watching the* SAMURAI. *Their eyes move from right to left.*

51. Medium close-up of another SAMURAI, *walking towards camera. Pan right as he comes nearer.*

52. Close-up of YOHEI *and* MANZO *looking left. People in the street pass in front of and behind them as they turn their heads to the left.*

53. Medium close-up of the two SAMURAI *walking along the street. Someone comes past them, obscuring them from view for a moment. Pan left as they stride along the street.*

54. Close-up of RIKICHI *and* MOSUKE *watching them. A* GIRL *comes past them in the foreground, obscuring them from view for a moment.*

55. Medium close-up of a SAMURAI *walking through the streets, partly obscured by other people walking by, in both directions. Pan right with him as he looks round, slightly suspicious.*

56. Close-up of RIKICHI *and* MOSUKE, *watching closely.*

57. Close-up of YOHEI *and* MANZO, *also watching.* GIRLS *and* WOMEN *walk past them in the foreground.*

58. Close-up of RIKICHI *and* MOSUKE.

59. Close-up of MANZO *and* YOHEI *watching, their eyes moving first to the left and then to the right. Pan slightly right as* YOHEI *goes behind* MANZO *and they look towards the right.*

60. Close-up of RIKICHI *and* MOSUKE *also looking towards the right. People go past continually, obscuring them from view.* RIKICHI *looks back at* MOSUKE *then darts out of shot. The others follow, camera panning slightly left to right, holding as they stop. Music out.*

61. Wipe to an open square in the town, with houses in the background. A crowd of people gathered in the square begin to scatter in all directions, screaming and shouting, away from a scuffle taking place in the middle.

62. Medium shot of RIKICHI *rolling in the dust with women and children screaming and cowering up against the houses behind him. Pan left to right as he slowly gets up onto his knees, watched by the three other farmers. (Still on page 34)*

63. Low angle medium shot: RIKICHI *is in the foreground on his knees, bowing down in front of a* SAMURAI *who stands over him holding his spear. The crowd of townsfolk surround them, standing well back.*

SAMURAI : Look, farmer, poor as I am, I'm a samurai, not a beggar! *Camera tracks in slightly as the* SAMURAI *starts to walk forward towards camera, passing* RIKICHI *who is bowing down almost prostrate.*

SAMURAI : Fool! *Pan left to right and tilt up as the* SAMURAI *passes, coming into low angle medium shot. Pan further left to right with the* SAMURAI *as he goes out of shot in very low angle medium close-up.*

64. Slight high angle medium close-up of RIKICHI *bowing down on the ground, only his back visible. (Still on page 34) His shoulders are shaking with silent sobs. A choir begins a monotonous and very mournful humming, over.*

65. Big close-up of MANZO.

MANZO *muttering* : I told you so.

66. Big close-up of MOSUKE. *He looks in the direction of*

MANZO *who is out of shot. He frowns and then looks down.*
67. *Low angle medium shot of* RIKICHI *still bowed down on the ground, with* MOSUKE, MANZO *and* YOHEI *standing behind him and women and children watching in the background.* MOSUKE *goes up to* RIKICHI *and bends over him, brushing the dust off his clothes as* RIKICHI *slowly lifts his head. People begin to walk past in front of them again, with only the lower part of their bodies in frame as* RIKICHI *slowly gets to his feet. Fade out.*

68. *Fade in to a medium shot looking along a road, with the verandah of a house on the left in the foreground. Rain is falling steadily. Two people are walking up the road away from camera, splashing through puddles.*
69. *Medium long shot of the four farmers in a small open space between some houses.* RIKICHI *is drawing water from a well. It is pouring with rain and the farmers are wearing straw hats and matting on their backs to keep themselves dry. In the foreground can be seen a few ears of ripening barley. (Still on page 34) Suddenly* MOSUKE *rushes forward followed by* MANZO *and* YOHEI, *coming into medium shot. They look down at the barley, fingering the ears.*

MOSUKE : Look, it's almost ripe.
MANZO : Naturally. We've been away ten days now.
YOHEI : What will we do?
70. *Big close-up of* RIKICHI.

RIKICHI : This barley is early. Mountain barley like ours is later.
He turns and walks away, camera panning right with him as he walks towards one of the houses into medium shot.
71. *Medium shot of* RIKICHI, *back to camera, going into the house, which is a rough sort of inn. Camera pans slightly right to follow him. Two labourers, stripped to the waist, come into shot from the right.*

FIRST LABOURER : I'm soaked to the bones.
The first LABOURER *runs past camera, going off; a third comes in. He and the second man turn towards* RIKICHI *as he passes.*
THIRD LABOURER : Hey . . . *Camera holds with one man in the foreground, the other beyond him, both looking towards* RIKICHI,

who stands looking back at them . . . you found any samurai yet —
strong, willing and cheap?

The two men laugh and run out of shot. RIKICHI *stands for
a moment, back to camera, taking his hat off. The humming
begins again, over.*

*72. Wipe to a long shot of the farmers standing on a patch
of grass with a low bridge and a fast-running stream in the
foreground. It is a sunny day.* RIKICHI *and* MANZO *are
quarrelling and fighting.* MOSUKE *is trying to stop them.*

MOSUKE : Rikichi! Stop it, Manzo!

73. Medium shot of the farmers, with RIKICHI *struggling on
the ground nearest camera, trying to free himself from* YOHEI,
and MOSUKE *holding* MANZO *back in the background.*

MANZO *shouting to* RIKICHI : You said you wanted to go home
but . . .

74. Reverse, medium shot with MOSUKE *holding* MANZO
back in the foreground, and YOHEI *sitting down holding*
RIKICHI *down in front of him.*

RIKICHI : I said I wanted to go home. I didn't say I wanted to
bargain with the bandits.

75. Low angle medium close-up of MANZO *and* MOSUKE.

MANZO : But what else can we do? We can't find any samurai.
We'll bargain all right, whether we like it or not.

76. Reverse high angle medium close-up of RIKICHI, *held down
by* YOHEI. *The stream runs by in the background.*

RIKICHI : All right. *He suddenly stops struggling.*

The low humming continues, over.

77. High angle big close-up of RIKICHI. *He looks up calmly.*

RIKICHI *sneering* : But what will we offer them? How about your
daughter? Shino's pretty enough. It may work.

78. Low angle big close-up of MANZO, *horrified.*

79. Medium shot of the four farmers. RIKICHI *gets up, walks
towards camera, and stands thoughtfully in the foreground.*

80. Wipe to a medium shot of the four of them. RIKICHI *and*
MANZO *are washing their faces in the stream in the foreground,
the other two standing on the path, watching them.* MOSUKE,
*who is standing on the end of the bridge, looks up suddenly
and camera tracks back through the gateway of a house,
revealing two men coming out, back to camera. The farmers*

41

stand in the background, watching the men come towards them.

81. Medium shot of MOSUKE *and* YOHEI *standing on the bridge, in back view. Through the large gatehouse of a prosperous country house comes a crowd of people. Pan right and track in past* YOHEI *and* MOSUKE *as a* SAMURAI, *followed by a* PRIEST *and another man, the* OWNER *of the house, walk down to the edge of the stream.* RIKICHI *and* MANZO *stand by the stream in back view in the foreground. The* SAMURAI, KANBEI, *puts down his sword, then turns and takes a knife out of his belt.*

82. Low angle medium close-up of KANBEI *with the* OWNER *and the group of onlookers behind him. He lifts the knife to his head and cuts loose his samurai top-knot. There is a gasp from the crowd because the top-knot is one of the samurai's distinguishing features.* KANBEI *tucks the knife back in his belt. One of the men pushes through the crowd behind him and passes a razor to the* OWNER, *who hands it to* KANBEI. KANBEI *passes it to the* PRIEST *who is standing on his other side, camera panning slightly right as he does so to include the* PRIEST. *Then* KANBEI *sits down cross-legged, camera tilting down with him. He begins to wash his head in the stream.*

83. Medium close-up of the PRIEST *holding the razor. He looks at it nervously, then up at the people.*

84. Medium long shot across the stream, of the crowd of people (including the farmers) standing on the bank and the bridge. They all crane forward as the PRIEST *begins to shave* KANBEI'S *head.*

85. Close-up of KANBEI, *his face impassive, as the* PRIEST'S *hands shave his head. (Still on page 34)*

86. Medium close-up of the OWNER *and the other* MAN *watching, with others in the background, craning forward. The two men in the foreground look at each other in amazement and the second* MAN *turns away.*

87. Medium close-up of the MAN, *back to camera, as he pushes his way back through the crowd. They all turn to watch him as he goes to look back through the archway. Many of the crowd are carrying clubs and pitchforks. The* MAN *turns and comes back again.*

88. Medium close-up of the OWNER. *The* MAN *comes and joins him again.*

89. Medium close-up of another group of onlookers jostling one another to get a better view.

90. Medium close-up of others in the crowd, carrying pitchforks and scythes.

91. Medium shot of a group of people, including the four farmers and another MAN *and a* WOMAN. *They are all watching intently.* MOSUKE *leans forward, then turns to the* WOMAN *next to him.*

MOSUKE : What's happening?

WOMAN : There's a thief in that barn.

At that moment a young SAMURAI, KATSUSHIRO, *appears behind them, watching and listening silently.*

WOMAN : They found him and he ran in there.

MOSUKE *rushes out of shot, followed by the other three farmers.* KATSUSHIRO *stands watching with a slight frown, then follows them.*

92. Medium long shot of the barn with its thatched roof. The wind blows the dust up in the yard.

93. Long shot of the barn through the gateway, with two villagers standing looking towards it in medium long shot. The four farmers, followed by KATSUSHIRO, *pass through the gateway from the foreground, back to camera.*

94. Medium shot from the side of the two villagers standing at the gateway. KATSUSHIRO *comes up and stands by them, furthest from camera, and the farmers gather behind. They all stare forward.*

KATSUSHIRO : How many are there?

VILLAGER : Just one.

95. Medium close-up of the VILLAGER *and* KATSUSHIRO, *with* MANZO *and* RIKICHI *visible behind them.*

KATSUSHIRO *incredulously* : One? But there are so many of you.

VILLAGER : We can't do anything. He took a child in with him. If we try to get him he says he'll kill it. *Just then a* CHILD *is heard crying.* There, hear that?

96. Medium long shot of the barn. The CHILD *can be heard screaming above the noise of the wind.*

43

97. *Medium shot of the four farmers with the villagers and* KATSUSHIRO *at the gateway, listening.*

SECOND VILLAGER : Oh, the poor thing. And he's only seven.

98. *Medium shot of the group at the gateway from behind. The* SECOND VILLAGER *turns towards camera. Pan slightly right as he walks towards camera and the farmers surround him sympathetically.*

SECOND VILLAGER : His parents must be frantic.

MOSUKE : But who is that samurai?

SECOND VILLAGER : Nobody knows. We asked him to save the child and he agreed. Then he asked for two rice balls. *He goes off.*

FIRST VILLAGER, *coming forward* : Then he had his head shaved like that and asked the priest to lend him his robes. I don't know what he intends to do.

As the FIRST VILLAGER *finishes speaking, they all walk past camera going off in the foreground, leaving* KATSUSHIRO *looking back at the barn. Then he follows them off, leaving the deserted yard in view. A pause; then a* WOMAN *runs out of the house by the barn in long shot, carrying a dish. She pauses for a moment as the* CHILD *screams again, and then turns and runs towards camera, which tracks back through the archway. Pan right with her as she comes under the gateway, holding as she pushes her way through the crowd and disappears from view.* KATSUSHIRO *and the farmers move past camera.*

99. *Medium shot of* KATSUSHIRO *and the four farmers coming round behind the crowd to get a better view of* KANBEI *on the river bank. Pan right with them and hold as they stand, back to camera, in the foreground. Kneeling on the ground in front of them is another* SAMURAI, KIKUCHIYO. *He looks up at* KATSUSHIRO, *who is just behind him, and stands up, giving them all a dirty look. The farmers back off slightly, and* KIKUCHIYO *settles down again to watch* KANBEI.

100. *Medium shot of* KANBEI, *back to camera, his head completely shaved, with the* PRIEST *beside him. He has dressed himself in tattered priest's robes. On the other side of the stream,* KIKUCHIYO *can be seen crouching down watching,* KATSUSHIRO *and the farmers directly behind him and the group of villagers looking on. (Still on page 34)* KANBEI *turns*

as the PRIEST *hands him a belt, then turns back again to put it on.*

101. *Low angle close-up of* KANBEI *looking across the stream.*

102. *Close-up of* KIKUCHIYO *staring back.*

103. *Low angle close-up of* KANBEI *(as 101). He turns away, and then looks up again.*

104. *Close-up of* KIKUCHIYO *(as 102). He scratches his neck.*

105. *Low angle close-up of* KANBEI *(as 101), staring towards* KIKUCHIYO. *He lowers his eyes and turns his back as camera pans slightly right to include the* PRIEST. *Pan back slightly to* KANBEI, *losing the* PRIEST. KANBEI *stares across the stream again.*

106. *Close-up of* KIKUCHIYO *looking up, a puzzled frown on his face.*

107. *Low angle close-up of* KANBEI, *looking across impassively; he turns away. Pan left with him as he takes a few paces forward to where the* WOMAN *is holding out her dish with two rice balls on it. (Still on page 34) He takes it and walks past her, camera panning further left and tilting up slightly as he starts to go through to the gateway.*

108. *Long shot, looking along the stream to the bridge. The crowd hurry through the gateway, disappearing from view as they follow* KANBEI.

109. *Long shot of the gateway from the other side, with* KANBEI *coming through and the crowd following.*

110. *Medium shot of the* PRIEST *with* KATSUSHIRO *standing beside him. They stop with the crowd pressing up behind. Then* KIKUCHIYO *pushes his way between them.*

111. *Medium shot of the* OWNER *with his* WIFE *and the other* MAN *standing watching.* KIKUCHIYO *pushes his way past them and comes into the foreground, standing in low angle medium close-up.*

112. *Medium shot of* KANBEI *from behind, approaching the barn in his priest's robes.* KIKUCHIYO *comes into shot in the foreground, only the lower half of his body in shot. He stops in low angle medium close-up, kicks over a barrel and sits down on it. The* CHILD *can be heard screaming from inside the barn, and the* THIEF *begins yelling hysterically, off, as* KANBEI *comes up to the barn door.*

45

113. Medium shot of KANBEI *outside the barn door. He places the dish of rice balls on a stone outside the barn.*

THIEF *off* : So you've come. Well don't come any nearer or I'll kill the boy. You hear me.

KANBEI : I'm a priest.

114. Medium shot of KIKUCHIYO *sitting on the barrel, watching, with the villagers lined up by the gatehouse in the background.*

115. Medium shot of KANBEI *looking through the bamboo struts of the barn wall, back to camera.*

THIEF *off* : Don't come in, I'm warning you !

KANBEI : I'm not. I just thought the child might be hungry.

As he speaks KANBEI *slides the barn door open.*

THIEF *hysterically, off* : Don't come in !

KANBEI *kneels down at the door holding out the rice balls, one in each hand.*

KANBEI : I've brought some rice. One is for you.

116. Medium shot of KIKUCHIYO *watching closely with the crowd looking on, motionless, in the background.*

KANBEI *off* : Here, take it. It's all right.

117. Medium shot of the OWNER *and his* WIFE *and the other* MAN *with the villagers in the background, including* KATSUSHIRO *and the farmers.*

118. Medium shot of KATSUSHIRO *standing by the* PRIEST *with the villagers crowding round behind them.*

119. Close-up of KIKUCHIYO *watching.*

120. Medium shot of KANBEI *holding out the rice balls through the open door of the barn.*

THIEF *off* : Throw them in !

KANBEI *throws the rice balls through the doorway. The* CHILD *screams, off.*

KANBEI : All right. There you are.

KANBEI *stands up again, rubs his hands together. A slight pause. Then he rushes through the barn door.*

121. General shot of the crowd in the yard shifting and murmuring with KIKUCHIYO *in medium shot in the foreground, the* CHILD'S *parents behind him and the villagers all crowded together in the background.*

122. Medium shot of the outside of the barn; the CHILD'S

screaming can be heard from inside. The wind blows up the dust. Then suddenly the THIEF *staggers through the door.*

123. *General shot of the watching crowd (as 121). They all stare and some of the villagers cower back fearfully.*

124. *Medium shot of the* THIEF *running past the stockade in slow motion.*

125. *Resume on the crowd (as 121). The villagers are huddling together. In the foreground* KIKUCHIYO *rises slowly to his feet.*

126. *Medium shot of the* THIEF *staggering in agony.*

127. *Same shot of the watching crowd (as 121).* KIKUCHIYO *is now standing up, staring in amazement.*

128. *Medium close-up of the* THIEF *from the side, his eyes staring and his mouth open. He sways slightly.*

129. *Medium shot of* KIKUCHIYO *in the foreground with the villagers in the background.* KIKUCHIYO *is leaning forward staring. Suddenly the* CHILD'S MOTHER *behind him screams and runs towards camera, going out of shot.*

130. *Medium shot of the* WOMAN *running across to where* KANBEI *is standing in the background holding the* CHILD, *who is still crying. Pan right to include the* THIEF *in the foreground, swaying backwards and forwards with a fixed expression. The* WOMAN *grabs the* CHILD *as* KANBEI *throws down his sword.*

131. *High angle close-up of* KANBEI'S *sword lying on the ground, its point bloodstained. (Still on page 34)*

132. *Medium close-up of the* THIEF *from behind; he is almost bent double. He sinks to the ground in slow motion.*

133. *Medium shot of* KIKUCHIYO *in the foreground with the villagers and the* CHILD'S FATHER *and the other* MAN *edging forward slightly to see what has happened.* KIKUCHIYO *takes a couple of steps towards camera.*

134. *High angle medium shot of the dead* THIEF, *the wind ruffling his clothes. (Still on page 34)*

135. *Long shot of the courtyard, with the* THIEF *lying on the left and* KANBEI *standing on the right, with the* MOTHER *clutching her* CHILD *on her knees in front of him. In the background,* KIKUCHIYO *and the villagers stand watching.* KIKUCHIYO *strides forward and leans over the* THIEF'S *body as the* CHILD'S FATHER *comes up to comfort his* WIFE *and* SON.

KANBEI *starts to walk away, watching* KIKUCHIYO. KIKUCHIYO *prods the body and then looks back at* KANBEI. *As* KANBEI *walks away,* KIKUCHIYO *picks up the sword, leaps over the body of the* THIEF *and dances about, brandishing the sword and shouting for joy. At the same time all the villagers rush forward, crowding round* KIKUCHIYO, *who stands triumphantly with one foot on the corpse's back.*

136. Medium long shot of KANBEI *in profile, standing with the* PRIEST; KATSUSHIRO *is in the background, watching with the farmers.* KANBEI *starts to remove the priest's robes. The* PRIEST *holds out his sword sheath.*

137. Medium close-up of KATSUSHIRO *looking on with admiration, with the four farmers in the background.*

138. Medium close-up of the four farmers watching the proceedings. RIKICHI *looks excited. He looks back at the others, smiling slightly.*

139. Wipe to medium shot of KANBEI *from behind, walking along a road, silhouetted against a cloudy sky. Music in: the 'Seven Samurai' theme. Camera tracks along behind him, up a slight incline.*

140. Medium shot, from behind, of the four farmers; KANBEI *is beyond them in the background. Camera tracks behind them as they follow him along the road. (Still on page 35)*

RIKICHI *looking back to* MOSUKE: I think we ought to try him, don't you?

MOSUKE: Yes, let's talk to him before he reaches town and we lose him.

RIKICHI: Right.

He begins to run towards KANBEI, *but at that moment,* KIKUCHIYO *appears in the foreground and runs past the three farmers after* RIKICHI, *also going towards* KANBEI. *Camera continues to track along behind them.*

141. Medium close-up tracking along beside RIKICHI. KIKUCHIYO *comes up, running past* RIKICHI *and elbowing him out of the way. They both stop, then* KIKUCHIYO *rushes out of shot, leaving* RIKICHI *staring after him.*

142. Medium long shot of KANBEI, *back to camera on the brow of the hill, silhouetted against the sky. He looks back and* KIKUCHIYO *runs into shot from the foreground, back to camera.*

48

KIKUCHIYO *runs up to where* KANBEI *has stopped on the road and leaps into the air with a manic chuckle, (Still on page 35) then stands facing him, looking him up and down, with his samurai sword balanced on his shoulder. They stand looking at each other, both silhouetted against the sky.*

KANBEI : What is it?

KIKUCHIYO *says nothing but scratches his head, and then circles round in front of* KANBEI, *camera panning slightly right with him.* KANBEI *also circles round till they are facing one another again. At that moment* KATSUSHIRO *runs up from the foreground.*

143. *Low angle medium shot of* KANBEI *and* KIKUCHIYO *standing silhouetted against the sky;* KATSUSHIRO *kneels and bows down in front of* KANBEI. *(Still on page 35)*

KATSUSHIRO : Please listen to me. My name is Katsushiro Okamoto. Please take me as one of your disciples.

144. *Low angle medium shot of* KANBEI *with* KIKUCHIYO *in the foreground, three-quarters back to camera, looking at him.* KANBEI *looks down and rubs his bald head, then smiles.*

KANBEI : Disciple? My name is Kanbei Shimada . . .

Pan slightly left as KIKUCHIYO, *still in back view, circles round in front of* KANBEI *and looks at him from the other side.*

KANBEI : . . . I am only a ronin, not a samurai, and I have no disciples . . .

Pan right as KIKUCHIYO *circles round again to the other side and he and* KANBEI *both look down at* KATSUSHIRO *who is still out of shot.*

145. *Medium close-up of* KATSUSHIRO *still on his knees, staring up at* KANBEI, *whose head is out of frame.* KIKUCHIYO *stands beside* KANBEI, *behind* KATSUSHIRO, *also with his head out of frame.*

KATSUSHIRO : Please take me as your disciple.

146. *Close-up of* KANBEI *smiling, leaning down towards* KATSUSHIRO, *who is out of shot.*

KANBEI : Stand up so that we can talk properly.

147. *Low angle medium shot of* KANBEI *turning away and beginning to walk along the road again.* KIKUCHIYO *watches him, while* KATSUSHIRO *gets to his feet, then runs to join* KANBEI *as he walks away in back view over the brow of the*

hill. KIKUCHIYO *continues to circle round as if not knowing what to do.*

148. Medium long shot of the four farmers, back to camera, standing on the road where they have been watching. The music comes up louder, as KANBEI *and* KATSUSHIRO *are seen walking away over the hill in the background.* KIKUCHIYO *stands watching them, circling round with his samurai sword on his shoulder. He and the farmers begin to follow* KANBEI.

149. Wipe to a low angle medium shot of KANBEI *in profile with* KATSUSHIRO *nearest camera beside him. Track sideways with them as they walk along the road.*

KANBEI: But you're embarrassing me. I'm not all that good.

KATSUSHIRO: But you are.

KANBEI: Listen. I have nothing particular to teach you. I've just had a lot of experience fighting. That's all. So just forget about becoming a disciple, and stop following me. It's for your own good.

KATSUSHIRO *runs round and faces* KANBEI.

KATSUSHIRO: No, I have made up my mind. *They stop. Hold on a low angle medium shot of the two.* I'll follow you even if you never accept me.

KANBEI *sternly*: I forbid you to. KATSUSHIRO *looks crestfallen.* I cannot afford to have a disciple. *He starts to walk away.*

150. High angle long shot looking down the road towards a town. In the foreground the four farmers stand looking at one another. In the background KATSUSHIRO *stands facing camera as* KANBEI *walks away towards the town.* RIKICHI *then hurries after* KANBEI, *but at this moment* KIKUCHIYO *runs into shot in the foreground, pushing past the three other farmers and going into long shot as he passes* KATSUSHIRO. *The music changes to* KIKUCHIYO'S *theme.*

151. Medium shot with KANBEI *in the foreground,* KATSU-SHIRO *behind him and the three farmers in the background.* RIKICHI *is running towards* KANBEI *but* KIKUCHIYO *runs up behind him and pushes him out of the way. (Still on page 35)* RIKICHI *goes off, while* KIKUCHIYO *comes up and stands in front of* KANBEI, *who looks at him impassively.*

KANBEI: What is it?

KIKUCHIYO *scratches his head in embarrassment and walks round towards camera, coming into the foreground. Pan slightly with him until he stands back to camera facing* KANBEI, *with his samurai sword on his shoulder. All the others stop and watch them in the background.*

KANBEI : What do you want?

KIKUCHIYO *lopes round again and stands facing* KANBEI *in his former position. He does not reply.* KATSUSHIRO *takes a few steps forward, and then runs up and stands next to* KANBEI. *He stares at* KIKUCHIYO *who is still leering at* KANBEI.

KATSUSHIRO : Insolent fellow!

152. Medium close-up of KANBEI *and* KATSUSHIRO, *in back view, with* KIKUCHIYO *facing camera between them. He bends his head slightly and stares, frowning, at* KATSUSHIRO. *(Still on page 35)*

KIKUCHIYO : Mind your own business.

153. Low angle medium close-up of KATSUSHIRO *and* KIKUCHIYO *facing each other in profile, with* KANBEI *between them facing camera.* KANBEI *takes a step forward towards* KIKUCHIYO. *There is a tense pause.*

KANBEI *smiling slightly* : Are you a samurai?

154. Close-up of KIKUCHIYO *facing camera, seen over the shoulder of* KANBEI, *who is in back view in the foreground.* KIKUCHIYO *grins stupidly and then looks down, frowning again.*
155. Low angle medium shot of KATSUSHIRO, *three-quarters back to camera, with* KANBEI *beside him in profile, both facing* KIKUCHIYO. *Behind them can be seen the town square.* KIKUCHIYO *grins, lifts his sword from his shoulder and digs the point in the ground, holding it proudly at the hilt.*

KIKUCHIYO : Of course I'm a samurai!

156. Close-up of KANBEI *looking at* KIKUCHIYO, *out of shot, through narrowed eyes.*

KANBEI : I wonder. *He looks round towards* KATSUSHIRO. *The music returns to the samurai theme.*

157. Low angle medium shot of KANBEI *putting a hand on* KATSUSHIRO's *shoulder to lead him on.* KIKUCHIYO *watches in fury, still holding his sword.* KATSUSHIRO *looks back at him angrily, then he and* KANBEI *begin to walk away.* KIKUCHIYO *turns away to watch them go. He takes a few steps towards them and aims a furious kick in their direction. Then he strides back towards camera, still looking back at them over his*

shoulder and scratching his neck. He circles round, grimacing.
158. Camera tracks after KATSUSHIRO *and* KANBEI *in low*
angle medium close-up as they walk through the town square.
KATSUSHIRO *looks back, but* KANBEI, *with a hand on his*
shoulder, urges him on. Track slightly right as they walk
towards the corner of the square, then hold as KATSUSHIRO
looks back again, and stops.

KATSUSHIRO : Who was that? KANBEI *also stops and looks round.*

159. Long shot of KIKUCHIYO *standing by the side of the road.*
A small stream runs along beside it. In the background the
four farmers stand in a group staring at KIKUCHIYO.

160. Medium shot of KATSUSHIRO *and* KANBEI *still looking*
back towards KIKUCHIYO. KANBEI *looks at* KATSUSHIRO.

KANBEI : Don't pay any attention to him.

They turn away again and walk on, camera tilting down
slightly as they go.

161. Long shot of KIKUCHIYO *(as 159). Furiously, he picks*
up a stone and hurls it into the stream, watched in amazement
by the farmers. RIKICHI *looks at him nervously, and then runs*
along the road towards camera.

162. Medium long shot of KANBEI *and* KATSUSHIRO *in back*
view walking along the road. RIKICHI *runs into shot in the*
foreground, back to camera, and runs along behind them. Pan
to the right as RIKICHI *catches up with* KANBEI *and* KATSU-
SHIRO, *runs round in front of them and goes down on his knees*
in the road in front of KANBEI. *They are seen framed by the*
roof and wooden supports of a roadside verandah. Music out.

RIKICHI : Please . . .

163. Wipe to medium shot inside a cheap roadside inn. Three
of the farmers are kneeling on a low bench with heads bowed.
KATSUSHIRO *sits next to them, by some barred windows that*
look out onto the street. On the left, and beyond the farmers,
KANBEI *can be seen staring through a window into the street.*
They are all in back view.

164. Low angle medium close-up of the bamboo window bars.
People can be seen walking by in the street outside. Then in
the foreground, KANBEI *comes into shot, back to camera, as*
he stands up.

KANBEI : No, it's impossible.

KATSUSHIRO *off* : Sir . . .

165. Low angle medium close-up of KANBEI, *back to camera, as* KATSUSHIRO *comes into shot beside him, in three-quarter front view, looking at him earnestly.*

KATSUSHIRO : They could fight them with bamboo spears.

KANBEI : I'd thought of that.

KATSUSHIRO : And . . .

166. Low angle medium close-up of KANBEI, *three-quarters back to camera. He turns his head to face* KATSUSHIRO, *who stands in three-quarter back view in the foreground.*

KANBEI : This isn't a game, you know.

Pan slightly right as KANBEI *passes in front of* KATSUSHIRO *and turns round. He stands looking down, with his back to the window, then goes off.*

KANBEI *off* : Though they are only bandits, there are forty of them.

167. Low angle medium long shot of KANBEI *standing near the entrance to the inn, facing camera. Beside him, two of the farmers can be seen sitting in back view, their heads bowed dejectedly, and behind them, still standing by the window, is* KATSUSHIRO.

KANBEI : Two or three samurai would be no match for them.

168. High angle medium shot of the three farmers from the side with RIKICHI *in the foreground,* MANZO *in the centre and* MOSUKE *furthest from camera. (Still on page 35)*

169. Low angle medium close-up of KANBEI *looking down at the farmers, who are out of shot. He turns away; pan right with him as he goes over and leans on one of the wooden partitions, back to camera. Hold as he speaks.*

KANBEI : Defence is much more difficult than aggression. *He turns suddenly to face the farmers.* Did you say there were hills at the back of your village?

170. High angle medium shot of the three farmers. They all look up towards KANBEI, *who is out of shot.*

RIKICHI : Yes, sir.

171. Low angle medium close-up of KANBEI *looking down at them.*

KANBEI : Can horses get over them?

172. High angle medium close-up of the farmers (as 170).

RIKICHI : Yes, sir. *He smiles hopefully.*

173. Low angle medium close-up of KANBEI *(as 171). He looks down thoughtfully, (Still on page 35) then turns away; pan right with him as he paces along beside the wooden partition, thinking aloud.*

KANBEI: I see. There are fields in front, then, and so the village is wide open until they are flooded for planting.

Hold as he stops, standing in profile and leaning one arm on the partition.

KANBEI: We'd need guards. One for each direction, that means four.

He turns to face camera, looking down at the farmers, who are out of shot. Pan back to the left as he paces back along the partition, still talking to himself.

KANBEI: Two more for reserve. So you'd need . . . seven — including myself.*

174. High angle medium shot of the three farmers, MOSUKE *in the foreground, beside one of the upright wooden pillars, and* MANZO *and* RIKICHI *kneeling on the other side.* RIKICHI *is smiling happily.* KANBEI *can be seen pacing up and down in the background.*

RIKICHI: But can we afford seven?

MANZO: He told us to get four of them.

RIKICHI: Maybe we could do it with three.

KANBEI: Wait. I haven't said I will. KANBEI *begins to pace forward again, camera panning left with him.* It isn't easy to find that many reliable samurai. *Hold on a high angle medium shot of* KANBEI, *with* KATSUSHIRO *in the foreground.* And the reward will only be three meals a day and the fun of it, if you want to put it that way.

Track in slightly as KANBEI *walks forward and stands in front of* KATSUSHIRO *in profile, looking at the farmers who are out of shot.*

KANBEI: Besides, I'm tired of fighting. I'm probably getting old.

KANBEI *leans down, and picks up his sword and scarf;* KATSUSHIRO *also gathers up his belongings. There is a muffled sound of weeping, off.*

175. High angle medium close-up of RIKICHI *bending down and weeping, his head turned away from camera. Low*

---

* End of reel 1. 35 mm, British released version.

humming begins, over.

176. Medium shot of KANBEI *and* KATSUSHIRO *in front of the barred window, looking towards the farmers who are out of shot. Suddenly there is a burst of raucous laughter, off.*

177. Medium shot of three labourers leaning over the wooden partition; the one in the middle is laughing and swinging a wine bottle. They come round the partition into the foreground.

LABOURER : I'm glad I wasn't born a farmer.

178. Medium shot of the three labourers settling themselves down on one of the benches with the farmers visible behind them, and KANBEI *and* KATSUSHIRO *standing in front of the window.*

LABOURER : Even a dog has a better life than that.

One of the labourers suddenly jumps up and runs back to where the farmers are sitting. He bends over them.

LABOURER *derisively* : You can take it from me, just you go and hang yourselves. You'll be a lot happier. *He comes back grinning and joins the other two labourers.*

As the LABOURER *sits down he reveals* KANBEI *and* KATSUSHIRO *standing watching in the background.*

KATSUSHIRO : You watch what you're saying.

LABOURER : What's wrong? I'm just telling the truth.

KATSUSHIRO : The truth! Then you ought to be sorry for them.

LABOURER : Don't make me laugh.

The three labourers laugh and nudge one another, then the one who was speaking turns back to KATSUSHIRO.

LABOURER : How about you? Are you sorry for them?

KATSUSHIRO : What?

LABOURER : Yes . . . if you were sorry for them — really sorry — then you'd help them, wouldn't you?

179. Big close-up of KATSUSHIRO. *He looks down, then up. Suddenly he moves.*

180. High angle close-up of KATSUSHIRO's *sword lying on the bench. His hand comes into shot and grabs it. Tilt up to low angle medium close-up of* MANZO *and* MOSUKE *with the labourers visible behind them. One of the labourers stands up in alarm. The farmers rush out of the way as the other labourers stand up.*

181. Medium close-up of KANBEI *with the farmers trying to get out of the way behind him.* KANBEI *moves towards* KATSUSHIRO, *camera panning slightly right with him.*

LABOURER *off* : Oh, you're going to fight are you?

KANBEI : Stop!

KATSUSHIRO *lunges forward in front of* KANBEI. *Quick backward track and pan left as* KATSUSHIRO *darts across the benches, losing* KANBEI. KANBEI *comes into shot again in the foreground, back to camera. Pan left as* KANBEI *circles round after* KATSUSHIRO *and the three labourers scurry across frame in the foreground, escaping from* KATSUSHIRO. *Hold on a low angle medium shot of the group,* KANBEI *restraining them all.*

KANBEI : Fools!

182. Close-up of KANBEI. *He looks from left to right.*

183. Close-up of one of the labourers cowering behind one of his mates, whose shoulder and arm only are in shot. The LABOURER *runs round behind his friend, camera panning left with him, until he almost bumps into* YOHEI *coming in with a bowl of rice. Hold on a slight high angle medium shot of them. The* LABOURER *grabs the bowl of rice, pan further left as he approaches* KANBEI *and holds out the bowl to him. Hold on low angle medium shot of them both, with* KANBEI *nearest camera. (Still on page 35)*

LABOURER : Yes, look at it. It's for you. Go on. But do you know what they eat, those farmers? They eat millet. They're giving you their rice and eating millet themselves.

KANBEI *looks silently over to where the farmers are standing, out of shot.*

184. Medium shot of the farmers cowering against the door.

185. Low angle medium close-up of KANBEI *in the foreground, with the* LABOURER *holding out the bowl of rice to him.*

LABOURER : They're giving you everything they have.

KANBEI *looks down at the* LABOURER *and takes the bowl of rice.*

KANBEI : All right. I understand.

LABOURER *puzzled* : What?

186. Medium shot of the farmers cowering in the corner, RIKICHI *in back view. In the foreground,* KANBEI's *hand holds the bowl of steaming rice. The humming reaches a climax.*

KANBEI *off* : I understand. I accept your sacrifice.

56

The hand is withdrawn from the shot, and RIKICHI *turns and sinks down on his knees with a look of gratitude and relief. He bows down. Fade out, and end of music.*

187. Fade in to medium shot of the open space in the centre of the farmers' village. People are running from the foreground away from camera, gathering excitedly in a group.
188. High angle medium shot of the crowd of villagers surrounding MANZO *and* MOSUKE. *Track in to a high angle medium close-up of* MOSUKE *and* MANZO *in the centre of the group with villagers, including several of the leading men, pressing round them.*

GOSAKU : Look, Menzo's back!
ANOTHER VILLAGER : Where are Rikichi and Yohei?
MANZO : Still in town, looking for more samurai.
SAMPEI : More samurai?
MOSUKE : We have to find seven of them. *There is a gasp from the crowd.*

189. Medium shot of a group of villagers, repeating the number to each other, astounded.
190. Low angle medium shot from behind of a SAMURAI, *walking past camera in the town. Horn music in. Track along behind him as* RIKICHI *runs into shot, shouting.*

RIKICHI : Hey! Hey!

191. Medium shot from behind of YOHEI *and* KATSUSHIRO *inside the inn, watching* RIKICHI *and the* SAMURAI *who can be seen in the background through the doorway. As* RIKICHI *bows down to the* SAMURAI *in the distance,* KATSUSHIRO *moves across to the door.*
192. Medium shot of KATSUSHIRO *watching at the doorway, with* YOHEI *also watching, in the foreground.*
193. Medium shot of the SAMURAI *facing* RIKICHI *who is bowing down to him, back to camera.*

RIKICHI : Please sir . . .
SAMURAI : What is it? A fight?

194. Medium shot of KATSUSHIRO *and* YOHEI *watching at the door of the inn.*

KANBEI *off* : Katsushiro!

KATSUSHIRO *turns back and looks into the dark interior. Pan right with him as he goes in and stands back to camera. The music changes to the samurai theme. In the background, sitting cross-legged on one of the benches, is* KANBEI. *He holds out a stout stick.*

195. Medium close-up of KATSUSHIRO *looking surprised.* YOHEI *stands at the doorway behind him, looking out.*

196. Medium shot of KANBEI *holding up the stick. He swings it and hits the floor.*

KANBEI: You hide behind the door — and hold the stick up high.

197. Medium close-up of KATSUSHIRO *(as 195) looking rather uncertain.*

198. Medium shot of KANBEI *(as 196). He holds out the stick.*

KANBEI: When the samurai comes in, hit him as hard as you can.

199. Medium close-up of KATSUSHIRO *(as 195) with* YOHEI *visible behind him at the doorway.*

YOHEI: He's coming now! KATSUSHIRO *looks round hurriedly.*

Shot 200. Medium shot of KANBEI *holding up the stick impatiently.*

201. Medium close-up of KATSUSHIRO *looking rather nervous. He bends down.*

202. Low angle medium shot of KATSUSHIRO, *with* KANBEI'S *head in the foreground, back to camera.* KATSUSHIRO *takes the stick.*

KANBEI: Now, hit as hard as you can.

203. Close-up of YOHEI *at the door. Pan right with him as he runs and hides behind one of the wooden partitions. Camera picks up* KATSUSHIRO *and pans back to the left as he goes over and hides behind the doorpost.*

204. Medium shot of YOHEI *watching him from behind the partition.*

205. Medium shot of KANBEI *sitting cross-legged, waiting quietly. He picks up a small twig and fiddles with it.*

206. Medium shot of YOHEI *(as 204).*

207. Medium shot of KATSUSHIRO *behind the doorpost. He raises the stick in both hands, above his head.*

208. Medium shot of the SAMURAI *approaching along the street, followed by* RIKICHI. *Pan slightly right as he walks.*

209. Close-up of KATSUSHIRO *holding up the club and peering round the doorpost.*

210. Medium shot as the SAMURAI *comes through the entrance. Camera tracks back in front of him, revealing* KATSUSHIRO *behind the door with his stick raised.* RIKICHI *follows at a safe distance. Hold on a medium shot as* KATSUSHIRO *brings down the stick with a great shout — but the* SAMURAI *is too quick for him and wards off the blow. Music out.*

211. Medium close-up of the SAMURAI, *who has grabbed hold of* KATSUSHIRO *from behind. He pushes him violently away.*

212. Medium shot of the interior of the inn. Continuing his movement, KATSUSHIRO *staggers into shot in the foreground and slithers across the benches, landing in a heap in the corner. Pan slightly left to include* KANBEI *who stands up, looking pleased. Pan right with him as he walks across to where the* SAMURAI *is standing, very much on his guard.*

KANBEI: That was splendid. Please forgive us. *Pan slightly right as the* SAMURAI *steps back.* My name is Kanbei Shimada. I am looking for good fighters like yourself, I'm sorry this happened but it had to be done. *He bows.*

SAMURAI: Why did you do this?

213. Medium close-up of KATSUSHIRO *getting to his feet, rather shaken. Tilt up with him as he stands up.*

SAMURAI *off*: I'm very angry.

214. Medium long shot of KANBEI *standing facing the* SAMURAI, *holding out a placating hand.*

KANBEI: Please forgive us. I needed someone like you. You see, we're about to start a campaign against a band of brigands.

SAMURAI *interested*: I see. What clan do you belong to?

KANBEI: Well, as a matter of fact, this is rather unusual. Our employer is a group of farmers — a whole village.

SAMURAI: Farmers?

KANBEI: That's right. We don't get any land or anything as a reward but we do get three meals a day while we fight.

215. Medium close-up of KANBEI, *back to camera, with the* SAMURAI *in medium shot, facing him, and seen over his shoulder.*

SAMURAI *disdainfully*: Stupid — I can do better than that.

216. Wipe to medium close-up from the side of a SAMURAI *walking along the street. Horn music in. Track to the right, following him as he walks. As he goes out of shot, camera tracks left with another* SAMURAI *walking in the opposite direction, carrying a spear. Track left to right again as a third* SAMURAI *comes into shot in the foreground and strides past the second* SAMURAI. *As he goes out of shot, camera picks up a* RONIN, *walking in the other direction, and pans back with him, left to right.*

KANBEI *off* : Try him.

217. Medium long shot of the RONIN *walking along the middle of the street. He walks into medium shot as* RIKICHI *comes out of the inn in the background. Pan right with the* RONIN. *He walks along the street and round the corner, to where a group of children are playing. Hold as he walks towards them, in back view, to watch their game.* RIKICHI *runs into shot again.*

RIKICHI : Please, sir !

218. Medium shot of KANBEI *inside the inn. Behind him,* KATSUSHIRO *and* YOHEI *stand at the doorway, looking out into the street.* KANBEI *walks towards camera and* KATSUSHIRO *comes and stands behind him, looking over his shoulder. Samurai theme in.*

KATSUSHIRO : Like the last time?

KANBEI *smiles slightly, and turns towards* KATSUSHIRO.

KANBEI : Yes — and try hard. It's good training for you.

219. Close-up of YOHEI, *looking worried. Pan right with him as he goes and hides behind the partition again, camera holding on him for a moment.*

220. Medium shot of KATSUSHIRO *at the door with* KANBEI *resuming his position cross-legged on the bench.* KATSUSHIRO *peers round the doorpost.*

221. Medium long shot of the RONIN, *whose name is* GOROBEI, *and* RIKICHI, *walking towards camera along the street.*

222. Medium shot of KATSUSHIRO *(as 220), with* KANBEI *sitting in the background.* KATSUSHIRO *ducks out of sight behind the door.*

223. Medium shot of KATSUSHIRO *hiding behind the door. He raises the stick at the ready.* RIKICHI *appears in the street outside, and bows and stands aside to let* GOROBEI *approach first. (Still on page 36)* GOROBEI *hesitates, then stops just outside the door, looking through into the inn. He smiles.*

224. Close-up of GOROBEI *smiling, then laughing.*

60

GOROBEI : I see . . . it's a joke!

225. Medium shot of KANBEI *in the inn. He smiles and slaps his knee, then starts to get up. Tilt up with him as he stands up and comes forward into low angle medium close-up.*

KANBEI : Please forgive us!

226. Wipe to medium shot of KANBEI *standing in the inn with* GOROBEI *back to camera in the background. The latter paces up and down beside the window thoughtfully, and then comes back to face* KANBEI. *He smiles.*

GOROBEI : Well, it sounds interesting. KANBEI *bows slightly.* I know what the farmers have to put up with, but it's not because of them that I accept. It's because of you. KANBEI *grins and rubs his head. Music out.*

227. Wipe to medium shot of the entrance to the inn from the inside. Smiling happily, KANBEI *approaches in the street outside.*

228. Medium long shot of KATSUSHIRO *standing by the windows as* KANBEI *comes in through the door. He is followed by his old friend* SHICHIROJI, *who is carrying a yoke on his shoulders. He puts it on the floor as* KANBEI *speaks.*

KANBEI : But this is wonderful. It is so good to find you alive. I'd given you up for lost. How did you get away?

KANBEI *goes out of shot and* SHICHIROJI *prepares to sit down, taking off his hat.*

229. Medium shot of KANBEI *sitting down and* SHICHIROJI *in the foreground, also seated.*

SHICHIROJI : Well, I lay right down in the ditch there, in the water. But when the castle finally burned down and then almost fell on me, I thought I was gone. *He wipes his chest with a cloth.*

KANBEI : How did you feel?

SHICHIROJI : Oh, not too bad.

KANBEI : Are you ready for another fight?

230. Close-up of SHICHIROJI, *with* KATSUSHIRO *standing in the background.* SHICHIROJI *smiles. Music in.*

231. Medium shot of KANBEI *and* SHICHIROJI *(as 229). They smile at each other understandingly.*

232. Wipe to low angle medium close-up of GOROBEI *in the street, rubbing his chin. Tilt down slightly as he turns and walks towards a roadside food stall with seats, and the* STALL

KEEPER *preparing food.*

233. Medium shot from behind of GOROBEI *sitting down in the stall, watching the crowds of people going past in the street. The* STALL KEEPER *comes into shot and presents him with a tray. He takes a bowl from it and the* STALL KEEPER *leaves the tray on the seat beside him. Track back slightly as they speak. Music out.*

GOROBEI : I never knew they were so few.

STALL KEEPER : What is it you're after, sir?

GOROBEI : Samurai.

STALL KEEPER : Samurai?

GOROBEI : Yes.

STALL KEEPER : Well, there's one at the back of my house, though I don't think he's a very good one. He kept asking me to give him something to eat. Then he said he'd cut my firewood for me because he had no money. *They both laugh.*

There is a yell, then the sound of wood being chopped, off. The STALL KEEPER *goes out into the road.*

234. Low angle medium close-up of the STALL KEEPER *looking towards the sound of chopping.*

STALL KEEPER : Still, he seems honest enough.

Pan slightly right as GOROBEI *appears and stands in front of the* STALL KEEPER, *looking in the same direction. The* STALL KEEPER *goes off.*

235. Medium shot of a huge pile of logs. Every now and again there is a shout and the noise of an axe on wood. GOROBEI's *head appears over the pile of logs and camera tracks back as he walks round and over the heap, and stands looking down. Track continues to include a* SAMURAI *chopping wood. At every downward stroke he gives a bloodcurdling yell. His sword lies on the grass beside him. Hold on medium shot of him with* GOROBEI *in the background. (Still on page 36) The* SAMURAI, HEIHACHI, *looks back to where* GOROBEI *is standing watching him, and then continues. Grinning,* GOROBEI *sits down on the logs to watch. Without a word,* HEIHACHI *picks up his sword, and moves it away to his other side, a safe distance from* GOROBEI. *Music in.* HEIHACHI *is about to split another log when he turns away to face* GOROBEI.

HEIHACHI : Haven't you ever seen anyone cut firewood before?

GOROBEI : You seem to enjoy it.

HEIHACHI : That's just the way I am. Yah! *He chops another log.*

GOROBEI *laughing* : You're good!

236. High angle medium shot of HEIHACHI, *with* GOROBEI's *head and shoulders in back view in the foreground.*

HEIHACHI : Not really. It's a lot harder than killing enemies. Yah! *He splits another log.*

237. Low angle medium close-up of GOROBEI *leaning forward and grinning.*

GOROBEI : Have you killed many?

238. High angle medium shot of HEIHACHI *in back view, preparing to chop another log, with* GOROBEI *back to camera in the foreground.* HEIHACHI *turns towards him slightly.*

HEIHACHI : Since it's impossible to kill them all — yah! *He splits another log and then turns back to* GOROBEI *again* — I usually run away.

239. Low angle medium close-up of GOROBEI.

GOROBEI *grinning* : A splendid principle.

240. High angle medium shot of them both (as 238).

HEIHACHI : Thank you. Yah! *He chops a log and sets up the next, raising his axe and preparing to strike.*

GOROBEI : Incidentally — are you interested in killing twenty or thirty bandits?

HEIHACHI *misses the log completely and turns round in surprise. 241. Wipe to medium shot of* KANBEI *and* KATSUSHIRO *walking towards camera in the town square. Music out. They come into the foreground and go off. 242. Medium long shot of* KANBEI *and* KATSUSHIRO *in the street looking at a group of people who have gathered to watch something. 243. High angle long shot, over the heads of the group of people, of two samurai in the grounds of a temple, preparing to start a practice bout with long bamboo staffs.* KANBEI *and* KATSUSHIRO *appear in the foreground, backs to camera, and also stand and watch. 244. Medium shot of the two samurai, cutting bamboo shoots off their staffs. The taller of the two lays down his sword.*

TALL SAMURAI : Let's begin.

The second SAMURAI, KYUZO, *also lays down his sword as the*

TALL SAMURAI *comes forward into low angle medium close-up. He circles round.*

245. *Long shot of the two* SAMURAI *with the crowd watching; other people are running along the road on the other side of the temple wall to join them. Pan right to left as the* TALL SAMURAI *backs off and* KYUZO *comes forward. The crowd press round an opening in the temple wall with* KANBEI *and* KATSUSHIRO *in their midst, all watching. Hold as the* TALL SAMURAI *raises his staff, then slowly* KYUZO *also raises his staff and they both pause, at the ready.*

246. *Medium close-up of* KANBEI *and* KATSUSHIRO *with other men behind looking over their shoulders.* KANBEI *and* KATSUS-HIRO *take a few paces forward. Other people can be seen pushing forward in the background to get a better view.*

247. *Medium shot of the* TALL SAMURAI *holding his staff, one knee bent.*

248. *Medium close-up of* KANBEI *and* KATSUSHIRO *looking left. They turn their heads slightly and look right.*

249. *Medium shot of* KYUZO, *with one knee bent.*

250. *Medium close-up of* KANBEI *and* KATSUSHIRO. *Their eyes move from right to left.*

251. *Medium shot of the* TALL SAMURAI *flexing his muscles. He raises his staff over his head and yells.*

252. *Medium close-up of* KANBEI *and* KATSUSHIRO *(as 250).*

253. *Medium close-up of* KYUZO. *He steps back and holds his staff back at the ready.*

254. *Medium close-up of* KANBEI *and* KATSUSHIRO.

255. *Medium shot of the* TALL SAMURAI *edging forward, with his staff above his head.*

256. *Quick medium shot of* KYUZO *ready to take the blow.*

257. *Medium shot of the* TALL SAMURAI *(as 255).*

258. *Medium close-up of* KANBEI *and* KATSUSHIRO. *There is a sustained yell, off.*

259. *Medium long shot of the two* SAMURAI. *The tall one rushes towards* KYUZO, *yelling, watched by the crowd in the background. Pan right with him and hold as he strikes* KYUZO; KYUZO *parries the blow and they remain motionless for a moment, staffs locked.*

260. *Medium shot of the two* SAMURAI *locked together,* KYUZO

in back view. (Still on page 36) They step back slightly and the Tall Samurai *strikes* Kyuzo's *staff in a gesture of triumph.* Kyuzo *steps back, and walks out of shot.*

Tall Samurai : Too bad — a tie.

261. Medium shot of Kyuzo *standing impassively.*

Kyuzo : No.

262. Close-up of the Tall Samurai: *he grins and then stares in amazement.*

263. Close-up of Kyuzo.

Kyuzo : I won.

264. Close-up of the Tall Samurai, *incredulous.*

265. Close-up of Kyuzo *moving away; pan right with him.*

266. Close-up of the Tall Samurai *looking at him angrily.*

Tall Samurai : That's preposterous !

267. Low angle medium shot of the two Samurai, *backs to camera.* Kyuzo *walks away watched by the other man. He stops and turns back. (Still on page 36)*

Kyuzo : If it had been a real sword you would have been dead.

Then he walks on. The Tall Samurai, *furious, throws down his staff and strides after him.*

268. Medium long shot of the two Samurai *approaching the temple steps where they left their swords. The* Tall Samurai *grabs his sword. The crowd begins to move forward in the background.*

Tall Samurai : Well all right then. Let's use swords.

Kyuzo : There is no need.

Tall Samurai : What?

Kyuzo : If I use a sword I'll kill you. It's stupid.

Enraged, the Tall Samurai *runs across into the open space, camera tracking left with him. Hold on two men facing each other. The crowd presses forward in the background. The* Tall Samurai *draws his sword defiantly.*

Tall Samurai : Hey ! Don't you run away. Draw !

The crowd stops in its tracks. Kyuzo *stands motionless for a moment, then slowly drops his hat on the grass and draws his sword, coming forward slightly.*

269. High angle medium shot of the crowd backing hurriedly out through the opening into the road again.

270. Medium shot of the Tall Samurai, *back to camera in the*

foreground, with KYUZO *facing him, and* KANBEI *and* KATSU-
SHIRO *visible in the background. All the rest of the crowd have
now retreated.* KYUZO *and the* TALL SAMURAI *start to circle
round each other.*

*271. High angle medium long shot of the crowd behind the
wall, pressing forward again. A bird sings, off.*

*272. Medium long shot of the two samurai holding out their
swords,* KYUZO *facing, and the other* SAMURAI *still back to
camera, with the crowd in the background. The* TALL
SAMURAI *runs backwards holding his sword above his head,
ready to charge; pan right with him and then hold. He yells.*

273. Medium shot of KANBEI *and* KATSUSHIRO *watching
intently with the crowd a little way behind them.*

KANBEI : How senseless. It's obvious what will happen.

274. Medium long shot of the two men, KYUZO *on the left still
holding his sword out in front of him, the* TALL SAMURAI *on
the right holding his sword above his head, and the crowd in
the background.* KYUZO *takes one step forward, the other
takes one step back. Then* KYUZO *steps back and holds his
sword back at the ready, as he did with his staff in the previous
fight.*

275. Medium long shot of KANBEI *and* KATSUSHIRO *standing
tensely, with the crowd motionless behind them. The* TALL
SAMURAI *begins to yell.*

276. Medium shot panning left to right with the TALL SAMURAI
*as he bounds forward yelling. (Production still on page 36)
Hold as he reaches* KYUZO *who swiftly brings his sword up
and round onto the other's neck. The* TALL SAMURAI *stops
dead in his tracks.*

277. Medium close-up of KANBEI *and* KATSUSHIRO *taking a
step forward. The crowd shifts behind them.*

*278. Medium shot of the two swordsmen; they stand absolutely
still for a moment (Still on page 36) — then the* TALL
SAMURAI *sinks to the ground in slow motion. (Still on page 36)*

279. Medium close-up of KANBEI *and* KATSUSHIRO. KANBEI
does not look surprised at the outcome but KATSUSHIRO *is
obviously overwhelmed.*

280. Close-up of KATSUSHIRO *dumbfounded.*

281. Wipe to a general shot of the street. The samurai theme comes in, low. KANBEI *and* KATSUSHIRO *are walking along. Camera pans slightly right as they walk, picking up* GOROBEI *who comes up and joins them.*

GOROBEI : Have any luck?

KANBEI *looking at* KATSUSHIRO : Missed one — a fine swordsman.

GOROBEI *laughing* : The fish that gets away always looks big.

KANBEI *seriously* : No. I watched him kill a man. *An excited crowd rushes along the street in the opposite direction having obviously heard about the fight.* Yet he's not interested in killing, only in perfecting his skill. Sure enough, he refused.

GOROBEI : That's too bad.

They move towards the inn, camera panning with them.

KANBEI : I told him where to find me though. *Music out.*

282. Wipe to close-up of KYUZO *at the door of the inn. It is night.*

GOROBEI *off* : So now we'll need two more.

HEIHACHI *off* : Just one more, I think.

KANBEI *off* : What? Oh!

283. Medium close-up of KANBEI *standing up, smiling delightedly. Pan right with him as he goes across to the door of the inn where* KYUZO *is standing. (Still on page 36) Samurai theme in.*

KANBEI : You've consented to come. Thank you very much.

KYUZO : When do we leave?

KANBEI : Tomorrow.

284. High angle medium shot of HEIHACHI, GOROBEI *and* SHICHIROJI *sitting together. They look at each other in surprise. Tilt up with* HEIHACHI *as he stands up.*

HEIHACHI : Tomorrow?

285. Medium shot of KANBEI *and* KYUZO. KANBEI *turns with a smile.*

KANBEI : That's right. Let's forget about the seventh. We have no time to lose.

KANBEI goes off, and KYUZO *moves forward.*

286. Medium long shot of the samurai sitting and standing in relaxed positions in the inn. A figure can be seen running past the window outside.

287. Close-up of KATSUSHIRO *grinning happily.*

288. Medium shot of KYUZO *sitting on a bench behind one of*

the wooden partitions, undoing his shoe straps. Behind is the
dark doorway looking onto the street. Music out. One of the
labourers runs in, shouting for attention, camera tracking with
him, till he faces the samurai, seen between SHICHIROJI, *in back*
view in the foreground, and KANBEI. *They look at the*
LABOURER.

289. Close-up of the LABOURER.

LABOURER *excited*: I've found a really tough samurai. We had
this big fight with him and he really beat us up. I've never seen
anyone as tough as he is. Like a wild dog. We drank together afterwards and became friends though. I asked him. He's coming.

290. Medium shot of the group of samurai with the LABOURER
in back view in the foreground. They look at each other.

291. Close-up of KANBEI *in the foreground with* KATSUSHIRO
in medium close-up behind him.

KATSUSHIRO *grinning*: Shall I do it again?

KANBEI *turns his head to look at* KATSUSHIRO. *He looks away*
again and rubs his head, smiling.

292. High angle close-up of KATSUSHIRO's *hand grabbing his*
stick.

293. Medium close-up of KATSUSHIRO *from the side. Pan*
right with him as he moves forward.

294. Medium shot of the LABOURER, *dumbfounded; pan as he*
runs over to KATSUSHIRO. *Hold with the* LABOURER *by the*
open door and KATSUSHIRO *in his usual position, hiding behind*
the doorpost.

LABOURER : What are you doing?

KATSUSHIRO *raises the stick above his head.*

295. Low angle medium shot, through the bars of the partition,
of KANBEI *and the other samurai sitting down in a group. The*
LABOURER *rushes forward and points at* KANBEI.

LABOURER : That's not fair. Look . . .

KANBEI : Just watch. If he's really such a strong samurai he'll dodge
easily enough.

LABOURER : But he's drunk !

KANBEI : A strong samurai would never get so drunk.

Pan left to right as the LABOURER *runs back and crouches down*
by the window. Sound of confused shouting outside. Hold on
the dark doorway, including KATSUSHIRO *back to camera*

68

with his stick raised. The other two labourers appear outside the door with KIKUCHIYO.

SECOND LABOURER: Here it is. No, no. Here. Look where you're going. Come on, this way.

KIKUCHIYO *staggering and shouting*: What, what? Where?

KATSUSHIRO *lunges forward with a yell.*

296. Close-up of the FIRST LABOURER, *horrified. A sickening thump, off. He swallows nervously.*

297. Medium shot, with the partition in the foreground, of KATSUSHIRO *looking down in horror as* KIKUCHIYO *slumps to the floor at his feet. The two other labourers watch amazed in the doorway.* KIKUCHIYO *bends double on his knees, clutching his head.*

298. Close-up of the SECOND LABOURER *staring in amazement.*

299. Close-up of the FIRST LABOURER. *His mouth has dropped open and his eyes are popping as he stares at* KIKUCHIYO.

300. Low angle medium shot of KIKUCHIYO *in the foreground, holding his head and whimpering. The* FIRST LABOURER *rushes forward and kneels beside him, putting an arm round his shoulders. (Still on page 37)*

FIRST LABOURER: That wasn't fair at all.

KIKUCHIYO *pushes the* LABOURER *away roughly and he falls to the ground out of sight.*

301. Medium close-up of KIKUCHIYO *sitting up, with* KATSU-SHIRO *just visible in the background. Pan slightly to reveal* KATSUSHIRO *in full, staring down at* KIKUCHIYO *who is swaying drunkenly.* KIKUCHIYO *leans forward, coming in to close-up.*

KIKUCHIYO: Which one of you hit me like that? *A pause.*

302. Close-up of KANBEI *laughing, with* HEIHACHI *and* SHICHIROJI *behind him, also laughing. (Still on page 37)* KANBEI *suddenly stops laughing and looks closely at* KIKUCHIYO, *who is out of shot. He has recognised him.*

303. Close-up of KIKUCHIYO *with an evil expression on his face. (Still on page 37) He leans back. Pan slightly as* KATSUSHIRO *comes up and bends over him worriedly. He has also recognised* KIKUCHIYO. *Grunting furiously,* KIKUCHIYO *pulls himself to his feet.*

304. Low angle medium close-up of KATSUSHIRO, *three-quarters back to camera, seen between the wooden bars of the partition. In the background* KIKUCHIYO *has got to his feet. Fast pan to the left as he lunges towards* KATSUSHIRO, *who dodges out of the way. Hold on* KATSUSHIRO *and* KIKUCHIYO, *seen over the partition. In the background one of the labourers stands watching.* KIKUCHIYO *sways and grins nastily as* KATSUSHIRO *dodges away again. Infuriated,* KIKUCHIYO *staggers round after him supporting himself on the partition, camera panning with him. He drops down in a stupor, camera tilting down with him, one arm dangling over the lower bar of the partition. The other samurai can be seen through the partition in the background.* KIKUCHIYO, *in back view, heaves slightly, looks up and then points towards* KANBEI. *Pan slightly further to include all the other samurai.* KIKUCHIYO *begins to crawl towards them.*

305. Medium close-up of KANBEI, *back to camera, with* KIKUCHIYO *facing him on all fours. He pulls himself closer and stares at* KANBEI *from under beetling brows.*

KIKUCHIYO : Oh, it's you, is it? *He runs his hand over* KANBEI'S *shaved head.* I remember your head. You had the nerve to ask me if I was a samurai. Didn't you? I never forget a face. Look, I'm a real samurai, all right.

306. Medium shot of GOROBEI, HEIHACHI *and* SHICHIROJI *laughing uncontrollably.*

307. Medium shot of KIKUCHIYO *leaning back against the partition.*

KIKUCHIYO : Here. I'm going to show you something. Just look at this.

He stands up and backs away, camera tilting up slightly. He turns round and drunkenly fumbles inside his clothing to find something that is concealed there. He turns back, holding out a scroll. (Still on page 37)

KIKUCHIYO : There, just you look at this. It's been handed down in my family for generations and generations. And you asked me if I were a samurai! Look at this, just look at this!

He lurches towards camera, but trips on his sword and falls back against the partition.

308. Medium shot of the group of samurai. KIKUCHIYO *staggers across in the foreground and slumps down next to* KANBEI, *throwing down his sword as he does so. He unrolls the long scroll.* KANBEI *picks it up and looks at the part that* KIKUCHIYO *has indicated. The others lean forward.*

KANBEI : I see. And so this Kikuchiyo is you?

KIKUCHIYO : That's right.

KANBEI : You were born, let's see . . . on February 17th, the Second Year of Tensho. *He begins to roar with laughter.*

KIKUCHIYO : What's so funny?

KANBEI : You don't look thirteen.

KIKUCHIYO *suspiciously* : What's that?

KANBEI : Where did you steal this scroll?

KIKUCHIYO : What? Stole it? Now, look here, just who do you think you are?

HEIHACHI : Just thirteen, eh?

KIKUCHIYO : You just shut your mouth, you there.

KIKUCHIYO *grunts and sways even though he is sitting down.* KYUZO, *who is sitting opposite him, watches him carefully. He picks up his own sword and puts it out of sight.* KIKUCHIYO *lunges towards his sword; rapid pan as* KYUZO *swiftly grabs it and passes it back to* KATSUSHIRO, *who is standing by the partition behind him.* KATSUSHIRO *takes the sword and dashes off, camera panning quickly with him. Hold as he darts round between the partitions and out of sight.*

309. High angle medium shot of KATSUSHIRO *running between the wooden uprights of the stable in the inn.* KIKUCHIYO *dashes up in the background, shouting, but* KATSUSHIRO *dodges out of the way, camera tracking left with him.* KIKUCHIYO *charges forward and leans against the partition as* KATSUSHIRO *appears in the foreground, holding up the sword.* KIKUCHIYO *grabs a stick that is leaning against one of the posts and runs round to* KATSUSHIRO's *side of the partition, camera panning with him, but* KATSUSHIRO *dodges away.*

310. Low angle medium close-up of the two labourers still at the doorway, seen from outside. They get out of the way as KIKUCHIYO *runs past inside and camera pans right along the outside of the windows, following him. Hold on* KIKUCHIYO, *back to camera, on the other side of the bamboo slats. At that moment, he steps back, as* HEIHACHI *is seen taking the sword from* KATSUSHIRO, *and falls against the bamboo slats which collapse under his weight. He falls backwards into the street.*

(Still on page 37) He staggers to his feet again as HEIHACHI *approaches holding the sword.*

HEIHACHI : Steady, thirteen-year-old!

KIKUCHIYO *grabs hold of the bamboo bars.*

311. Close-up of KIKUCHIYO *through the bars. He holds onto them and shakes them violently.*

312. Medium shot of KIKUCHIYO *holding onto the bars.* HEIHACHI *stands inside watching him with the other samurai in the background. As* KIKUCHIYO *lunges forward and through the opening he has made in the wall,* HEIHACHI *dashes out of shot, followed by the infuriated* KIKUCHIYO. *Music in:* KIKUCHIYO'S *theme.*

313. Medium close-up, panning left to right with HEIHACHI *as he dashes past, still carrying* KIKUCHIYO'S *sword.*

314. Medium close-up of KIKUCHIYO *dashing past on the other side of the partition, camera moving with him.*

315. High angle medium shot of HEIHACHI *jumping down through an opening into the kitchen of the inn. He stands looking through the partition.*

316. Medium shot of KIKUCHIYO, *who has fallen over, grabbing a wooden tub which he hurls in the direction of* HEIHACHI. *He gets to his feet and plunges forward again, camera panning with him. Hold on the entrance to the kitchen;* HEIHACHI *dodges out. of sight and* KIKUCHIYO *staggers down into the kitchen area.* HEIHACHI *comes forward again and taps him on the shoulder, but* KIKUCHIYO *is so drunk he cannot catch him, and hangs on to a post to keep his balance, shouting.*

317. Medium close-up, panning right with HEIHACHI, *who is still rushing round and round the same part of the inn.*

318. Medium close-up, panning right with KIKUCHIYO, *who is stumbling along, hauling himself from post to post. He gets onto the wrong side of the partition, coming into the foreground, and dives towards* HEIHACHI *who is on the other side, but he is stopped by the wooden rails. Camera holds on him. He hurls himself back the other way, camera panning left with him.*

319. Low angle medium shot of HEIHACHI *looking over the partition.* KIKUCHIYO *appears in the foreground. He has almost had it. Pan slightly as* HEIHACHI *leans forward, and*

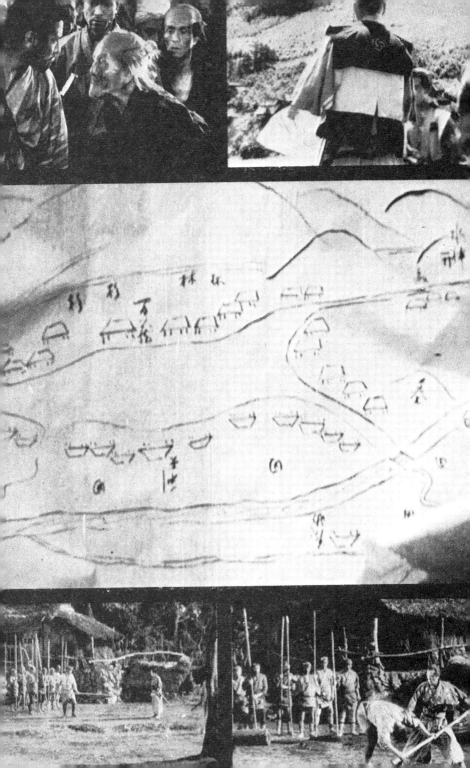

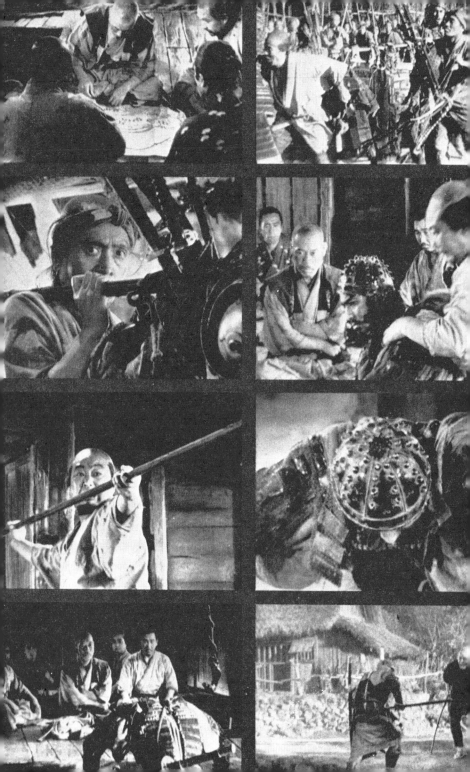

pats KIKUCHIYO *on the shoulder, over the partition.*

HEIHACHI : Brace up, Sir Kikuchiyo!

With a great roar, KIKUCHIYO *pulls himself up again, camera panning as* HEIHACHI *steps back prudently.*

320. Low angle medium close-up of KIKUCHIYO *stepping back from the partition. He leans back against a post, camera holding after a slight pan to the right.* HEIHACHI's *arm appears over the partition and taps him on the shoulder.*

HEIHACHI : Courage, thirteen!

KIKUCHIYO *makes another desperate lunge over the partition, camera panning slightly with him, but again* HEIHACHI *dodges out of the way. He tries to climb over, and camera pans further and tilts up to reveal* HEIHACHI, *laughing, on the other side of the partition with* KIKUCHIYO, *back to camera, in the foreground. He can hold on no longer and loses his grip, dropping down out of sight at the bottom of frame. Tilt down following his limp arm against the partition. Hold as he falls onto a bed of straw, muttering to himself.*

KIKUCHIYO : Blasted samurai!

321. Medium shot of HEIHACHI *looking over the partition and laughing. He steps forward and looks over.*

322. High angle medium close-up of KIKUCHIYO *who has fallen asleep in a drunken stupor on the straw. (Still on page 37) Music out as he begins to snore.**

323. Medium close-up of HEIHACHI *leaning over the wooden barrier, looking at* KIKUCHIYO, *who is out of shot. Pan left with him as he moves away, laughing loudly. Pan further and hold as he joins the others who have come up on the other side of the partition. They all laugh with* HEIHACHI.

KATSUSHIRO : Do you think he's a real samurai?

KANBEI : Well, he thinks he is.

As they all turn away, laughing, and go back to the main room of the inn, the FIRST LABOURER *comes up from the shadows in the foreground and stares over the partition towards* KIKUCHIYO, *puzzled and dismayed.* KIKUCHIYO *snores, off.*

324. Wipe to a low angle shot of the dawn sky, looking up over the roof of the inn. A cock crows. Music in.

---

* End of reel 2.

325. *Medium shot of the samurai inside the inn, getting ready to leave.* KANBEI *is in the foreground, fastening his cloak, and the others are busy behind him fixing their clothes or weapons. (Still on page 37) They all get up and file out to the left until only* HEIHACHI *remains. Pan with him as he bends down and picks up* KIKUCHIYO's *scroll. Swift circular pan and tilt up as* HEIHACHI *goes round the wooden partition carrying the scroll.*

HEIHACHI : Hey, Kikuchiyo!

Camera tilts down as he tosses the scroll over the bar and it unrolls on both sides.

HEIHACHI : Take good care of this.

Quick track in towards the lower bars of the partition to reveal KIKUCHIYO *behind them, sitting up. He grabs the scroll, tearing it in half. Track in closer as he kneels up, and stares between the bars in the direction of* HEIHACHI. *(Still on page 37)*

KIKUCHIYO *desperately*: Wait! Take me with you! *He shakes the wooden bars angrily, and grits his teeth as he glares after* HEIHACHI.

326. *Long shot of the samurai coming towards camera in the deserted town square. In the foreground,* RIKICHI *and* YOHEI *are waiting for them, seen from behind. As the six samurai walk towards them, the two farmers turn towards camera and walk forward, both smiling happily. They go off in the foreground and camera holds on the samurai following them.*

327. *Very high angle long shot of the farmers' village from the top of the hill. Nothing moves.*

328. *Medium shot of the entrance of a house, looking through the doorway. Inside, a* YOUNG GIRL *is kneeling down, back to camera, her head bent forward.*

329. *Medium shot of the* GIRL, *back to camera. She is washing her long hair in a small stream which runs through the back of the house. Suddenly she turns her head and looks round towards camera. It is* SHINO. *Music out.*

330. *Low angle medium close-up of* SHINO *looking away from camera, still kneeling on the floor.* MANZO, *her father, stands at the threshold, silhouetted against the light.*

331. *High angle medium close-up of* SHINO *looking up over her shoulder. (Still on page 38)*

SHINO : What's the matter?

She turns away to continue washing her hair. A pause. She looks round again.

332. Low angle medium shot of MANZO *looking down at her fearfully. He takes a few paces forward.*

333. High angle medium close-up of SHINO *(as 331). Tilt up with her as she stands up and turns to face camera. Her wet hair hangs down over her shoulder.*

SHINO : Why are you looking at me like that?

334. Medium long shot of SHINO, *back to camera, with* MANZO *facing her, still standing in the doorway. He takes a step towards her.*

335. Low angle medium close-up of MANZO, *staring at* SHINO, *out of shot. He takes a cut-throat razor out from inside his robe.*

MANZO : Shino. You must cut your hair.

336. Low angle medium close-up of SHINO. *She looks at* MANZO *nervously and instinctively puts a hand up to her hair.*

337. Resume on MANZO *(as 335).*

MANZO : So you can look like a boy.

338. Medium close-up of SHINO *(as 336). She looks down at her long wet hair and holds it protectively against her head.*

SHINO *frightened* : But why?

339. Resume on MANZO *(as 335).*

MANZO : It's for your own good.

340. Medium long shot, through the thin wall of the house, of MANZO *striding towards* SHINO. SHINO *backs away.*

MANZO *shouting* : Samurai are coming here! They are dangerous! *Fast track along the outside wall as* SHINO *runs backwards, still holding onto her hair, pursued by* MANZO *brandishing the razor.*

SHINO *screaming* : No, please!

MANZO *shouting* : I'll cut it myself.

She runs away through the house and camera tracks back along the outside wall again as MANZO *chases after her. They are just visible through the wall. Hold beside the entrance as* SHINO *rushes out, closely followed by* MANZO. *Tilt down and pan as she runs across to a nearby house.* MANZO *almost catches her but she manages to get away and camera pans right with them as she runs back into the middle of the village square, followed by* MANZO. *She ducks under a wooden rail and then trips. (Still on page 38)*

341. High angle medium close-up of SHINO *as she falls face down on the ground, raising a cloud of dust. Pan slightly as* MANZO *comes up and grabs her. She tries to get away, screaming, her wet hair flying about her shoulders. Tilt up as he tries to drag her off, screaming and crying, as* MOSUKE *and another* FARMER *are revealed coming towards camera behind them. Other villagers have gathered to watch in the background.* MANZO *manages to drag* SHINO *away, going off in the foreground. Hold on the watching villagers.*

342. Wipe to a medium shot of the entrance to MANZO'S *house from inside.* MOSUKE *ducks under the low doorway and comes in. Pan with him as he runs over and stops in three-quarter back view, looking at* MANZO, *who is revealed sitting cross-legged on the floor in the middle of the room. In the background,* SHINO *is lying face down, sobbing.*

343. Medium shot of SHINO *lying on a low bed, crying bitterly. Branches of blossom can be seen through the open window behind her.*

344. High angle close-up of SHINO *sobbing. Her hair has been cut short.*

345. Medium shot of MOSUKE *still standing, in three-quarter back view, with* MANZO *seated in front of him.*

MOSUKE : You really are a fool.

Pan slightly right as MOSUKE *sits down in front of* MANZO.

MOSUKE : Now you've got the whole village in an uproar. All the girls are terrified. What are we to do? Those samurai are coming any day now. *He gets up and faces* MANZO, *who does not move.* We'll go and see old Gisaku.

Pan left with MOSUKE, *now back to camera, as he rushes back to the doorway, where a crowd of onlookers has gathered. Track in and hold on* MOSUKE, *in back view, with the crowd in the background.*

MOSUKE *waving his arms* : It's nothing, go on home. *They do not move.*

Pan left with him as he runs towards camera to a barred window high in the wall, where another group are looking in from outside. He looks through at them, still in back view.

MOSUKE : Go away!

He turns back towards MANZO, *who is out of shot, and moves away. Hold on the crowd, still looking anxiously through the window.*

MOSUKE *off* : Well, if we're going to do something we should do it before the samurai get here.

346. High angle medium shot of the samurai, led by RIKICHI *and* YOHEI, *striding towards camera along a country road, with hills in the background. Samurai theme in — horns. On the crest of the hill behind them,* KIKUCHIYO *can be seen following. They all stop and look round towards him. He also stops.*

HEIHACHI : Still following us!

In the background KIKUCHIYO *begins to pace across the track. Music changes to* KIKUCHIYO's *theme on the cut.*

347. Low angle medium long shot of KIKUCHIYO *standing on the brow of the hill, silhouetted against the sky, with his sword balanced on one shoulder. He is looking towards the others. He turns round, and then crouches down on the verge, still looking towards them.*

348. High angle medium shot of the samurai and the two farmers, all in back view, looking back up the road towards KIKUCHIYO. HEIHACHI *picks up a stone and pretends to throw it.* KIKUCHIYO *stands up again in the background. As he does so, they all laugh and then turn back towards camera, walking out of shot at the bottom of frame. Hold on* KIKUCHIYO, *who starts to follow them — cautiously at first, then striding quickly forwards.*

349. Wipe to low angle long shot of the samurai, silhouetted against the sky. They are seated on some rocks at the top of a roaring waterfall, eating their midday meal. (Still on page 39) Music louder. HEIHACHI, *who is sitting on the rock nearest the water, stands up and points towards the bottom of the fall, which is out of shot.* KATSUSHIRO *stands up as well and the others look at* HEIHACHI.

350. Low angle long shot looking towards the waterfall. In the background the samurai can be seen sitting on the rocks at the top. In the foreground, KIKUCHIYO *appears from the bottom of frame as he stands up. Occasionally glancing up at the watching samurai, he takes off his robe and stands wearing only a loin cloth. Tilt down and pan left to right as he throws down his robe and turns away, picking his way through boulders to the stream. Smoke from a small fire blows across. The waterfall roars down in the background. Hold on him standing legs apart, bending down with his hands on his knees in the middle of the stream. He studies the water closely, then walks forward, the water swirling round his knees.*

351. Low angle medium long shot of the samurai sitting or standing on the rocks by the waterfall, looking down.

352. Medium shot of KIKUCHIYO, *in three-quarter back view, thigh-deep in the racing stream. He bends down, peering at the murky water. He turns away, and very carefully bends down towards an outcrop of rock on the other side of the stream. Very slowly, he lowers himself into the water until he is almost submerged. A pause. Then suddenly he leaps up, with a gleeful shout, holding a fish. Pan right with him as he leaps through the stream, then turns towards camera, coming up onto the nearer bank again, smiling broadly. Hold on him as he turns and looks up at the samurai, waving the fish. Laughing, he crouches down on his haunches, camera tilting down with him. He fixes the fish on the end of a twig; pan slightly right to reveal the small fire. Satisfied, he begins to toast the fish, blowing up the flames as he does so. (Still on page 39)*

353. Wipe to a medium shot of the samurai, backs to camera, walking through a forest. Music softer. Sunlight streams through the branches of tall trees on either side of the track. Camera tracks behind them as they walk along. Then HEIHACHI, *at the back of the group and nearest camera, turns round and walks backwards a couple of steps before stopping.*

HEIHACHI : He doesn't seem to be coming.

All the others stop and turn round, looking back the way they have just come. GOROBEI *comes forward and stands by* HEIHACHI, *smiling.*

GOROBEI : Finally gave up, did he?

HEIHACHI : Funny though, he followed us all this time, now I sort of . . . miss him !

They all laugh, then turn back to continue up the sloping path.

Suddenly, with a yell, KIKUCHIYO *jumps down from a high bank on the left, landing on the path ahead of them. Music louder. With a high-pitched giggle he points up the path through the trees and shouts down at them.*

KIKUCHIYO : This way, this way!

Laughing, he turns and strides on up the path, going out of sight. The samurai in the foreground look at one another, laughing in amazement, then turn to follow him. Music changes to a quiet tune on a wipe to the next shot.

354. Wipe to a high angle very long shot looking down onto the village, with the brow of the hill in the foreground. RIKICHI *runs in from the bottom of frame and stops on the edge of the steep slope, back to camera, as* YOHEI *follows with the samurai.* RIKICHI *points excitedly down at the village.*

355. Low angle medium shot of KANBEI, *furthest from camera, with* HEIHACHI, GOROBEI *and* SHICHIROJI *nearest camera, all in profile. Track with them as they stride down the slope, picking up* RIKICHI *and* YOHEI *in the background. They all stop and look down into the valley. Track on slightly as* KIKUCHIYO *passes them all in the foreground and stands insolently in front of* HEIHACHI, *also looking down.*

HEIHACHI : So that's our castle, is it?

KIKUCHIYO : I'd hate to die in a dung heap like that.

HEIHACHI *looking down at him* : Nobody asked you to help.

KIKUCHIYO *looks up at* HEIHACHI *as* RIKICHI *runs further down the slope in the background, camera panning left with him, losing the others.* RIKICHI *stops on the edge of the steep drop. He shouts and waves his hat, and the pan continues across the hillside until the village is revealed below. (Still on page 40) Music out. As* RIKICHI'S *voice echoes round the valley, the few people who are visible in the village square disappear rapidly into the houses.*

356. Wipe to medium long shot of the samurai with RIKICHI *and* YOHEI *standing in the village square, looking round. It is late afternoon. The square is completely deserted.* RIKICHI *runs forward, dropping his hat, shouting again.* YOHEI *follows him.*

RIKICHI : I'm back! I brought the gentlemen with me.

Pan left with RIKICHI *as he runs across to the houses on the far side of the square, followed by* YOHEI. *The samurai watch him in the background.*

RIKICHI : The samurai are here!

Pan right as he runs back past the samurai, stopping to shout desperately.

RIKICHI : What's the matter? Come out!

Pan left as he runs back to the samurai.

357. Medium shot of RIKICHI *from the side, shouting through cupped hands, watched by* KATSUSHIRO, GOROBEI, HEIHACHI *and* KYUZO *on one side, and* KIKUCHIYO, *who is sitting up on a wooden railing on the other side. (Still on page 40) He laughs as there is no response to* RIKICHI'S *shouts.* RIKICHI *runs forward again, camera panning with him as he goes and stands on some raised ground in front of* KIKUCHIYO. YOHEI *comes running up to him anxiously. Then* SHICHIROJI *and* KANBEI *appear in back view in the foreground. A noise off makes them all turn towards camera.*

358. Medium shot of the door of a house, partly obscured behind a straw fence. The door opens slightly and two faces peer out through the crack. Then the door closes again quickly.

359. Medium shot of KANBEI *and* SHICHIROJI *still looking over their shoulders towards camera, with* RIKICHI *and* YOHEI *facing camera standing up on the mound. In the background stand* HEIHACHI *and* KYUZO, *with* KIKUCHIYO *still sitting on the fence. Then* KATSUSHIRO *and* GOROBEI *move forward. They all look up towards* RIKICHI. HEIHACHI *goes up onto the mound and stands beside him, looking round the deserted village.*

RIKICHI *embarrassed* : I don't know what's happened.

HEIHACHI : A real welcome, I'd say.

KIKUCHIYO *laughs again.* KANBEI, *still standing in the foreground, addresses* RIKICHI.

KANBEI : What does this mean? RIKICHI *spins round desperately.*

360. High angle medium shot of RIKICHI *shouting through cupped hands, and* YOHEI *next to him looking frightened. In the foreground,* KIKUCHIYO *sits perched on the fence in three-quarter back view.*

RIKICHI : Come out. What's the matter with you? Welcome your guests! *(Still on page 40)*

KIKUCHIYO *laughs heartily, pointing at* RIKICHI. *In the back-*

ground MOSUKE *is running towards camera.* RIKICHI *sees him and runs off towards him.*

361. Medium long shot of RIKICHI *with* MOSUKE *at the edge of the deserted square. They confer and then run back.*

362. Medium shot of RIKICHI, *panning left with him as he races up to where the samurai are still standing. Hold on the whole group except* KANBEI *and* KATSUSHIRO, *then pan slightly further to include the latter.* MOSUKE *joins them.*

RIKICHI : Well . . . let's go and see old Gisaku.

KANBEI : Gisaku ?

MOSUKE : He makes all our decisions for us.

HEIHACHI : The village patriach ?

RIKICHI *and* MOSUKE : Yes sir, yes.

HEIHACHI *ironically* : So we're to have an audience. What an honour.

    KIKUCHIYO *guffaws again.*

RIKICHI : Shall we go ?

Pan slightly right as they all follow RIKICHI *and* MOSUKE. *Laughing,* KIKUCHIYO *remains sitting on the fence then gets down and strides after them. He stops on the edge of the bank and yells after them, then mockingly scrapes his foot several times on the ground. (Still on page 40)*

363. Wipe to close-up of GISAKU *in the mill, his head bent and his eyes closed. (Still on page 40) The sound of the waterwheel can be heard throughout this sequence. He raises his head slightly and looks left. The low, humming chorus begins over as camera starts a circular track round him until* KANBEI *is included, in front view, with* GISAKU *in three-quarter back view in the foreground.* GOROBEI *and* HEIHACHI *stand in the background behind* KANBEI. *They look bored.*

364. Low angle medium close-up of GOROBEI *with* KYUZO *and* KATSUSHIRO *visible behind him, and in the background* YOHEI *and* RIKICHI, *with heads bent. Track back until* GISAKU *is revealed, three-quarters back to camera. They sit motionless, looking down or with arms folded. Then* GISAKU *turns his head towards camera and looks round.*

365. Medium shot of MOSUKE *and* MANZO *sitting in a corner with their hands on their knees. Track back to reveal* KANBEI *sitting cross-legged on one side, and* GISAKU *sitting opposite him. The two farmers can be seen between them, watching carefully in the background.* GISAKU *groans.*

GISAKU : They are just foolish, you see. *He looks up towards* KANBEI. They are farmers; they're afraid. Afraid of everything : rains, droughts, winds. They wake up afraid, they go to bed afraid. Today is no different.

366. Close-up of KANBEI *with* SHICHIROJI *and* HEIHACHI *behind him, seen over his shoulders.*

KANBEI : But why are they afraid of us? What do they think we'll do to them?

367. Big close-up of GISAKU. *He closes his eyes tightly. Suddenly the wooden alarm clapper sounds loudly off.* GISAKU *looks up, his eyes open wide with alarm.*

368. Close-up of YOHEI, *his mouth open, very frightened. He turns and rushes out of shot.*

369. Medium shot of YOHEI. *Pan with him as he rushes through the mill.*

370. High angle medium close-up of MOSUKE *and* MANZO *looking round nervously as the alarm clapper continues, off.*

371. Long shot focussed on part of the village square. As the alarm clapper sounds off, the villagers, screaming and yelling, rush out of their houses and congregate in the middle of the square. Pan left across the square as they gather together in panic.

372. Low angle medium long shot of the mill. Pan right as the samurai and the farmers run out of the mill doorway, led by KYUZO. *The samurai theme comes in, loud. Pan with them as they rush along the river bank.*

373. Medium close-up tracking with KYUZO *as he runs.*

374. Medium close-up tracking with HEIHACHI.

375. Medium close-up tracking with SHICHIROJI.

376. Quick medium close-up tracking with GOROBEI.

377. Quick medium close-up tracking with KANBEI.

378. Quick medium close-up tracking with KATSUSHIRO.

379. High angle long shot of the panicking villagers in the square.

380. Long shot of the samurai rushing across a small bridge with the paddy fields stretching out behind them and the hills rising up in the background.

90

YOHEI *shouting, off* : Help! The bandits! The bandits are coming. *The samurai, led by* KYUZO, *race towards camera and go off in the foreground followed by the farmers. Last to cross the bridge is* YOHEI *who pauses for a moment in medium long shot as the uproar continues off. Then he runs off in the foreground.*

381. Medium long shot tracking with KYUZO *and* HEIHACHI *as they dash towards the village square. Hold as they reach the crowd, who immediately surround them, shouting hysterically.* HEIHACHI *pushes his way through, shouting and waving his arms, trying to quieten them down. Pan further left as all the samurai push through and get up onto the raised ground, looking down on the villagers who jostle for position below them.*

HEIHACHI *shouting* : Shut up!

382. Medium close-up of KANBEI *with* SHICHIROJI *just behind him.*

KANBEI *fiercely* : Calm down now. Just calm down. Listen! *He begins to move towards the crowd.*

383. High angle medium shot, with KATSUSHIRO *in back view in the foreground and* HEIHACHI *beside him. Pan with* KANBEI *as he goes to the edge of the raised bank to address the crowd, who are gathered round facing camera in the background. Hold on* KANBEI *as he stops in back view, with* HEIHACHI *and* GOROBEI *behind him, facing camera.*

KANBEI : First, which direction are they coming from?

Pan with KANBEI *as he crosses from right to left, looking round as the crowd shifts and many conflicting voices answer him.*

VOICES : From the mountains . . . The main road . . . No, no, the mountains . . .

KANBEI *turns back to another part of the crowd.*

384. Medium close-up of KANBEI *continuing his movement until he faces camera with* GOROBEI *behind him. Pan right with him as he strides past* KATSUSHIRO, *shouting.*

KANBEI : Now, who saw them? Come on, step forward. Who saw them? No one? *Pan left as he paces back, still facing camera.* Then who rang the alarm?

KIKUCHIYO *off* : I did!

KANBEI, *startled, looks towards the voice. Behind him,* KATSU-

SHIRO *turns as well.*

385. Long shot of KIKUCHIYO *standing on a raised pathway in front of a house, seen over the heads of the crowd. The other samurai stand in back view on the left. They all look towards* KIKUCHIYO *who beats the wooden alarm clapper. Then he leaps down from the terrace and runs towards them, stopping in front of the crowd. He laughs at the crowd as they back off fearfully.*

386. Medium shot of KIKUCHIYO *surrounded by the crowd, with* RIKICHI *next to him. He laughs again and pulls faces at the crowd, which edges back further. Music changes to* KIKUCHIYO's *theme.*

KIKUCHIYO : Don't be scared! *He laughs again and strides backwards and forwards, camera panning with him so that he remains in the centre of the shot.* No bandits are coming! *He laughs, swings round, and then beats the top of the clapper again.* Look, you idiots. We come all this way and then look at the welcome you give us! Yet when I knock on your alarm a few times . . . *He turns towards camera, squinting and mimicking the hysterical villagers in a high-pitched voice.*

387. High angle medium shot of KIKUCHIYO *prancing up and down, surrounded by villagers. On the left, the six samurai look down at him from the bank.* KIKUCHIYO *rushes at the crowd and makes a final gesture of disgust.*

KIKUCHIYO : . . . You all rush out screaming for us to help you! Stupid!

388. High angle medium close-up of KIKUCHIYO *with some villagers behind him. He laughs derisively and bangs the clapper again, then turns and looks up towards the samurai. The villagers look at one another uncomfortably.*

389. Low angle medium shot of the samurai looking down at KIKUCHIYO *with* HEIHACHI, GOROBEI *and* KANBEI *in the foreground. They are all laughing.*

390. Medium shot of KIKUCHIYO, *in back view, prancing about proudly with villagers facing camera behind him. Some of them look towards the right.*

391. High angle medium shot of GISAKU *making his way through the crowd and looking up towards the samurai, who are out of shot. Pan with him as he shuffles along, leaning on a stick, until he reaches* KIKUCHIYO. KIKUCHIYO *bends over **him**, watched in amazement by* RIKICHI, *who is behind them. (Still on page 73)*

KIKUCHIYO : Have you any objections, old man?

GISAKU : No. Everything's all right.

KIKUCHIYO *nods emphatically and turns grinning towards the other samurai.*

392. Low angle medium close-up of GOROEEI *and* HEIHACHI, *who burst out laughing. Pan slightly right as* HEIHACHI *moves forward to stand beside* KANBEI, *with* KATSUSHIRO *and* SHICHIROJI *behind them.*

HEIHACHI : Well, I guess we're really seven now.

They all laugh. Fade out.

393. Fade in on high angle long shot looking down over the village with hills in the background. Music in. KANBEI *appears in the foreground holding a map, and stands back to camera as* KATSUSHIRO *and* GOROBEI *join him. (Still on page 73)*

394. High angle close-up of the map of the village. (Still on page 73)

KANBEI *off* : Well, if you were them, where would you attack?

GOROBEI'S *hand comes into shot and indicates the hills **marked** on the map. He withdraws his hand.*

GOROBEI *off* : I'd come down from the hills.

KANBEI'S *hand comes into shot and points at a road at the top of the plan.*

395. Big close-up of KANBEI'S *finger indicating the road.*

KANBEI *off* : I see. And you'd probably take this road.

His finger traces the road to the west.

*396. Long shot of a group of villagers carrying a huge tree trunk down a path towards camera. Another group of **men** follow with an equally huge log.* SHICHIROJI *is directing the operation. Pan slightly left as the first group dump their log on the grass by the path and collapse exhausted on the ground. The second group come along behind and let go of their log.*

397. High angle medium long shot of the men as the log hits the ground. SHICHIROJI *stands back to camera in the foreground, with the first group of men lying on the ground **in** front of him. The second group sink to the ground as well.* SHICHIROJI *strides about among them, instructing them.*

SHICHIROJI : All right now, remember. A war is mostly *run*. We run whether we are defending or attacking. If you can't run in a war then it's already over.

398. Big close-up of the southern section of the map.

399. Long shot of KANBEI, GOROBEI *and* KATSUSHIRO *coming towards camera through a field of ripening corn. A barn stands in the foreground to one side, and there are trees in the background silhouetted against the sky.*

400. High angle medium close-up of KANBEI *and* GOROBEI *in back view with* KATSUSHIRO *just beyond them, in three-quarter front view, with the corn behind them.* KANBEI *waves his hand over the corn.*

KANBEI : Right after the harvest we'll flood this section.

GOROBEI : I can see why, but will we have enough time, I wonder?

KANBEI : I wonder.

KANBEI *turns to walk away.*

401. Medium shot of KANBEI, *continuing his movement as he walks away, followed by* GOROBEI *and* KATSUSHIRO. *Pan slightly right as they go.*

402. Long shot of KYUZO *training a group of farmers who are all armed with bamboo spears.* MOSUKE *stands in front of the others facing* KYUZO *with his spear lowered, ready to attack. (Still on page 73)*

KYUZO : Well, spear me. Look, I'm a bandit.

As he speaks, KANBEI, GOROBEI *and* KATSUSHIRO *walk past.* KANBEI *and* GOROBEI *go off;* KATSUSHIRO, *without stopping, turns back to watch.*

403. Medium long shot of KANBEI *and* GOROBEI, *followed by* KATSUSHIRO, *going round behind a fence.* KANBEI *and* GOROBEI *go off, as* KATSUSHIRO *turns back again to look at* KYUZO.

404. Low angle medium long shot of KYUZO, *back to camera, with* MOSUKE *in front of him, spear lowered. The other men are lined up behind him, watching.* MOSUKE *makes an awkward lunge at* KYUZO, *but the samurai sends him flying. (Still on page 73)*

405. Medium close-up of KATSUSHIRO *watching admiringly.*

406. Medium long shot of KYUZO *with* MOSUKE *still lying on the grass at his feet. He tosses the spear away and turns back* to the line of men.

KYUZO : All right. Next.

407. Medium close-up of KATSUSHIRO. *He stands looking for a moment and then runs off.*

408. High angle big close-up of the eastern section of the map. KANBEI's *hand comes into shot and he points at a bridge.*

409. Medium shot of KANBEI *and* GOROBEI *looking at the map with* KATSUSHIRO *behind them, looking over* KANBEI'S *shoulder. They are standing on the bridge.*

KANBEI : If we destroy this bridge . . . *pointing* . . . we can defend this area a lot easier.

KANBEI *hands the plan to* KATSUSHIRO *and they walk towards camera, going off in the foreground.*

410. Long shot of a small group of houses on the other side of a field, with the hills rising up behind them. The three samurai appear in the foreground and stand in back view, looking towards the houses.

GOROBEI : But what about those houses over there?

Pan left as they walk across and stand looking across the fields to the mill.

411. Medium close-up of KANBEI *and* GOROBEI *looking at each other.*

KANBEI : They'll have to be evacuated. *They turn away and begin to walk back towards the bridge.*

GOROBEI : The mill too? *They both stop and look back in the direction of the mill.*

KANBEI : Yes. *They turn again and walk on.*

GOROBEI : That old man is stubborn, you know.

KANBEI *rubs his head ruefully.* GOROBEI *walks off across the bridge followed by* KANBEI. KATSUSHIRO *follows them, back to camera.*

412. Medium long shot of HEIHACHI *sitting on the wooden railing of a verandah, under a thatched roof. In the foreground a group of villagers sit round looking up at him. (Still on page 74)*

HEIHACHI : So you're afraid of the enemy. Well, that's only natural . . . But remember, they're afraid of you too !

As he speaks, KANBEI, GOROBEI *and* KATSUSHIRO *pass along the street behind him.* HEIHACHI *and his audience all laugh happily together.*

413. High angle long shot of KANBEI, GOROBEI *and* KATSU-SHIRO *coming round from behind a house towards camera, up a side street in the village.*

414. Medium long shot of KIKUCHIYO, *back to camera, striding along in front of a parade of farmers who are standing to attention holding bamboo spears. (Still on page 74) He looks at each one in turn, then turns back towards camera, folds his arms and shambles forward. He squats on his haunches and scratches his leg. Music out.*

KIKUCHIYO : Oh, you're all just splendid. Standing there like a line of scarecrows. *He stands up and yells at them.* Only, remember, these bandits aren't crows — and they're not sparrows either. *As he speaks* KANBEI *and the other two walk past behind the line of cowering recruits.*

As KIKUCHIYO *continues to speak, track round and back slightly until a large group of children is revealed watching avidly in the foreground.* KIKUCHIYO *and his line of recruits are now seen from the side over the heads of the children.*

KIKUCHIYO : Hey you, stop chewing the cud.

415. Medium close-up of one of the farmers holding his spear. His jaw moves regularly. He swallows, stops chewing, and blinks nervously.

416. Medium close-up of KIKUCHIYO *(Still on page 74)*

KIKUCHIYO : This isn't a cow barn.

KIKUCHIYO *takes a couple of steps backwards and puts his hands on his hips. He looks at his recruits then suddenly draws his sword.*

417. Long shot of KIKUCHIYO *continuing his movement as he draws his sword. He is seen over the heads of the children who are watching, backs to camera in the foreground. The line of recruits backs away nervously as* KIKUCHIYO *waves his sword.*

KIKUCHIYO : You there. That's right. You. Step forward.

418. Medium shot of YOHEI *standing holding his spear at the end of the line, next to three other farmers. He looks towards* KIKUCHIYO *who is out of shot. (Still on page 74) The others look at* YOHEI.

419. Medium close-up of KIKUCHIYO *pointing with his sword.*

KIKUCHIYO : I mean you !

420. Medium shot of YOHEI *(as 418). He steps out sideways from the line, very uncertainly; pan right with him.*

421. Medium shot of KIKUCHIYO *with his sword on his shoulder, and the scabbard in his other hand. He brings down his sword and lets it hang in his hand, mimicking* YOHEI, *shuffling towards camera, and drooping at the knees with the other hand dangling. (Still on page 74) The children laugh, off.*

422. Medium shot of the crowd of children laughing.

423. Long shot of KIKUCHIYO *shambling towards camera, seen over the heads of the children. The line of farmers stand in the background with* YOHEI *in back view in front of them. The children continue to laugh.* KIKUCHIYO *goes towards them, gesturing.*

KIKUCHIYO : Hey you! I'm going to start charging you admission! *He puts his sword back in its scabbard.* YOHEI *looks nervously towards the children, as* KIKUCHIYO's *back is turned, but he turns away again quickly when* KIKUCHIYO *walks up to him.*

424. Medium close-up of KIKUCHIYO *coming up and facing* YOHEI. *The other men are seen behind them.* KIKUCHIYO *takes* YOHEI's *spear and looks at the spearhead. It is not bamboo, but a proper samurai spear.* KIKUCHIYO *gives it back to* YOHEI.

KIKUCHIYO : What's this?

YOHEI : Why, it's a spear.

KIKUCHIYO : I know that, idiot. I'm asking you where you got it. *Pause.* Well, speak up. Found it growing on a bush? *He walks away, then turns back to* YOHEI *who looks very unhappy.* I know. You don't get spears like that unless you take them — from dead samurai. If you have this one then you must have others. *Shouting at all of them.* Where — are — they? *He stamps on the ground and shakes his fist.*

425. High angle medium long shot of KANBEI *and* GOROBEI, *with* KATSUSHIRO *beside them, standing on a grassy bank by a stream. (Still on page 74) They are surrounded by trees and the ground rises slightly behind them. They are in the forest, on the lower slopes of the hills round the village.*

426. High angle big close-up of the northern section of the map, marked as forest. KANBEI's *hands indicate something on it.*

427. *High angle medium close-up of* KANBEI *and* GOROBEI, *in three-quarter back view, with* KATSUSHIRO *standing nearer camera with his back to them. The stream trickles by in the background. Sunshine streams through the branches and flowers grow in profusion at their feet.*

KANBEI : It looks so peaceful here, but it's our weakest spot.

KANBEI goes off, followed by GOROBEI. KATSUSHIRO *turns and looks up the stream, back to camera. He begins to walk away.*
428. *Medium long shot of* KATSUSHIRO *on the other side of the stream, back to camera, running up to a small tree in blossom. He picks a sprig of blossom and looks at it tenderly. Then he runs back towards camera, jumping over the stream. Pan with him as he runs through the trees and goes out of sight.*
429. *High angle long shot of* KANBEI *and* GOROBEI *walking slowly along through the trees, accompanied by* KATSUSHIRO. *The grassy forest floor is covered with flowers.* GOROBEI *holds the map as he and* KANBEI *study the surrounding terrain.* KATSUSHIRO *does not seem to be taking much notice of them. He runs up the slope towards camera, still holding the sprig of blossom. The two older men stand below him in a pool of sunlight.*

KANBEI *calling* : Katsushiro, we're leaving.

KATSUSHIRO turns and looks back. The two samurai begin to walk back the way they came, but KATSUSHIRO *looks up and then goes down on one knee to smell the flowers at his feet. (Still on page 74) The older men stop and watch him.*
430. *Medium shot of* KANBEI *and* GOROBEI *looking up. They both smile. (Still on page 74)*

KANBEI *laughing* : He's still a child.

431. *Medium shot of* KATSUSHIRO *walking through the trees with flowers growing all round him, so that he is only visible above the waist. Pan left with him as he climbs the slope.*
432. *Medium long shot of* KATSUSHIRO *among the trees and flowers. He gazes round and then goes on up the hill.*
433. *Long shot of* KATSUSHIRO *walking along the top of a steep slope surrounded by trees, with the stream in the foreground at the foot of the bank.* KATSUSHIRO *runs down the bank to the edge of the stream. Camera tilts down with him to*

reveal the stream more clearly; he sits down beside it in a patch of sunlight. *Music begins over — a quiet theme associated with* KATSUSHIRO *and the forest — as he starts to lie back.*
434. High angle close-up of KATSUSHIRO *lying back on a carpet of small white flowers. He looks up and smiles contentedly. (Still on page 75)*
435. Low angle medium long shot of the branches overhead, from KATSUSHIRO'S *viewpoint. The afternoon sun shines through them and a breeze flutters the leaves. Pan across the branches.*
436. High angle close-up of KATSUSHIRO *(as 434). He closes his eyes, with the sunlight on his face. A pause. Suddenly he sits up.*
437. Medium shot continuing the movement as KATSUSHIRO *sits up and quickly turns round, getting to his feet at the same time and beginning to scramble up the bank, looking back over his shoulder.*
438. Long shot of the clearing with the stream in the foreground. KATSUSHIRO *can be seen on one side of the stream as a figure appears running towards the stream on the other.*
439. Medium shot of SHINO, *back to camera, holding a large bunch of wild flowers. She is dressed as a boy, with her hair tied back in a short pigtail. She stands amid a carpet of flowers, staring at* KATSUSHIRO, *who stands motionless halfway up the bank on the other side of the stream staring back at her. (Still on page 75) A pause.*
440. Medium close-up of KATSUSHIRO *on the bank. He puts his sword, which he has drawn, back into his belt.*

KATSUSHIRO : Who are you? Are you one of the villagers?

441. Medium close-up of SHINO. *She shifts from one foot to the other, then nods nervously. (Still on page 75)*
442. Medium close-up of KATSUSHIRO. *He goes down the bank a little way; tilt down with him.*

KATSUSHIRO : Are you a girl?

443. Medium close-up of SHINO. *Now very afraid, she shakes her head vigorously.*
444. Medium close-up of KATSUSHIRO. *He looks puzzled.*

KATSUSHIRO : If you're a boy why aren't you out drilling with the others? Picking flowers . . .

445. Medium shot of SHINO *looking nervously at her flowers.*
KATSUSHIRO *off* : . . . at a time like this!

446. Medium close-up of KATSUSHIRO *waving his sprig of blossom at her to emphasise his words. He suddenly realises what he is doing and, embarrassed, tosses away the blossom.*
KATSUSHIRO : Just you come here! *He turns and goes out of shot.*

447. Medium shot of SHINO, *in back view, holding her flowers behind her back;* KATSUSHIRO, *on the opposite bank, starts to climb up, then stops to shout back at her.*
KATSUSHIRO : I'll make you march!

She does not move, and he starts back down the bank towards her. She turns quickly and runs off in the foreground.

448. Long shot of the clearing with the stream in the fore-ground. SHINO *disappears through the trees, pursued by* KATSUSHIRO.

449. High angle medium shot tracking with SHINO *as she plunges through the undergrowth down a slope. Hold as she ducks round between two trees, running away as* KATSUSHIRO *comes up behind her.*

450. High angle medium long shot tracking with SHINO *through the trees and undergrowth.* KATSUSHIRO *appears, running after her. Track with them, then hold as* SHINO *trips and falls and* KATSUSHIRO *makes a grab at her.*

451. Medium shot of KATSUSHIRO *and* SHINO *struggling in the undergrowth. (Still on page 75)*

452. High angle medium shot of SHINO *on the ground pushing at* KATSUSHIRO, *who is holding her down. He grabs at her chest and she pushes him off, holding her robe closely across her chest. Pan right with him as he jumps away in horror, looking down at her. He realises she is a girl.*

453. Medium close-up, panning left with SHINO *as she crawls away through the flowers, adjusting her robe.*

454. High angle medium shot of SHINO, *in three-quarter front view, holding her robe close across her breasts.* KATSUSHIRO *kneels among the flowers in the background, watching her anxiously. (Still on page 75)*

455. Medium shot of KATSUSHIRO *among the flowers and undergrowth, looking towards* SHINO.

456. High angle medium close-up of SHINO *holding her robe,*

100

surrounded by flowers and seen through twisted undergrowth.
457. High angle medium close-up of KATSUSHIRO *staring towards her. He looks away in embarrassment.*
458. Long shot of KATSUSHIRO *and* SHINO *sitting some yards apart, partly obscured by flowers and undergrowth.**

459. High angle medium shot of KANBEI *facing camera, with the other samurai (except* KATSUSHIRO *and* KIKUCHIYO*) grouped round him. They are in* RIKICHI*'s house, with the map spread out in front of them. (Still on page 76)*

[KANBEI: Now this place here would be all right. But so would this one. The question is, which? . . .]†

A strange noise, off. They all look towards the doorway.
460. Medium long shot of KIKUCHIYO, *in complete samurai armour, leading a large group of farmers all armed with spears. They are running towards* RIKICHI*'s house, led by* YOHEI *and* MANZO, *who are carrying between them a long pole slung with a heavy load.* YOHEI *and* MANZO *come past camera in the foreground, revealing that the load consists of armour, helmets, bows and arrows and spears. (Still on page 76)* KIKUCHIYO *motions the other men to stop as* YOHEI *and* MANZO *trot off, camera panning slightly with them.*
461. Medium shot of YOHEI *coming towards camera, carrying the end of the pole on his shoulder, with* MANZO *behind.* KIKUCHIYO *comes up behind them. They go into the outer room of* RIKICHI*'s house.* KIKUCHIYO *hangs up his sword.*

KIKUCHIYO *triumphantly*: Look what I've found. Just look what I've got!

KIKUCHIYO *comes over to* YOHEI *and picks up a complete suit of armour which is hanging over the end of the pole. Pan with him as he goes through the doorway into the main room. He squats down on his haunches and puts the armour down on the floor. Hold to include* KANBEI *three-quarters back to camera, with* GOROBEI *behind him. They look surprised.*

KANBEI: What's this?
KIKUCHIYO: It's all samurai stuff.

---

* End of reel 3.

† This dialogue is not heard in the version of the film released in England.

462. High angle medium shot of KANBEI *with* GOROBEI, KYUZO, SHICHIROJI *and* HEIHACHI *sitting round behind him.* KIKUCHIYO's *helmeted head is visible in the foreground. They all stare at him in amazement.*

KANBEI : Where did you find it?

463. Medium close-up of KANBEI, *in back view, with* KIKUCHIYO, *smirking, seen over his shoulder. In the background* YOHEI *looks on anxiously.*

464. High angle medium shot of the samurai (as 462).

KANBEI : Here in the village?

465. Medium close-up of KANBEI *and* KIKUCHIYO *(as 463).*

KIKUCHIYO : At Manzo's house.

466. Medium shot of the samurai (as 462). They are all staring at KIKUCHIYO *as they realise that the farmers must have killed samurai to obtain the weapons and armour.*

467. Low angle medium close-up of MANZO, *the pole on his shoulder, almost obscured by the load of weapons. He looks frightened and shifts uneasily. (Still on page 76)*

468. Medium shot of the samurai (as 462). KANBEI *folds his arms but says nothing.*

469. Medium close-up of KIKUCHIYO *(as 463). He looks uncomfortable and throws the suit of armour forward in front of* KANBEI.

470. Medium shot of the samurai facing camera, with KIKU-CHIYO *in profile in the background.*

KIKUCHIYO : Here, isn't this nice? Look at that there. That's a really fine helmet. *He taps the helmet.*

The samurai sit silently, not looking at the armour.

KIKUCHIYO : Well, what's the matter? We need it, don't we? Armour, spears, bows and arrows. That's why I brought them.

SHICHIROJI *suddenly stands up; tilt up with him as he shouts down at* KIKUCHIYO.

SHICHIROJI : Shame! And you call yourself a samurai!

Quick pan to the right and then to the left as he runs round the others and comes into the foreground, kneeling behind KIKUCHIYO. KANBEI, KYUZO *and* HEIHACHI *can be seen in the background, watching.* SHICHIROJI *grabs* KIKUCHIYO's *shoulders and points at the armour.*

SHICHIROJI : Don't you know how they got these? They were taken from samurai!

KIKUCHIYO : I know that.

SHICHIROJI *shakes him violently. (Still on page 76)*

SHICHIROJI : Then how dare you . . .

KANBEI *intervening* : That's enough now.

SHICHIROJI : But . . .

KIKUCHIYO *and* SHICHIROJI *both turn towards him.*

KANBEI *to* SHICHIROJI : I understand. But someone who has never been hunted down after the battle by bamboo spears wouldn't understand.

A pause, then SHICHIROJI *pushes* KIKUCHIYO *away roughly. Tilt up as he stands up, in three-quarter back view. Hold as he moves away. In the foreground is the shaft of a samurai spear.* SHICHIROJI *suddenly turns back and grabs the spear, lowering it threateningly. (Still on page 76)*

471. Medium close-up of MANZO *still holding the pole. He looks terrified. Fast pan as he shuffles backwards out of the way of the door.*

472. Medium close-up of SHICHIROJI *hurling the spear towards camera.*

473. Medium long shot of the group of farmers still standing outside RIKICHI'S *house, on the other side of the small stream.* RIKICHI *is coming towards the door as the spear flies through and lands at his feet. He looks through the door in some trepidation, then rushes back to the men, shooing them away. They scatter quickly.*

474. Medium shot of MANZO *and* YOHEI *crouching on the floor with the load of weapons in front of them. They look frightened and ashamed. A bundle of arrows rests against a wooden pillar between them.*

475. Medium close-up of KIKUCHIYO *bending forward and looking up, his eyebrows bristling, with his back to the other samurai who are visible behind him.* SHICHIROJI *also has his back to the others.* HEIHACHI *stabs at the floor with a knife.*

KYUZO : I'd like to kill every farmer in this village.

KIKUCHIYO *and* KANBEI *turn towards* KYUZO *who is sitting right at the back. They turn back without speaking. A pause. Suddenly* KIKUCHIYO *yells in fury and starts to get up.*

476. Close-up of KIKUCHIYO, *continuing his movement as he stands up and stares down at the others. He takes a step forward.*

KIKUCHIYO *laughing bitterly*: Well, what do you think farmers are? Saints? *He steps back again.* They are the most cunning and untrustworthy animals on earth.

Fast pan to the right, tilting down as KIKUCHIYO *bends down and seizes the suit of armour. Fast pan back again as he hurls it away from him.*

477. High angle medium close-up of the armour landing in the stream which runs along under one wall of the house, which is raised on stilts above it.

478. High angle medium close-up of KIKUCHIYO *staring down at the other samurai.*

KIKUCHIYO: If you ask them for rice, they'll say they have none. But they have.

Pan slightly right as KIKUCHIYO *strides forward again. Hold on big close-up of him as he speaks.*

KIKUCHIYO: They have everything. Look in the rafters, dig in the ground. You'll find it. Rice in jars. Salt. Beans. Sake. *He laughs mirthlessly, then walks away, pointing through the window.* Look in the mountains, hidden farms everywhere. And yet they pretend to be oppressed. *Pan with* KIKUCHIYO *as he strides backwards and forwards, still haranguing the samurai.* They are full of lies.

479. High angle medium shot of the five samurai with KANBEI *in the foreground, all staring up at* KIKUCHIYO.

KIKUCHIYO *off*: When they smell a battle they make themselves bamboo spears. And then they hunt. But they hunt the wounded and the defeated.

480. Medium close-up of KIKUCHIYO. *As he begins to speak again, camera pans slightly right with him, then holds as he comes forward into close-up again.*

KIKUCHIYO: Farmers are miserly, craven . . .

481. Medium close-up of MANZO *and* YOHEI *listening, petrified.*

KIKUCHIYO *off*: . . . mean, stupid . . .

482. Close-up of KIKUCHIYO *shouting.*

KIKUCHIYO: . . . murderous! You make me laugh so hard I'm crying. *He turns his back to camera and walks away; then he turns back to them again, his eyes brimming with tears.* But then, who made animals out of them? You! *He comes forward into big close-up, yelling at the others.* You did — you samurai! All of you damned samurai!

He turns away; pan with him as he grabs something and hurls it away from him.

483. Quick medium shot of several arrows sticking into wooden beams.

484. Medium close-up of KIKUCHIYO *panning with him as he bends down to pick up more arrows.*

485. Closer medium shot of more arrows flying past and sticking in the beams or falling to the floor.

486. Medium close-up of KIKUCHIYO *staring down at the samurai again. Pan left then right as he strides about, shouting at them again.*

KIKUCHIYO : And each time you fight you burn villages, you destroy the fields, you take away the food, you rape the women and enslave the men. And you kill them when they resist. *He comes into close-up.* You hear me — you damned samurai!

Tilt down as KIKUCHIYO *suddenly sinks to his knees, bending his head. (Still on page 76) He begins to sob uncontrollably.*

487. Medium shot of the five samurai sitting facing camera, with KIKUCHIYO *in the foreground, his head bowed and his shoulders shaking with sobs. (Still on page 76) A pause then* KANBEI *unfolds his arms and looks down at the palms of his hands.*

488. Close-up of KANBEI, *head bowed, with* HEIHACHI *and* SHICHIROJI *visible behind him. They are all very moved.* KANBEI *looks up, tears in his eyes.* KIKUCHIYO *can be heard sobbing quietly, off.*

KANBEI *quietly* : You're a farmer's son, aren't you?

489. High angle close-up of KIKUCHIYO, *his head bowed and his face obscured by his helmet. He looks up and then turns and gets to his feet. Hold on a medium close-up of his legs and feet at the doorway, dust blowing about on the path outside.*

490. Medium shot of KIKUCHIYO *running out from the house. Pan slightly right with him, and hold as he stops and looks up at* RIKICHI *and old* GISAKU *who are coming towards him, in the background.* KIKUCHIYO *picks up the spear which is still lying where it landed earlier, and dashes off, watched with some surprise by* RIKICHI *and* GISAKU. *(Still on page 76) Pan with them as they shuffle towards the door of the house.*

491. Medium shot of MANZO *and* YOHEI, *heads bowed, backs to camera, sitting against a wooden rail which is in the foreground. The outer room of the house is visible beyond them.* RIKICHI *and* GISAKU *come in, pausing to look down at the two farmers, who raise their heads. Then* GISAKU *goes through to the main room, leaning on his stick, followed by* RIKICHI.

492. Medium close-up of KANBEI, *back to camera, with* GISAKU *bending over and facing him.* RIKICHI *can be seen behind him, looking back over his shoulder.*

GISAKU : Is anything the matter?

KANBEI *rubbing his head* : No, nothing.

493. High angle medium shot of the five samurai, with KANBEI *in the foreground. Some of them smile slightly.*

494. Long shot, looking up the village street. Music in. Pan slightly left as KATSUSHIRO *comes bounding down the road towards camera then stops dead, looking at something out of shot. Music out as he stops. Pan right with him as he tiptoes round until* KIKUCHIYO *is revealed in the foreground, sitting on the ground looking disgruntled. The wind is blowing up the dust.* KIKUCHIYO *has his back to* KATSUSHIRO *and does not notice him at first.* KATSUSHIRO *grins to see* KIKUCHIYO *in his full samurai armour and comes a few steps closer, studying him interestedly. Then* KIKUCHIYO *looks up, sees him and angrily pushes him away with the spear.* KATSUSHIRO *backs away, puzzled.* KIKUCHIYO *gets up; circular pan right as he stumps away from* KATSUSHIRO, *who remains in the foreground watching him. Sound of children's voices, off. Hold as a group of children run towards* KIKUCHIYO *but stop in confusion as he turns and menaces them with his spear.* KIKUCHIYO *walks off, watched by the children.* KATSUSHIRO *also looks back over his shoulder, as he begins to walk towards camera. Fade out.*

495. Fade in to medium shot of GOROBEI *at the door of* RIKICHI'S *house, seen from the outside. He is kneeling and looking up. It is pouring with rain. Behind him in the house* KANBEI *sits cross-legged on the floor, and* HEIHACHI *is sewing in the background.*

496. Medium close-up of GOROBEI, *with* KANBEI *and* HEIHACHI *visible behind him.* KIKUCHIYO *can be seen lying on his back beside* HEIHACHI.

GOROBEI : It's so quiet.

KANBEI *looking up* : Isn't it?

GOROBEI : On a day like this it doesn't seem possible that those mountains are full of bandits.

KIKUCHIYO *suddenly begins to move in the background.*

497. High angle medium close-up of KIKUCHIYO *continuing his movement as he rolls over in a somersault. Tilt up with him as he sits up on his haunches, revealing* HEIHACHI *behind him, sewing away.*

KIKUCHIYO : Hey, there are women in the village you know.

HEIHACHI *looks at him.*

498. Medium close-up of KYUZO *sitting with his back against a wooden pillar. He looks round rather disdainfully in the direction of* KIKUCHIYO, *then looks away. Suddenly he starts to rise.*

499. Medium shot of the room, with RIKICHI *sitting on the floor in the background. In the foreground, continuing his movement,* KYUZO *gets to his feet, holding his sword. Pan right with him as he walks through the room to the door, losing the others and revealing* SHICHIROJI, *mending a long-bow, and* KATSUSHIRO, *leaning up against the doorpost, looking out.*

SHICHIROJI : Where are you going?

KYUZO : Up towards the hills.

SHICHIROJI *standing up in surprise* : The hills?

KYUZO : To practise. *He goes out, watched by* KATSUSHIRO *and* SHICHIROJI.

500. Medium shot of KIKUCHIYO, *kneeling and scratching his knee, with* HEIHACHI *beside him.*

KIKUCHIYO : You won't find many women in the hills.

501. Jump cut to close-up of KATSUSHIRO *at the doorway. He looks round guiltily, then down in embarrassment.*

502. Medium shot of KIKUCHIYO *and* HEIHACHI *(as 500).* HEIHACHI *laughs.*

HEIHACHI : Sometimes you almost sound intelligent.

KIKUCHIYO : What are you making?

HEIHACHI : A banner.

KIKUCHIYO : A banner? *He picks up the free end of the banner and looks at it.*

HEIHACHI : Something to hold up, hoist high — you know. Something to stir our fighting spirit.

He stands up; tilt up with him and track back slightly to reveal the long narrow banner with circles and symbols on it. Track back further to include RIKICHI *in the foreground, then* KANBEI, GOROBEI *and* SHICHIROJI *who gather round to examine the banner.* HEIHACHI *has drawn six circles, one triangle, and, at the bottom, the Japanese character* ta.

KIKUCHIYO *pointing at it* : What's that?

HEIHACHI : That? You read it as ' farmer ', but actually it means this village.

KIKUCHIYO : Oh? And the circles?

HEIHACHI : That's us.

KIKUCHIYO : But there's only six. What about me?

HEIHACHI : You're so special that I made you a triangle.

They all laugh at this, particularly SHICHIROJI. *(Still on page 77)* KIKUCHIYO *looks bashful, and scratches his cheek.*

503. Medium close-up of KATSUSHIRO *at the doorway, smiling at the others. He steps forward, still looking towards them, then discreetly backs out and runs out of the door into the pouring rain.*

504. Medium long shot of KYUZO *in the forest with the rain pouring down. A small stream runs down towards camera.* KYUZO *stands at the edge of the stream shuffling his feet in the wet ground. Then he suddenly lunges wtih his sword across the stream. He does it again. Then, with sword erect, he abruptly crosses the stream and strides off through the dripping forest.*

505. Medium shot of KYUZO *with his sword in one hand coming along a path towards camera. The trunk of a tree stands on one side in the foreground. He stops by the tree and stares towards camera.*

506. Medium shot of KYUZO, *back to camera, leaning against the tree trunk. In the background,* SHINO *appears from out of a rough wooden hut; she stands in the rain for a moment looking up the track towards the village.*

507. Medium shot of SHINO, *in back view, standing outside the hut. Music in. She involuntarily puts a hand up to her hair, then bends down, camera tilting down with her, and begins to comb her hair, looking at her reflection in a puddle.*

508. Medium shot of KYUZO *by the tree trunk, watching closely.*

509. Medium shot of SHINO *crouching down, tidying her hair. She looks round and then starts to straighten up.*

510. Medium shot of KYUZO *by the tree trunk, watching with interest. He puts his sword back in its scabbard, moves further behind the trunk and looks round, but keeps almost out of sight. Pan slightly right with him.*

511. Medium long shot of SHINO *at the entrance to the hut. In the distance* KATSUSHIRO *is splashing along the muddy track from the village. He pauses as he reaches* SHINO, *then ducks down to go into the hut.*

512. Medium shot of KATSUSHIRO, *back to camera, continuing his movement as he ducks under the low entrance to the hut, with* SHINO *beside him. She goes in and they face one another just inside. He holds out a carefully wrapped parcel and she smiles happily. (Still on page 77)*

KATSUSHIRO *in a low voice* : It's rice. Go ahead. Eat.

SHINO : But —

KATSUSHIRO : Look, I tasted that millet you all eat. It's terrible. Go on, take it. *He gives it to her.*

Tilt down with them as SHINO *kneels down and* KATSUSHIRO *squats beside her. She holds the rice as if it were something very precious.*

KATSUSHIRO : If you don't want to eat in front of me, I'll go and come back later.

He gets up and goes outside the hut; tilt up and pan left with him. She gets up too and stands on the threshold. KATSUSHIRO *turns towards her.*

SHINO : I won't eat it.

KATSUSHIRO : Why not? *He turns right round, back to camera.* I brought it specially for you.

SHINO : It was very nice of you. It's not that. I'll take it over to Kyumon's grandmother.

KATSUSHIRO : Kyumon's grandmother?

SHINO : Yes.

513. Medium shot of KYUZO *by the tree, watching.*

514. Medium shot of KYUZO, *back to camera, looking up the track to the hut.* KATSUSHIRO *comes out, followed by* SHINO. *They walk away back towards the village, and he takes her arm as she slips in one of the puddles.* KYUZO *leaves his hiding-place and starts to follow them.*

515. Wipe to medium shot of all the samurai and RIKICHI *seated round a low table having dinner. It is evening. A cauldron of rice hangs from a hook in the roof and* RIKICHI *sits by it serving the samurai.* GOROBEI *passes his bowl to* RIKICHI *for some rice.* RIKICHI *is about to serve* KATSUSHIRO *as well when* KATSUSHIRO *interrupts.*

KATSUSHIRO : Rikichi, I'm not hungry now. I'll eat later.

KYUZO : Go ahead, eat. I'll keep something back from my portion this time.

KATSUSHIRO *looks embarrassed.*

KANBEI : What's this? It sounds interesting.

KIKUCHIYO *eating* : What does?

516. Wipe to medium close-up of an OLD WOMAN, *Kyumon's grandmother, bending forward with her palms pressed together, a bowl of rice in front of her. (Still on page 77) Rain can be seen pouring down past an opening at the back of the hut.*

517. Medium shot of the OLD WOMAN *in the foreground, back to camera, with the samurai grouped together in front of her.* KATSUSHIRO *stands in front with* RIKICHI *and* KANBEI *beside him, the others in the background. They are all looking down compassionately. By contrast,* KIKUCHIYO *stands with his back to the others.*

KANBEI : But this is terrible. *Turning to* RIKICHI. Hasn't she any relatives?

RIKICHI : No, the bandits killed them all.

KANBEI : I see.

518. Close-up of the OLD WOMAN, *her head bowed. She looks up and speaks in a quavering voice.*

OLD WOMAN : I want to die.

519. High angle medium close-up of KANBEI *and* GOROBEI *looking down, with* KIKUCHIYO *pacing about bad-temperedly behind them.*

OLD WOMAN *off* : I don't want to live any more.

520. Low angle medium close-up of HEIHACHI *beside a beam, with* SHICHIROJI *and* KYUZO *behind him. They look down, listening sympathetically.*

OLD WOMAN *off* : But I'm afraid . . .

521. Close-up of KATSUSHIRO *and* RIKICHI, *in three-quarter front view, looking down.*

OLD WOMAN *off* : . . . the next world will be . . .

522. Big close-up of HEIHACHI *looking very upset.*

OLD WOMAN *off* : . . . terrible too . . . HEIHACHI *leans forward.*

523. Medium shot with the OLD WOMAN *back to camera in the foreground, and* HEIHACHI *on his knees leaning towards her, the other samurai behind him.*

HEIHACHI *trying to comfort her* : No, no. It's paradise, no bandits or anything. It's very nice.

KIKUCHIYO, *pushing through from the back* : How do you know? Ever been dead?

524. Medium shot of HEIHACHI, *only head and shoulders in frame, looking up at* KIKUCHIYO *who bends over him glaring, standing next to* KANBEI.

HEIHACHI : You needn't shout at me.

KIKUCHIYO : I hate misery. And I hate miserable people.

As he speaks, SHICHIROJI *gets up behind them, and* KYUZO *also comes forward.* KIKUCHIYO *stumps out of shot. The others watch him go.*

525. Medium shot of KIKUCHIYO *pacing about petulantly, arms folded, in the rough hovel. The roof leaks and rain drips through. The other samurai stand together on the left looking at him, backs to camera.*

KIKUCHIYO : Looking at a worm like her I get sick. Wretched, helpless. I never want to be like that. *He tosses a bunch of straw onto the ground.* I want to be reckless, daring . . .

KANBEI *stepping forward* : Then you just keep feeling like that until the bandits come.

KIKUCHIYO *folds his arms petulantly as* KYUZO *rushes out in the background.*

526. Low angle medium shot of KYUZO *coming out through the low doorway of the hovel. Pan and track slightly to the right as he comes forward and stands in the foreground in the*

111

rain, arms folded. KATSUSHIRO *appears at the entrance behind him. Pan slightly right as he hesitates, then comes forward beside* KYUZO. *(Still on page 77)*

KATSUSHIRO *stuttering* : Wait . . . you . . . you saw me today didn't you? I mean, with . . .

KYUZO : With the girl?

KATSUSHIRO : Yes . . . well — why didn't you say something?

KYUZO : What do you want me to say?

KYUZO *strides off, leaving* KATSUSHIRO *with his head bent with relief. Then he looks round after* KYUZO. *Fade out.*

527. *Fade in on high angle medium shot of ripening corn filling the whole frame, rippling in the breeze. Music in.*

528. *Medium shot of the outer room of* RIKICHI's *house. A crowd of children are pressed up against the bamboo walls outside and round the door, staring in.*

CHILDREN *shouting and clamouring* : We want rice, give us some rice !

Suddenly, they all run away. KIKUCHIYO *runs across the room and out through the door.*

529. *High angle medium long shot of* KIKUCHIYO *coming through the door, with the children scattering in front of him. He stands glaring at them, hands on hips. They all stop and turn to look back at him.*

KIKUCHIYO *shouting* : Shut up, you brats. We haven't got any.

A pause, then HEIHACHI *appears at the door carrying bowls of rice, followed by* KATSUSHIRO, KYUZO *and* SHICHIROJI, *all carrying bowls. All the children rush towards them, laughing and shouting.*

KIKUCHIYO *grinning broadly* : Don't shout so much ! If you feel that good, then why all this ' give us rice ' business? *He imitates them.*

530. *Medium shot of* KIKUCHIYO *holding a bowl of rice out of reach of several children who are crowding round him. In the background the other samurai listen, smiling.* KIKUCHIYO *holds up the bowl of rice and lectures the children in mock-seriousness.*

KIKUCHIYO : Now, you look here, this is all we can give you. If we give you any more we'll look like this. *He sucks in his cheeks and squints. (Still on page 77) The children laugh.*

531. High angle medium shot of the children looking up at KIKUCHIYO *who stands over them in the foreground, back to camera, only his head and shoulders in shot. They are all laughing at him.*

532. Medium shot of KIKUCHIYO *making faces, with the children, in back view, surrounding him and laughing. The four other samurai stand behind* KIKUCHIYO *laughing with them.*

KIKUCHIYO : So, you understand now, don't you? *He bends down. Wickedly:* Hey, haven't any of you kids got a pretty sister? Huh? *The children giggle and the other samurai look at him with mock disapproval.* HEIHACHI *makes a face and raises a hand to give* KIKUCHIYO *a friendly shove.*

533. Medium close-up of KIKUCHIYO *and* HEIHACHI *in profile, continuing the movement. The children laugh as* KIKUCHIYO *nudges* HEIHACHI *back, and then bends down to a small boy near him.*

KIKUCHIYO : Come on, haven't you? *The child giggles.*

534. Close-up of GISAKU *in the mill with a* WOMAN *behind him looking worried. They both look towards something off-screen. The* WOMAN *puts a hand on the old man's shoulder with a cry of distress.*

535. Medium close-up of MOSUKE *with* GOROBEI *just in shot beside him. He looks at* GOROBEI *fearfully. Other farmers are gathered behind him, open-mouthed with amazement.*

MOSUKE : You mean I have to leave my place?

536. Close-up of GISAKU, *with his* SON *and his* SON'S WIFE, *just behind him, frowning worriedly. The* SON *stands up but his* WIFE *pulls him down, looking away nervously.*

537. Medium shot of GISAKU *sitting in the middle of the room with* KANBEI, *his* SON *and his* WIFE *behind him and* GOROBEI *and* MANZO *beside him.* KANBEI *is holding a small child in his arms. Tilt up with him as he stands up, still holding the child. He paces backwards and forwards in the foreground, back to camera. The waterwheel makes its regular noise throughout the scene, emphasising the pauses.*

KANBEI : I know how you feel, but you have to. We can't defend these outlying farms.

113

KANBEI *continues to pace about. Suddenly the* WIFE *bursts into tears.*

538. High angle medium shot of some village men all armed with bamboo spears, sitting on the ground in a circle, with GOROBEI, KIKUCHIYO, HEIHACHI, KYUZO *and* SHICHIROJI *standing in the middle, looking at them. Circular track over the heads of the villagers, revealing* KANBEI *and* KATSUSHIRO *standing behind* GOROBEI *as he lectures the villagers.*

GOROBEI: Now, remember. Soon the barley will be ready for harvesting. The bandits will come right after that. So, let's be prepared for it. From the very beginning we're going to work in formation. We're going to harvest together and no one is going to go off and work by himself. From tomorrow on we're going to camp together, unit by unit. So, remember, from tomorrow on no one is going to do anything by himself.

The circular track continues as GOROBEI *steps aside and* KIKUCHIYO *addresses the men.*

KIKUCHIYO: So you just be sure you get all the individual action you need from your wives tonight, eh? *All the villagers laugh.*

539. Medium close-up of YOHEI *looking up and laughing. Two girls and three old women stand behind him* roaring with laughter.

540. Close-up of the toothless old women, rocking with laughter.

541. High angle medium shot of a group of villagers laughing with HEIHACHI *in three-quarter back view in the foreground. He slaps one of the men good-naturedly on the shoulder.*

542. High angle medium shot of SHICHIROJI, *with another group of villagers sitting behind him. They are all laughing.*

543. High angle medium shot of three old women, laughing coarsely, one of them clapping her hands with delight.

544. Medium shot of KANBEI *and* KATSUSHIRO, *with* GOROBEI *near them in the foreground, all laughing.* GOROBEI *turns to look at* KANBEI.

545. High angle medium long shot of the circle of villagers with the samurai standing in the middle. In the foreground, backs to camera, several children look down on the scene, perched on or leaning against a fence.

546. High angle medium shot of MOSUKE *suddenly standing*

114

up amid the villagers, with KANBEI, GOROBEI *and* KATSUSHIRO *in the foreground, backs to camera.* MOSUKE *throws down his spear angrily and the laughter suddenly tails off. Pan left with* MOSUKE *as he walks through to the edge of the circle.*

MOSUKE : Everyone who lives beyond the bridge, come here.

He runs away into the middle of the village square; pan with him, losing the crowd of villagers. Four or five other men, some carrying spears, come into shot following him. He stops, and turns to them.

MOSUKE : Now throw down your spears. It's useless to carry a spear to protect someone else's house when you can't protect your own. *The men drop their spears.* Come on. *He runs off, followed by the five others.*

547. *Medium shot of* MOSUKE, *back to camera, running away with his five followers. Camera tracks after them a little way.*
KANBEI *off* : Wait! *They all stop in their tracks and turn towards camera.*

548. *Medium shot of* KANBEI, *back to camera, with* MOSUKE *and the other men facing him in the background. (Still on page 78)* KANBEI *points to the ground behind him.*

KANBEI : You, pick up your spears, and return to your units. *He puts his hand to the hilt of his sword.*

549. *Medium shot of* KANBEI *continuing his movement as he draws his sword, waving it threateningly. The samurai theme comes in, loud. The other farmers and samurai rush round and start forming a line in the background.*

550. *High angle medium shot of* MOSUKE *and his five neighbours backing away nervously. Track forward with them and then round as they dodge past* KANBEI *and run across the open space. Circular pan with them as they mount a bank, running towards the other villagers, who are watching behind the other samurai in the background.* KANBEI *appears in back view in the foreground, chasing them. Pan further to the left as he goes and stands over them; they shamefacedly pick up their spears and move off to join the others, prodded and pushed by* KIKUCHIYO. KANBEI *walks round and then across the square, looking sternly at the parade of farmers. Then he gestures with his sword. At this the other samurai draw their swords and shout orders, and the village men rush across the square to*

115

form up in battle units. Pan right along the top of the bank in the foreground as they rush round nearer camera to form up in front of KANBEI, *who is now standing in the background. There is general confusion.*

KIKUCHIYO *shouting off* : Where's that fool Yohei?

Hold on the end of the line nearest camera where SHICHIROJI's *unit is forming up.* YOHEI *shambles up behind them, confused and lost.* KIKUCHIYO *runs along in front of the men, grabs* YOHEI *and drags him off to his own unit, camera panning left to show* KIKUCHIYO *manhandling* YOHEI *into his proper place, and revealing the whole parade from behind.*

551. Medium shot of KANBEI *still holding his drawn sword with* KATSUSHIRO *standing beside him. (Still on page 78)* KANBEI *steps forward, camera panning right with him, losing* KATSUSHIRO, *and revealing* GOROBEI. *Pan back with* KANBEI, *losing* GOROBEI *and picking up* KATSUSHIRO *again.* KANBEI *eyes the farmers, who are out of shot.*

KANBEI *sternly* : There are only three houses beyond the bridge and there are twenty in the village. We cannot endanger twenty because of three. *Pan left with* KANBEI *as he speaks, losing* KATSUSHIRO *and including* GOROBEI. And if the village is destroyed, those three will not be safe anyway. *Pan back as he goes back to stand by* KATSUSHIRO. *Hold as he shouts.* War is like that. If the defence is for everyone, each individual will be protected. The man who thinks only of himself, destroys himself. From now on such desertion will be punished.

He raises his sword and, running it between his fingers, replaces it in his sheath. He starts to walk forward.

552. High angle long shot, looking along the parade of farmers holding their spears erect, with the samurai captains each standing in front of their units. KANBEI *stands facing them, then walks towards them, passes through the men and goes on out of shot. No one else moves. The wind rises and blows the dust about in the open space. In the foreground* KIKUCHIYO *goes up to one of his men and fussily straightens his spear. Then he turns away and leans on his sword with his back to his unit. Music out. Fade out.**

---

* End of reel 4.

553. *Fade in on low angle medium close-up of corn being harvested by a* MAN, *his body half out of shot. Festival music in.*

554. *Medium close-up of a* WOMAN *harvesting corn.*

555. *Medium close-up of the* MAN's *hands gathering corn.*

556. *Medium close-up of the* MAN, *clad only in a loin cloth, harvesting corn.*

557. *Medium close-up of the* WOMAN *cutting corn.*

558. *Medium close-up of the* MAN *harvesting.*

559. *Medium long shot of four women in single file, three of them carrying sheafs of corn on their backs, and one of them carrying a yoke with bundles of corn hanging from each end. (Still on page 79) They trot in single file round the edge of the field that has already been harvested, coming towards camera along a grassy bank. Pan slightly left to reveal* KIKUCHIYO, *in low angle, on the edge of the next field. Yelling joyfully, he runs after the women as they go off in the foreground.*

560. *Low angle medium close-up of one of the women from the side, carrying a sheaf of corn on her back. She passes camera, going out of shot, followed by the other three women. Pan slightly left as they pass.*

561. *Close-up of* KIKUCHIYO *watching them, licking his lips. He comes towards camera with a surprised expression.*

562. *Medium long shot of women and girls working in the field, partly obscured by corn in the foreground.*

563. *Close-up of* KIKUCHIYO. *He turns away from camera, revealing the sword which he is carrying as usual over his shoulder.*

564. *Medium shot of three women gathering up the harvested corn. In the background others can be seen cutting more corn.*

565. *Close-up of* KIKUCHIYO, *back to camera, scratching his neck. He turns round.*

566. *Medium long shot tracking left with girls running along, carying yokes with sheafs of corn at each end, partly obscured by the uncut corn in the foreground.*

567. *Close-up of* KIKUCHIYO, *greatly excited by the number of women working in the fields.*

KIKUCHIYO : Now who would have thought that this village held

so many pretty girls! *He gives a delighted whoop and leaps away.*
568. Long shot looking over the fields with hills in the background, and waving corn in the foreground. KIKUCHIYO *runs towards camera just as* YOHEI *stands up from behind the corn in the foreground. He looks round at* KIKUCHIYO, *who comes and taps him on the shoulder.*

KIKUCHIYO *gesturing round* : Yohei, where have you been keeping these girls so long?

YOHEI *looks round and chuckles.* KIKUCHIYO *pushes him goodnaturedly. He looks up, laughs wildly and, elbowing* YOHEI *out of the way, runs out of shot.*
569. Low angle medium shot of a girl, with her backside prominently facing camera, as she bends down cutting corn. KIKUCHIYO *runs towards her from the background. Tilt up slightly as he comes up and stands beside the* GIRL, *looking down at her, with the hills and sky behind them. He giggles maniacally.*

KIKUCHIYO *to the* GIRL : Give me your sickle for a minute. *He hands her his sword to hold.* I'll cut three times as much as you can. You see, I'm friendly.

Pan slightly left as the GIRL *backs away from him in alarm; he steps closer and bends down, staring into her face. Then he playfully slaps her thigh and leaps off, giggling.*
570. High angle medium close-up of KIKUCHIYO *bounding up with a sickle and setting to work on the corn, three-quarters back to camera, giggling and chattering all the time.*
571. Medium shot of the GIRL *holding his sword and looking at it very nervously. In the background, two men stop work to watch. (Still on page 79)*
572. High angle medium shot of KIKUCHIYO *cutting the corn. He looks back at the* GIRL, *leaps up in the air, and then carries on.*
573. Medium shot, panning with KANBEI *and* GOROBEI *as they walk along by one of the fields. Women, carrying sheafs of corn, pass in the foreground.*
574. Medium shot of KATSUSHIRO *standing watching the work, three-quarters back to camera with his hands on his hips.* HEIHACHI *is standing on a rock, just beyond him.* RIKICHI *is working in the corn at his feet.*

HEIHACHI : Rikichi. RIKICHI *stops and stands up.* HEIHACHI *crouches* *on his haunches on the rock.* I see that married couples work a lot better than anyone else. *Grinning.* You ought to get married.

RIKICHI *turns away, suddenly angry. Music out. He walks towards camera and stands in the foreground with the other two behind him.*

HEIHACHI : Look, that was a joke. What is there to get angry about?

RIKICHI *turns and runs off. Surprised,* HEIHACHI *turns to* KATSUSHIRO.

HEIHACHI : You go after him. KATSUSHIRO *runs off after* RIKICHI. Why did he run away like that? He's supposed to be working.

575. Medium long shot of the field with a small barn in the foreground. RIKICHI *runs past, going off in the foreground.* KATSUSHIRO *follows him.* SHINO, *who has been working at the edge of the field near the barn, stands up.*

SHINO *calling* : Rikichi!

576. Medium close-up of SHINO. MANZO *stands up in the corn behind her.*

MANZO : Shino, stop dreaming!

577. Medium shot of MANZO. SHICHIROJI *appears in the foreground as he stands up, back to camera.* MANZO *gets back to work.* SHICHIROJI *turns back towards camera, looking stern. 578. Medium close-up of* SHINO, *looking back towards* SHICHIROJI *who stands in the background looking at her. She steps back and quickly gets on with her work.* SHICHIROJI *looks round thoughtfully.*

579. Wipe to medium shot of some of the samurai making their way through dense undergrowth of cut bamboo cane, which partly obscures them from view.

580. Medium shot of KATSUSHIRO *and* KIKUCHIYO, KYUZO *behind them and* HEIHACHI *and* SHICHIROJI *following, making their way into an area of bamboo cane that has been cut and trampled.*

KIKUCHIYO *to* KATSUSHIRO : What did this? A bear?

KYUZO, HEIHACHI *and* SHICHIROJI *come up and join them.*

KYUZO : It's been sickled.

HEIHACHI : Rikichi?

581. Medium shot of KATSUSHIRO *facing camera with the*

others facing him in back view.

KATSUSHIRO : I didn't see him do it. I was looking for him, then he came out from here. He was all sweaty.

HEIHACHI : I see.

They all look in amazement at the chaos of bamboo. KIKUCHIYO *turns towards camera in the foreground.* HEIHACHI *comes up to him.*

KIKUCHIYO : What did you say in the first place?

HEIHACHI : Nothing, only that he ought to get married.

KIKUCHIYO : Something's the matter with him. You can tell that just to look at him.

HEIHACHI : His lips were set tight. Just like this. Like a locked door.

KIKUCHIYO *with a gesture* : Why don't you try to open it?

582. Wipe to high angle medium long shot of RIKICHI *crouching down, back to camera, beside a blazing fire. (Still on page 79) It is night. He is holding a spear. Suddenly he jumps to his feet.*

RIKICHI : Who goes there?

HEIHACHI *off* : It's me. RIKICHI *turns towards camera.*

583. Low angle medium shot of RIKICHI, *back to camera, and* HEIHACHI *approaching on the other side of the fire. Houses can be seen dimly in the background.* HEIHACHI *comes and stands near* RIKICHI *who turns slightly, and they face one another across the fire.*

RIKICHI : Yes, sir.

HEIHACHI *comes towards camera and sits down.*

HEIHACHI *beckoning to* RIKICHI : Sit down. Let's talk for a while. *Samurai theme in, very quietly.*

584. Medium close-up of RIKICHI *and* HEIHACHI *sitting down.* HEIHACHI *looks at* RIKICHI *sympathetically.*

HEIHACHI : Talking is a good thing, you know. If you talk about something that's worrying you, it often goes away. Incidentally, you're a man of few words. If you've got anything bottled up, well, now is a good time to say it.

RIKICHI *not looking at* HEIHACHI : I don't have anything bottled up.

HEIHACHI *sighs and fiddles with a bit of string. (Still on page 79)*

585. Low angle medium shot of KATSUSHIRO *nearest camera,*

KANBEI *in the centre and* GOROBEI *beside him, lying asleep with their heads on head-rests.* KANBEI *opens his eyes and then sits up, pushing back his blanket. He puts on his jerkin and turns to* GOROBEI.

KANBEI : Well, shall we go out?

GOROBEI *sits up and picks up his sword.*

GOROBEI *looking towards* KATSUSHIRO : Shall we wake him?

KANBEI : No, let the child sleep. *They get up and go out.*

Hold on KATSUSHIRO, *still asleep. He stirs.*

586. Medium shot of KANBEI *and* GOROBEI *walking through the anteroom.*

KATSUSHIRO *off, mumbling*: Shino! *They turn and stop at the sound.*

GOROBEI : He just said ' Shino '.

KANBEI : Shino. That's a girl's name. *Pan slightly right as they walk on towards the door.*

GOROBEI *looking back and grinning*: Indeed. That's not a very childish remark for a sleeping child to make, is it? *They make their way out through the sacking that covers the doorway.*

587. Medium shot, panning with KANBEI *and* GOROBEI *as they come out of the house. Pan continues right till they stop by the small bridge across the stream.* KANBEI *turns to* GOROBEI.

GOROBEI : Where shall we start?

KANBEI : At our weakest point.

They both laugh and start towards the east border. Pan further as they walk away, backs to camera, and then along the village street.

588. High angle medium shot of KIKUCHIYO *lying on the ground, his head propped up against a log and his feet resting on another log. He is supposed to be on guard, but is sound asleep. A fire blazes behind him. His sword is stuck upright in a pile of logs beside the fire. Track back and tilt up to reveal* KANBEI *and* GOROBEI *coming along the dark street towards him. (Still on page 79)*

589. Medium shot of KANBEI *and* GOROBEI *stopping.* KIKUCHIYO's *sword sticks up in the foreground. They come forward as soft snoring can be heard, off.* KANBEI *picks up the sword and walks away, followed by* GOROBEI.

590. Low angle medium close-up of a small straw hut. KANBEI *appears looking over his shoulder. Pan slightly left as he hides behind the straw hut, followed by* GOROBEI. *They stand looking back towards* KIKUCHIYO, *then* GOROBEI *looks at* KANBEI, *and picks up a stone and throws it.*

591. High angle medium close-up of KIKUCHIYO *lying with the fire in the background. He wakes with a start at the sound of the stone falling into a stream. Tilt up with him as he half crawls, half runs backwards past the fire to the log pile where his sword had been.*

KIKUCHIYO : Who's there? *He feels for his sword behind him. (Still on page 79) Realising it has gone he circles round, and then grabs a log from the pile.* Who is it? Come out. *The two others appear behind him.*

KANBEI : Kikuchiyo. KIKUCHIYO *leaps round and faces them.* You're very lucky it was only us. If it had been the bandits . . . *He throws the sword back to* KIKUCHIYO . . . you probably wouldn't be wearing your head any more.

They walk away into the darkness. KIKUCHIYO *is so ashamed he cannot answer and sinks down onto his knees by the fire. Fade out.*

592. Music in; fade in to a medium shot tracking with a horse which is pulling a plough guided by YOHEI. *In the foreground, men, women and children are watching. The horse is being led by a* WOMAN, *and* KIKUCHIYO *is walking along beside them, urging them on with shouts. (Still on page 79) Hold as they reach the end of the furrow and the* WOMAN *begins to lead the horse round.*

593. Low angle medium shot of the horse passing in the foreground, as the WOMAN *leads it round to the next furrow revealing* KIKUCHIYO *and* YOHEI *behind it, with the crowd of villagers and some of the samurai watching in the background.*

KIKUCHIYO : Yohei. *In the background* HEIHACHI *stands up.*
YOHEI : Yes, sir.
KIKUCHIYO : What is that? *He points at the emaciated horse.*

594. Low angle close-up of YOHEI.
YOHEI : It's my horse.

595. Close-up of KIKUCHIYO.

KIKUCHIYO *sarcastically*: Horse? I thought it was a big mouse. *He turns away.*

596. Medium shot of YOHEI *holding the plough, three-quarters back to camera in the foreground, and* KIKUCHIYO *standing by the horse; he smacks its rump.* SHICHIROJI, KYUZO, HEIHACHI *and some of the villagers stand watching in the background, laughing.*

597. Wipe to medium shot of SHICHIROJI, HEIHACHI, KYUZO *and* KATSUSHIRO, *backs to camera, walking towards a field where villagers are working.*

598. Low angle medium shot of GOROBEI *and* KANBEI, *silhouetted against the sky. They look round as two villagers carrying a basket slung from a pole pass behind them. Pan left as they walk along through a field. They walk behind a man wearing only a loin cloth, who is digging a trench. (Still on page 79) Other men are revealed working on the same job.* KANBEI *and* GOROBEI *inspect the work. Hold as* KANBEI *crouches down beside one of the trenches and puts his stick into it to measure the depth. Men behind them are digging other trenches while women carry away the earth in baskets.*

599. Dissolve to high angle medium shot of water running through a narrow channel into a larger pool. Tilt up to reveal it as a flooded field surrounded by barricades of bamboo stakes.

600. Dissolve to medium shot of children running along past a house. Pan right with them as they run, singing, and climb over a low wall towards some men building a high barricade.

601. Medium shot of the children reaching the barricade and climbing up it. Pan slightly right and tilt up with them.

602. Dissolve to medium shot of YOHEI, MANZO, MOSUKE *and* RIKICHI *threshing corn with hand-threshers. They circle round, threshing rhythmically as they talk.*

YOHEI: No bandits seem to be coming.

MOSUKE: That's right.

YOHEI: And we went to all the trouble of hiring those greedy samurai. And now we have to feed them. What a waste! *Music out.*

603. Dissolve to long shot of a crowd of villagers roaring with laughter, as they stand on the bridge. The river runs down into the foreground. Pan left across the bridge to where YOHEI'S *horse is standing on the opposite bank.* YOHEI *stands by its tail, and* KIKUCHIYO *at its head. The wooded hills rise up behind. Hold as* KIKUCHIYO *argues with* HEIHACHI, *who is standing nearby with* KYUZO. KIKUCHIYO *prepares to leap onto the horse's bare back.*

604. Medium shot with YOHEI *back to camera in the foreground, and the horse in front of him.* KIKUCHIYO *jumps onto the horse watched by* HEIHACHI *and* KYUZO. *He gathers in the reins and the horse circles round.*

HEIHACHI: Now what do you want to do that for? You'll tire it out. Get off. You'll cripple it and that will make Yohei cry.

KIKUCHIYO: You just don't know how good I am. If the rider is good enough even the worst horse will run well, fly right up in the sky.

KIKUCHIYO *rides off through the stubble fields. Music in:* KIKUCHIYO's *theme. He is watched by* YOHEI, HEIHACHI *and* KYUZO *all in back view.*

605. Long shot panning right with KIKUCHIYO *on the horse as it gallops through the fields.*

606. Medium shot of YOHEI, HEIHACHI *and* KYUZO, *watching* KIKUCHIYO *who is off-screen. In the background, the crowd of villagers are watching.*

HEIHACHI: He seems to be doing all right.

607. Long shot tracking right with KIKUCHIYO *as he gallops along the riverbank with the fields in the foreground. He goes out of sight behind a tall fence and a house. The track continues past the house and along a second fence, picking up the horse as it trots out from behind the fence, riderless and tossing its head.*

608. Medium shot of YOHEI, HEIHACHI *and* KYUZO *looking towards the horse in amazement with the villagers behind them.* HEIHACHI *and* KYUZO *burst out laughing.*

609. Long shot focussed on the high fence on the riverbank. KIKUCHIYO *appears from behind it and limps along the path. Track right with him.*

610. Medium shot (as 608). Everyone is roaring with laughter and pointing.

611. Long shot of KIKUCHIYO *on the riverbank, tracking with him as he limps and stumbles along. He picks up a stone and hurls it off-screen after the horse, then staggers on. Track with him until he catches up with the horse, which stands on the riverbank tossing its head and waving its tail. Track further as he tries to catch it; it trots on, just out of reach. He throws another stone at its rump but it trots away unconcerned, waving its tail.*

612. Medium shot of a crowd of villagers on the riverbank, laughing and pointing, and clapping their hands with delight. One of them slips into the water, still laughing.

613. High angle medium shot of another group of villagers crowded together, roaring with laughter. Music out, as camera tilts up slightly over their heads to reveal KANBEI and GOROBEI approaching in the background.

614. Medium shot of KANBEI and GOROBEI in the road, smiling as they look towards the scene. They stop. The laughter and shouting continues, off, during their conversation.

GOROBEI : They're happy.

KANBEI : Yes.

GOROBEI : The threshing is all done. The bandits haven't come. They're beginning to think they've gone away.

KANBEI : Yes. But when everything seems so peaceful, that's the most dangerous time of all.

GOROBEI : Right.

KANBEI : Tell them to return to their posts. GOROBEI *goes off.*

615. Medium long shot, through twisting branches, panning left with KATSUSHIRO and SHINO as they run up a slope in the forest, laughing happily. A bird sings, off. SHINO stops, and KATSUSHIRO stops also and looks back at her. She sits down among the flowers and he comes back and sits down next to her. Music in.

616. Medium close-up of SHINO sitting up, and KATSUSHIRO nearest camera, lying back among the flowers. SHINO looks down at him, (Still on page 80) then looks away, absently fingering a flower.

SHINO : I wish I'd been born into a samurai family.

KATSUSHIRO : I know. A farmer's life is very hard. I've been lucky.

SHINO : I mean . . . you're a real samurai and I'm just a farmer's daughter, so . . .

KATSUSHIRO *starts to sit up.*

617. Close-up of SHINO, *in back view, and* KATSUSHIRO *also in back view continuing his movement as he sits up beside her. They look at each other, their faces very close.*

KATSUSHIRO : No . . .

SHINO : Don't think about it.

618. Very big close-up of SHINO *facing camera, with the back of* KATSUSHIRO's *head half in frame, in soft focus in the foreground.*

SHINO : I don't care about what happens.

She moves her face towards him as if for a kiss, and KATSUSHIRO's *head moves left across frame completely masking her for a moment; then she is revealed again on the right, her eyes staring at him searchingly. She moves her head away.*

619. Jump cut to high angle medium shot of KATSUSHIRO *and* SHINO, *continuing her movement as she lies back suggestively among the flowers. He looks down at her. She breathes very deeply and her legs are splayed apart. Her breathing comes out in gasping sobs and then turns into near-hysterical laughter.*

620. Close-up of KATSUSHIRO *looking down at her, startled. She continues to laugh, off.*

621. High angle close-up of SHINO, *her head surrounded by flowers. Her laughter turns into sobs and she suddenly covers her face with both hands.*

SHINO : You . . . you're not a real samurai. Not a *real* samurai.

622. Close-up of KATSUSHIRO *staring down at her in amazement. Suddenly a horse neighs in the distance, off. He raises his eyes fearfully.* SHINO's *sobbing continues, off. The horse neighs again.*

623. High angle close-up of SHINO, *her face covered with her hands. Music out. She lowers her hands over her mouth and her eyes stare up in terror. She begins to sit up.*

624. High angle long shot through the trees and undergrowth continuing SHINO's *movement as she sits up. Then she and* KATSUSHIRO *both stand up. She holds onto his arm.* KATUSHIRO *begins to climb the slope followed by* SHINO, *and they go off on the left.*

625. General shot of a clearing in the forest with the ground dappled with sunlight filtering through the leaves. In the background SHINO *and* KATSUSHIRO *appear through the undergrowth, then stop. Sinister drumbeats in. Tilt down to reveal three horses all saddled, standing below a tree in a small hollow.*

626. *Medium close-up of* KATSUSHIRO, *with* SHINO *looking over his shoulder. He moves forward slightly, parting the undergrowth in front of him, and stares down. (Still on page 80) They look at each other, then he pushes* SHINO *and they run back the way they came. Drumbeats out.*

627. *Medium shot of the outer room of* RIKICHI's *house.* SHICHIROJI *comes in through the low entrance. Pan left with him as he walks towards the main room and bows at the entrance, then hold as* KANBEI *and* GOROBEI *are revealed sitting on the floor.* KANBEI *stands up and walks over to* SHICHIROJI, *camera panning slightly right with him.*

SHICHIROJI : I saw three men near the west road.

GOROBEI *comes up, listening.*

KANBEI : I see. Has anyone else seen them? *He looks at* GOROBEI.

SHICHIROJI : No. *They hear a noise and look towards the entrance.*

628. *Medium shot of the outer room.* KATSUSHIRO *runs through to the three other men, camera panning left with him.*

KATSUSHIRO *breathlessly* : I saw three horses on the back hill. I think they belong to the bandits.

KANBEI *putting his sword into his scabbard* : I know.

KATSUSHIRO *looks up at them incredulously, then they all turn again towards the entrance.*

629. *Medium shot of the outer room (as 628).* KYUZO *comes in; pan left with him as he comes up to join the group.*

KYUZO : So, they finally came, did they?

KANBEI : How did you know?

KYUZO *standing back to camera, looking at the other four* : Anyone would. All this running around. *They all look towards the entrance again.*

630. *Medium shot (as 628).* HEIHACHI *and* RIKICHI *run through the door; pan left with them as they go through to the others.*

HEIHACHI *to* KANBEI : Where did they come from? The hills, or from the west?

KANBEI : The west.

HEIHACHI : I see.

The six samurai and RIKICHI *stand together for a moment, weighing up the situation.* KATSUSHIRO *looks very alarmed.* KANBEI, *back to camera, gives him a friendly pat on the shoulder and then makes for the door, followed by* SHICHIROJI. *631. High angle medium shot outside the house as* KANBEI *and* SHICHIROJI *run out, quickly followed by all the others. 632. Medium shot of two children playing on the ground near a house. In the background the samurai run down into the village square. A* WOMAN *comes into shot in the foreground and hustles the children away. 633. Medium shot of* KANBEI, *in the foreground, with the others behind him. They all stop to look at something off-screen. 634. Quick shot of several women gathering together outside a house.*

A WOMAN *in a hushed voice* : The bandits are coming!

635. Medium shot (as 633). The samurai look round, frowning worriedly. 636. Medium shot of several villagers running around outside their house, excited and frightened, as the news is passed around. 637. Medium shot (633). Everyone looks around. KANBEI *turns to* RIKICHI.

KANBEI : Tell them to keep quiet. There are only three bandits. Make them go to their houses. Keep them quiet.

RIKICHI : Yes, sir. RIKICHI *runs off.*

KANBEI *turning to the others* : Those three would be scouts. They mustn't know that there are samurai here.

SHICHIROJI *nods and rushes off, followed by* KANBEI *and the others. Semi-circular pan right as they run away from camera. 638. Medium shot of a group of women and children screaming at each other hysterically, in complete confusion.* RIKICHI *comes up, trying to calm them down. He manages to get them to disperse; then turns round, camera panning right with him as he runs across to another group of villagers including several men. He explains the situation to them and pushes them off to their houses, then runs off again, camera panning right with him as he goes over to another group, who gather round him for reassurance. Pan further as the villagers scatter, gathering their children and going to their homes.* RIKICHI *turns round the square and camera pans with him, picking up* KIKUCHIYO *who is leading along the horse with* YOHEI *and a group of children. Hold as he calls out to* RIKICHI.

KIKUCHIYO : What's happened? Bandits? *He claps his hands in delight as* RIKICHI *nods.* Oh, they've finally come, have they? YOHEI *hands him his sword, and he hands the horse's reins to* RIKICHI, *looking pleased.*

639. Medium shot of the wall of a house near the western barricade, with a straw fence in the foreground. Behind the fence some of the samurai can be seen creeping past very quietly, camera tracking left with them. Hold at the end of the fence as SHICHIROJI *appears, dropping down onto all fours. The other samurai quickly go into the house, camera panning right with them as they disappear inside.*

640. Medium shot of the family inside the house. Hearing the door open they all look up. Tilt up as they all leap to their feet and KANBEI *appears in the foreground, back to camera. The family rush back and cower together against the far wall.*

KANBEI : Keep quiet.

641. Medium shot of a window with KANBEI *going towards it in back view followed by* GOROBEI *and the other samurai. They crowd together, looking through the window. (Still on page 80)* SHICHIROJI *leans over* KANBEI's *shoulder.*

GOROBEI : Where?

SHICHIROJI : By that big tree.

Suddenly they all duck down below the level of the window ledge.

642. Medium close-up of the window bars in the foreground with pots and bowls on the window ledge. Outside can be seen the big western barricade with a hill rising up beyond it and three figures making their way downwards.

643. Medium shot of part of the barricade with the three bandits just visible on the other side, looking through.

644. Medium shot of the six samurai, bending down and look-ing through the window. KANBEI *kneels down and turns back to the others. Outside, the three bandits can be seen running*

129

along beyond the barricade.

KANBEI : They're scouts, all right.

GOROBEI : Looks like they're surprised to see our fence.

KANBEI : At any rate, they still don't know about us.

GOROBEI : They think they've got only farmers to contend with, then.

Just then the voice of KIKUCHIYO *is heard shouting loudly.*

KIKUCHIYO *off* : Hey, where did you all get to?

HEIHACHI : Oh, the idiot!

> HEIHACHI *gets up quickly; pan left, losing the others except* KATSUSHIRO, *as* HEIHACHI *goes over to a side window and looks through it.*

HEIHACHI *in a low voice* : Kikuchiyo!

> KIKUCHIYO *can be seen standing outside the window.* HEIHACHI *beckons to him then hurries off, as* KIKUCHIYO, *grinning, comes up to the window, watched by* KATSUSHIRO. KIKUCHIYO *looks through the window, giggling.*
>
> *645. Medium shot of* KIKUCHIYO *outside the house, by the doorway.*

KIKUCHIYO : Oh, there you are! Hey, what's this about the bandits finally coming here? Have they arrived at last?

> HEIHACHI'S *hands appear through the doorway. One clamps over* KIKUCHIYO's *mouth and the other drags him out of sight by the shoulder.*
>
> *646. Medium close-up continuing* HEIHACHI's *movement as he drags* KIKUCHIYO *into the house. In the background the other samurai look at him reproachfully.* HEIHACHI *and* KIKUCHIYO *stand facing one another angrily in the foreground. Behind them* KANBEI *suddenly stands up in front of the window.*

KANBEI : Now they know about us.

> *The other samurai crowd back round the window leaving* KIKUCHIYO *watching them petulantly.*
>
> *647. Medium shot of the barricade with the three bandits visible beyond it, running away up the hill.*
>
> *648. Medium shot from behind of the six samurai peering through the window, which is off-screen. They move away, camera panning slightly right, and look at each other worriedly.*

GOROBEI : They can't be allowed to rejoin the others.

KANBEI : Right.

KYUZO : I'll get them. The hills are my responsibility.

As KYUZO *moves he reveals* KIKUCHIYO *standing shamefacedly by the door.*

KIKUCHIYO : I'm sorry . . . I didn't know.

KANBEI : Don't apologise. Just go out and get them. And take the short cut.

KIKUCHIYO *grins with delight, hands his sword to* SHICHIROJI *and runs off rubbing his hands with glee.*

KYUZO : Right, we'll reach the horses first.

He turns and runs after KIKUCHIYO, *camera panning left with him, revealing* KIKUCHIYO *standing in the porch beckoning excitedly.* KATSUSHIRO *starts to follow* KYUZO *and camera holds on the doorway as he is about to go through. But* KANBEI *steps up to him.*

KANBEI : Katsushiro ! KIKUCHIYO *runs off as* KATSUSHIRO *turns to* KANBEI *who continues.* You can go, but just watch, don't fight. Understand ? *(Still on page 80)*

KIKUCHIYO *leaps back to the porch and pulls at* KATSUSHIRO, *then goes off again.*

KATSUSHIRO *to* KANBEI : Yes, sir. *He quickly follows* KIKUCHIYO.

649. Wipe to medium shot of the three horses standing among the trees in the forest. Drumbeats in, very softly. Tilt up through the trees, losing the horses, to reveal KIKUCHIYO, KYUZO *and* KATSUSHIRO *at the top of the rise, hurrying towards camera. One of the horses neighs, off.*

650. Medium shot of the three samurai peering through the foliage which partly obscures them in the foreground.

KIKUCHIYO *impressed* : They're very good horses.

KYUZO *looks around and then goes off. Pan right with* KIKUCHIYO *as he turns to follow.* KATSUSHIRO *follows him and the pan continues as they climb a short rise, till they rejoin* KYUZO, *who turns to* KATSUSHIRO.

KYUZO : You stay here.

KIKUCHIYO *and* KYUZO *make off up the hill and* KATSUSHIRO *starts to run down it towards camera. Fast pan right with him and hold as he stops to look back up the hill. Pan continues down and right past the base of a large tree trunk.* KATSUSHIRO *dodges behind it and then appears on the other side, looking round.*

651. Low angle medium close-up of KATSUSHIRO, *back to camera, looking up round the tree trunk. At the top of the slope* KIKUCHIYO *and* KYUZO *can be seen running through the trees; they go out of sight behind the tree trunk. Pan right with* KATSUSHIRO *as he edges round to the other side of the tree to look, but* KIKUCHIYO *and* KYUZO *have disappeared. A horse whinnies, off, and he ducks back behind the tree trunk, camera panning slightly right as he does so. Drumbeats, louder. He looks in the direction of the horses, then looks all round, very nervously. He plucks up courage and looks back up the hill in an attempt to catch sight of* KIKUCHIYO *and* KYUZO.

652. Low angle long shot looking up slope to the trees at the top. Flowers grow in profusion. For a moment nothing moves; a bird sings.

653. High angle medium close-up of KATSUSHIRO *peering round the tree trunk. He starts to move away, still looking up. Pan right with him and tilt down slightly as he runs down a short slope to where the horses are revealed standing under the trees. Pan right with him as he pushes his way through the undergrowth, and begins to crawl up the slope.*

654. High angle medium shot of KATSUSHIRO, *back to camera, crawling up the slope through the flowers and grass. Hold as he stops, pressed against the ground, and parts the flowers to get a better view up the slope. Drumbeats get gradually louder. Tilt up losing* KATSUSHIRO, *revealing the trees and grass on the crown of the hill.* KYUZO *can be seen near the base of a tree.*

655. Medium long shot of KYUZO, *partly obscured by the grass and flowers in the foreground, sitting nonchalantly at the base of the tree.*

656. Medium close-up of KATSUSHIRO *peering up through the flowers. He looks round then flattens some more flowers to get a better view, moving his head very slightly.*

657. Medium long shot (as 655). Suddenly KIKUCHIYO *appears about ten feet up in a nearby tree, pressing himself flat against one of the main branches. He picks a twig and throws it down towards* KYUZO, *who does not react.*

658. High angle medium close-up of KATSUSHIRO.

659. Medium shot of KYUZO *leaning against the tree trunk, relaxed and surrounded by flowers, his sword resting lightly across his knees. (Still on page 80) He plays with a flower; it is the only thing moving in the shot.*

660. High angle close-up of KATSUSHIRO *amid the flowers, staring up in amazement. (Still on page 80) His eyes move as he looks in the direction of* KIKUCHIYO.

661. Low angle medium shot of KIKUCHIYO *up in the tree, his body pressed flat along the branch. He looks round the branch and then crouches right down in the fork. (Still on page 80) Drumbeats even louder.*

662. Close-up of KATSUSHIRO *(as 660).*

663. Medium shot of KYUZO *fiddling with the flower at the base of his tree.*

664. High angle big close-up of KATSUSHIRO *looking up tensely. His eyes move from one to the other.*

665. Low angle medium long shot of the two trees with KYUZO *sitting at the base of one, and* KIKUCHIYO *high up on the branch of the other. Suddenly the three bandits appear, running up the slope towards the trees.*

666. High angle big close-up of KATSUSHIRO, *his eyes wide with apprehension. Drumbeats very loud.*

667. Medium long shot of the bandits running towards camera under KIKUCHIYO's *tree, with* KYUZO *visible sitting by the other tree. As they run* KIKUCHIYO *braces himself to jump and* KYUZO *very slowly starts to get up. He stands in front of the bandits impassively and they stop, off their guard, staring at him in amazement. Then, as* KIKUCHIYO *jumps down from the branch with a yell, pan slightly right as* KYUZO *steps forward to one of the bandits who has just drawn his sword. He fells the man with one blow (Still on page 80) and* KIKUCHIYO *falls on the second man. The third* BANDIT *tries to run away, coming towards camera. Fast pan right as* KYUZO *pursues him and, with a single sword thrust, runs him through at the base of a tree. Drumbeats out, abruptly. As he falls, pan back with* KYUZO, *who returns to where* KIKUCHIYO *and the other* BANDIT *are still struggling.* KYUZO *turns to where* KATSUSHIRO *is hiding, off-screen.*

KYUZO : Katsushiro! It's all over. You can come out now.
As he calls KIKUCHIYO *is pounding the* BANDIT *into the ground*

with obvious satisfaction.

668. Wipe to medium close-up of the head and shoulders of the surviving BANDIT, *lying on the ground, his arms bound tightly. (Still on page 145) People's feet can be seen in the background and the crowd shouts, off. The man rolls about, screaming for mercy. Track back to include* KIKUCHIYO *who is hanging onto the end of the rope that is tied round the* BANDIT. *(Still on page 145) Behind him the other samurai are holding back the villagers who are trying to get at the man, armed— men and women alike—with picks, hoes, spears or clubs.* KIKUCHIYO *is in very good spirits and every now and again gives the* BANDIT *a vicious kick. Suddenly some villagers break through the cordon in the foreground.*

669. Medium shot panning swiftly right as GOROBEI *rushes through with a spear to hold back some of the villagers.*

670. Medium close-up of SHICHIROJI *with a spear using all his strength to hold back another group of villagers, who are screaming and shouting hysterically.*

671. Medium close-up of HEIHACHI *holding back some men and women who are pushing and struggling to get through. Pan left as he manages to push them back with both arms outstretched.*

672. High angle medium close-up of KYUZO, *in back view, surrounded by villagers but holding them off with his sword which he is holding horizontally with both hands.*

673. Quick medium shot of KATSUSHIRO *struggling with other villagers.*

674. Medium shot of KANBEI, *back to camera, pushing back more villagers. Fast pan left with* KANBEI *as he turns away from them and runs towards camera.*

675. Medium close-up of KANBEI *panning left with him as he runs into the middle of the circle of screaming villagers.*

676. High angle medium long shot of KANBEI *standing surrounded by the angry villagers, who are still trying to get through to the* BANDIT, *waving and threatening with their weapons. The commotion has raised clouds of dust. (Still on page 145)*

KANBEI *shouting and waving his arms*: Listen! This man is a prisoner of war. *The villagers take no notice.* He gave himself up.

He's confessed. He is begging for mercy. We must not kill him!

The villagers take little notice and still try to break in while the samurai continue to fight to keep them back.

677. Medium shot of a group of villagers with HEIHACHI *trying to hold them back. In the foreground a man naked to the waist manages to break through. A woman next to him waves a pickaxe.*

678. Medium shot of another group with RIKICHI *in front holding a spear. He looks down towards the bandit, off-screen, his eyes wild.*

RIKICHI : Let me do it, let me.

The man next to him tries to pull his spear away, but RIKICHI *hangs onto it and pushes the man back. He comes forward, staring down, and raises his spear to strike. Pan right as* KANBEI *rushes up and grabs* RIKICHI *round the waist, pulling him back. (Still on page 145) Suddenly everyone stops and looks towards something off-screen; the noise dies down.*

679. Medium shot of the OLD WOMAN *(Kyumon's grandmother) coming up the edge of the crowd carrying a vicious-looking three-pronged hoe. Music and humming chorus in. (Still on page 145) Pan left with her as she shuffles past the crowd who stand staring at her, motionless and silent. Camera picks up* KANBEI *watching her pass and holds on him as the* OLD WOMAN *goes off.* RIKICHI *and* SHICHIROJI *stand behind* KANBEI. GOROBEI *comes up from one side, and* HEIHACHI, KYUZO *and* KATSUSHIRO *join them from the other. They all watch the* OLD WOMAN, *out of shot. Then old* GISAKU *appears in the foreground, leaning on his stick. The samurai look towards him as he begins to speak.*

GISAKU : Very good. Let her avenge her son's death in her own way. Make way there. Somebody help her!

RIKICHI pushes past KANBEI *and goes off, following the* OLD WOMAN. GISAKU *looks up at* KANBEI, *while more villagers run past him in the foreground, following* RIKICHI. *The samurai turn away dejectedly, then go off, pushing their way through the crowd. Hold on* GISAKU *as the villagers continue to crowd forward. Music out.*

680. Wipe to high angle medium shot of the samurai sitting in a circle in RIKICHI's *house with* RIKICHI *in the background.*

KIKUCHIYO *is lying with his feet propped up against a pillar.*

GOROBEI : According to what the bandit said, their fortress must be . . .

KYUZO : . . . Must be very easy to take.

KIKUCHIYO *rolling over and grinning* : Must be as full of holes as Yohei's trousers.

GOROBEI : If it is that easy . . .

KIKUCHIYO : I'd attack by night, I would.

HEIHACHI : There are forty of them. But we could march right in and fight.

KANBEI : Wait. If we lose one man we've lost . . . even if we kill five for that one.

> *In the background,* RIKICHI *gets up and gets on with some work.*

GOROBEI : That is true of any battle.

KYUZO : If three of us go we can kill ten of them easily.

KANBEI *calling* : Rikichi.

> RIKICHI *puts down what he is doing and comes to the edge of the group.*

RIKICHI : Yes, sir?

KANBEI : How far is it there?

RIKICHI : A good day's walk.

KIKUCHIYO : But we have horses, the ones we took from the bandits.

RIKICHI : On horseback it would take about half a day.

KANBEI : I see. *A pause as they all stare at* KANBEI *thoughtfully. (Still on page 146)* *

> *681. Close-up of* KANBEI, *his head bent forward. He looks up.*

KANBEI : It's decided then. If we leave now and ride all night long, we'll get there at dawn. Now, who will go? *He looks up.*

> *682. Medium close-up of* KYUZO *and* HEIHACHI *who have already got to their feet and are moving towards the door. Tilt down to reveal* KATSUSHIRO *also standing up.*

> *683. Close-up of* KANBEI *looking up.*

KANBEI : No, not you, Katsushiro.

> *684. Medium shot of* KATSUSHIRO *looking back, disappointed.* RIKICHI *is in the foreground, three-quarters back to camera, looking up at* KATSUSHIRO. KIKUCHIYO *gets to his feet beside*

---

* End of reel 5.

KATSUSHIRO.

KIKUCHIYO *pointing down to* KANBEI, *out of shot* : Well, I'm going. It's all decided.

As KIKUCHIYO *starts to go,* RIKICHI *jumps to his feet in the foreground.*

685. Medium close-up panning with RIKICHI *as he jumps forward and kneels beside* KANBEI. *Hold on them both,* KANBEI *in three-quarter back view,* RIKICHI *facing camera.*

RIKICHI *urgently* : Me too . . . you'll need a guide !

686. Medium close-up of KIKUCHIYO *adjusting his sword. He looks down towards* KANBEI.

KIKUCHIYO : But you can't. There aren't enough horses.

687. Medium close-up of HEIHACHI. *He moves towards camera,* KYUZO *behind him.*

HEIHACHI : There's Yohei's horse. You'll take it.

688. Quick close-up of KIKUCHIYO, *looking sick.*

HEIHACHI *off* : No one but . . .

689. Medium close-up of HEIHACHI *(as 687).*

HEIHACHI : . . . Sir Kikuchiyo can manage that animal. *He points, and he and* KYUZO *both laugh.*

690. Medium close-up of KIKUCHIYO, *grimacing, He rubs his nose with his finger.*

691. Wipe to a long shot of KYUZO, HEIHACHI *and* RIKICHI *galloping through the dark forest. Drumbeats in. Pan briefly right with them. Hold as they go off. A second's pause; then* KIKUCHIYO *appears, riding* YOHEI's *horse; it is moving rather reluctantly and in spite of* KIKUCHIYO's *shouts it stops and wheels round, heading for home.*

KIKUCHIYO : No, you idiot, not that way, this way !

692. Medium shot of KIKUCHIYO *on the horse, trying to pull it up. Pan slightly left with them and hold as* KIKUCHIYO *manages to stop the horse.*

KIKUCHIYO : Stupid ! No, no !

Pan further as he jumps off and faces the horse, pulling the reins hard. The horse pulls back the other way. (Still on page 146) KIKUCHIYO *continues to haul at the reins, pointing up the path in the direction he wants to go.*

693. Medium shot of KIKUCHIYO *pulling the reins. The horse tosses its head.*

KIKUCHIYO : Call yourself a horse? Shame on you!

KIKUCHIYO *picks up a stone and is about to remount when the horse jerks away and gallops off up the path past him. He gets up quickly and runs after it.*

KIKUCHIYO *shouting* : Wait, wait.

694. *Medium shot tracking with the horse as it gallops through the forest.*

695. *Medium shot of* KIKUCHIYO, *tracking with him as he runs after it.*

KIKUCHIYO *shouting* : Don't run off like that! I apologise! I'm sorry!

696. *High angle medium shot tracking through the forest with the horse.*

697. *High angle medium shot of* KIKUCHIYO *running after it waving his arms desperately.*

698. *Wipe to a very high angle long shot of the side of a mountain. Tilt down into the valley where the first three horses gallop by, followed by the fourth —* KIKUCHIYO *having now remounted. Tilt down further, into a deep ravine, losing the horses.*

699. *Wipe to medium shot of a waterfall in a gorge with a river running along in the foreground. Drumbeats in, very softly. In the background one of the horses, led by* RIKICHI, *appears round an outcrop of rock, followed by the others.*

700. *Medium shot from behind of the four men leading their horses along a ledge of rock behind the waterfall. (Still on page 146)*

701. *Medium shot from the side of the men leading the horses behind the waterfall.* KIKUCHIYO *is having difficulty in making* YOHEI'S *horse follow him. They leave their horses and start to move towards the river.*

702. *Medium shot of* RIKICHI *with* HEIHACHI *behind him.* KYUZO *and* KIKUCHIYO *come up and join them, and they peer forward through the darkness.* RIKICHI *points, then they all run forward, going off in the foreground.*

703. *High angle long shot looking up the river towards the waterfall. In the background the four men can be seen jumping down into the river and splashing towards camera in single file. (Still on page 146) Camera tilts down slightly as they*

138

climb the rocky bank in the foreground, led by KIKUCHIYO.
Track back slightly and pan right as KIKUCHIYO *and* RIKICHI
run along the bank. Track past some tethered horses as KIKU-
CHIYO *and* RIKICHI *run towards a group of buildings visible in
the background. They go out of sight behind the horses and*
KYUZO *and* HEIHACHI *can be seen following them. Track on
further, then back slightly as they run up to the largest of the
buildings.*

704. Medium close-up of RIKICHI *with* KYUZO *next to him
peering through cracks in the timber wall of the building.*
HEIHACHI *comes up between them and also peers through.*

*705. General shot of the interior of the bandits' hideout, seen
through the crack in the wall. Men and women can be seen
lying asleep in the gloom, in varying degrees of nakedness.*

*706. Medium shot of the bandits asleep on the floor or on raised
beds, partly covered by blankets or clothing that has been
strewn about. A woman's leg can be seen hanging down over
the edge of one of the high beds. Drumbeats louder.*

707. Medium shot of the three samurai and RIKICHI, *in back
view, peering through the crack. Pan left with* KIKUCHIYO,
*losing the others, as he goes to the corner of the house and
looks round it to the out-buildings. Pan back as he rejoins*
HEIHACHI *and* RIKICHI. *He taps* RIKICHI *on the shoulder.*

KIKUCHIYO *whispering* : Set fire to the huts.

Pan slightly to include KYUZO.

HEIHACHI : Then we'll kill them as they come out.

RIKICHI *looks round excitedly and then dashes away. The
others go back to look through the crack.*

708. Close-up of KIKUCHIYO *in profile peering through another
crack, looking amazed.*

*709. Medium shot of some bandits asleep; the woman's leg is
again visible hanging over the edge of the bed.*

710. Close-up of KIKUCHIYO. *He moves back a bit. Still looking
through a crack, he undoes his belt and winds it round his
forehead, tying it at the back of his head.*

*711. Medium shot of a bandit and a woman lying naked on
the floor, their bare legs entwined, partly covered by a blanket.*

712. Close-up of KIKUCHIYO *grinning; he looks through the
crack, as he finishes fixing the belt round his forehead.*

139

713. Medium shot of a man and a woman sleeping on a raised bed. One of the woman's arms is dangling over the edge. (Still on page 146)

714. Close-up of KIKUCHIYO *looking through. Suddenly he ducks down; tilt down with him as he looks through another crack in the wall.*

715. Medium shot of more bodies lying about—bare knees, bare arms, men, women; it is impossible to distinguish individual bodies. Drumbeats still over.

716. Close-up of KIKUCHIYO *grinning.* HEIHACHI *and* KYUZO *are visible beside him, also peering through.*

717. Medium shot of a corner of the building. A figure can be seen lying down behind gauze curtains. A single candle burns, its flame flickering in a slight draught. The figure sits up slowly. It is a beautiful YOUNG WOMAN. *A Noh flute begins to play over. The curtains stir in a slight breeze.*

718. Close-up of KYUZO, *nearest camera,* HEIHACHI *in the centre and* KIKUCHIYO, *beside him, all looking through cracks in the wall.*

719. Close-up of the YOUNG WOMAN, *staring sadly into space. Her head sways mournfully from side to side as the flute continues over. Then fast pan right as she suddenly pulls herself back, staring fearfully at something off-screen.*

720. Close-up of the three samurai (as 718). Suddenly they all turn their heads towards something they can see inside.

721. Medium shot inside the building with things strewn all over the floor and various cooking utensils and weapons hanging from the roof. Smoke is billowing up in the background. Suddenly a flame flares up and catches hold on the wooden wall.

722. Close-up of the three samurai outside. HEIHACHI *grins delightedly.*

723. Close-up of the YOUNG WOMAN *through the gauze curtains. Pan right with her as she backs away in horror. Suddenly she turns her head, camera re-framing slightly as she looks away. Then she turns back and looks through the curtain, camera re-framing again to keep her in close-up. She lowers her head, then raises her eyes again with a bitter little smile. Then very slowly she turns away.*

140

724. *Close-up of the three samurai (as 722). Their swords at the ready, they look at each other then back out through the crack in the wall. The flute stops, but the drumbeats continue over.*

725. *Long shot of* RIKICHI *dashing out of one of the outbuildings. Pan right as he runs along beside the main building and rejoins the samurai. The roof is now burning fiercely. The four men pair off and stand ready on either side of the door. Suddenly screams can be heard inside and several women appear at the door. (Still on page 147) Drumbeats out. The samurai push them out of the way, waiting for the men to appear, and as the first bandits rush out they cut them down.*

726. *Medium shot of* RIKICHI *and* HEIHACHI *fighting three or four bandits.*

727. *Medium long shot of the samurai outside the doorway beating off the men and pushing the women away as they come out.*

728. *Long shot focussed towards the building, which is now silhouetted by the flames on the roof. The three samurai and* RIKICHI *battle with the bandits, and women rush about hysterically. Many of the bandits and their women run towards camera, falling down the riverbank in the foreground. Horses neigh shrilly off.*

729. *Low angle medium long shot looking towards the entrance.* KYUZO *and* HEIHACHI *shove two women away who run towards camera. In the foreground two horses can be seen, bucking and plunging with fear, trying to break free.*

730. *Long shot from the other side of the river with the main building blazing on the left. Smoke billows across the clearing, obscuring most of the battle. Two women crouch in the foreground, near a tall, dead tree trunk.*

731. *Low angle medium long shot of the battle outside the house. More people rush out. Half-naked bandits fall screaming into the river in the foreground.* RIKICHI *kicks one of them roughly and then turns back to the battle as more men rush out.*

732. *Medium shot of* KYUZO *and* HEIHACHI *in back view, chasing two of the men who are running out of the house. (Still on page 147)* RIKICHI *joins them and he and* KYUZO *turn*

towards camera.

*733. High angle medium long shot looking down over the bank
into the river. Several bandits are wading along the river-bed
closely pursued by* HEIHACHI *and* KIKUCHIYO. KIKUCHIYO
*wades through the water, camera panning right as he comes up
onto the bank in the foreground at the base of the dead tree-
trunk. He crouches down beside a rock and* KYUZO, HEIHACHI
and RIKICHI *join him. He laughs as they watch the confusion
in the river.*

734. Medium close-up of HEIHACHI, *and* KIKUCHIYO *in back
view in the foreground. In the background the fort blazes
furiously. A few half-dressed bandits are running about on the
opposite river bank, now armed with swords, and one or two
with guns. They point across in the direction of the samurai.*

735. Medium close-up of KYUZO *and* RIKICHI *in the foreground, crouching behind the rock. The bandits can be seen
outside the blazing building in the background. Suddenly*
RIKICHI *looks round and stands up.*

736. Medium shot of the YOUNG WOMAN *appearing at the
entrance of the blazing house wearing a flowered kimono.
(Still on page 147) Her arms are folded and she looks round
calmly. Noh flute in again.*

737. Medium shot of RIKICHI *and* KYUZO *with the flaming
buildings in the background.* RIKICHI *suddenly runs off,
revealing* HEIHACHI *and* KIKUCHIYO *beside* KYUZO. *They all
watch him go in amazement.*

738. Medium long shot of RIKICHI, *back to camera, running
towards the* YOUNG WOMAN, *who is standing at the doorway
of the house.*

*739. High angle medium shot of the three samurai looking
towards* RIKICHI, *out of shot, with the river behind them.*

HEIHACHI *shouting*: Rikichi! Look out! Rikichi!

740. Medium long shot of RIKICHI, *back to camera, facing the*
YOUNG WOMAN, *who stands at the doorway, silhouetted against
the flames.*

741. Medium close-up of the YOUNG WOMAN. *She notices*
RIKICHI *and starts to run away terrified.*

742. Medium shot of the entrance from the side. The YOUNG
WOMAN *runs inside, dropping her shawl. Flute tune out.*

743. High angle medium close-up of KIKUCHIYO *in three-quarter back view, looking up in horror towards the house*

744. Medium shot of RIKICHI *from the side, running towards the doorway of the building. He reaches the threshold but staggers back from the leaping, roaring flames.*

745. Medium close-up of RIKICHI *in back view, silhouetted against the flames holding his sword. Pan left as he backs away.*

746. High angle medium shot of KIKUCHIYO, HEIHACHI *and* KYUZO *ducking behind the rock.*

747. Medium long shot of RIKICHI, *three-quarters back to camera, beside the burning doorway. He thrusts and lunges with his sword, but there is no-one else there. He backs away and loses his balance.*

748. Long shot of the blazing buildings. In the foreground the samurai, backs to camera, watch as RIKICHI *slips down the river bank opposite.* KYUZO *half-stands, shouting.*

KYUZO : Come back, Rikichi! Rikichi, come back!

RIKICHI *staggers to his feet and scrambles back up towards the house again. (Still on page 147) The air is filled with the noise of the fire and the bandits' shouts.* RIKICHI *staggers about waving his sword insanely.*

749. High angle medium shot of the three samurai by the river looking towards the buildings, off-screen. Suddenly HEIHACHI *gets up and rushes away. The other two watch him go in alarm.*

750. High angle medium close-up of KYUZO *in profile.*

KYUZO *shouting* : Heihachi!

751. Low angle medium shot of RIKICHI, *three-quarters back to camera, half-crawling, half-running towards the house.* HEIHACHI *appears and grabs his free arm. Pan right as* RIKICHI *rushes towards the doorway and plunges across the threshold. Pan left as* HEIHACHI *grabs him round the waist and pulls him out backwards. Track back slightly and tilt down as they both fall down the river bank into the water, still struggling. Pan further left as* HEIHACHI *manages to drag* RIKICHI *back, in spite of the latter's efforts to get back to the building. Suddenly a shot rings out. Rapid tilt down as* HEIHACHI *falls, landing heavily on the rocks at the edge of the water.*

752. Medium close-up of RIKICHI; *his mouth falls open in horror as he looks back down at* HEIHACHI *off-screen. Pan left and tilt down as he bends down to grab hold of* HEIHACHI.

753. Medium close-up of KIKUCHIYO *getting to his feet.*

754. High angle medium shot panning with KIKUCHIYO *and* KYUZO *as they run along the river bank towards* RIKICHI *and* HEIHACHI. *Hold as* RIKICHI *and* KIKUCHIYO *help* HEIHACHI *up. Pan back as they drag him to safety behind the rock.*

755. Long shot of the building completely enveloped in flames.

756. Very high angle long shot of the group of buildings blazing, smoke billowing upwards, with mountains just visible in the background.

757. High angle long shot of the blazing buildings with the horses tethered in the foreground. (Still on page 147)

758. High angle medium shot, panning right with RIKICHI *and* KIKUCHIYO *as they drag* HEIHACHI *through the river. Tilt up as they climb onto the opposite bank, followed by* KYUZO, *going away from camera towards the waterfall.*

759. Medium shot of KIKUCHIYO *and* RIKICHI *laying* HEIHACHI *on the bank in front of the waterfall.* KYUZO *joins them.*

KIKUCHIYO *slapping* RIKICHI : You idiot! It's your fault. Who was that woman?

RIKICHI *sobbing* : My wife! *He throws himself forward.*

760. Medium long shot of the four men on the riverbank near the waterfall, the river flowing past into the foreground. Continuing his movement, RIKICHI *throws himself onto the ground. Suddenly* HEIHACHI *lurches forward onto his face, hanging over the river bank. The samurai theme comes in softly.*

KYUZO *quickly bending over him* : Heihachi!

KIKUCHIYO *and* RIKICHI *immediately jump up to help.*

KIKUCHIYO : Heihachi! Brace up!

RIKICHI *sobs.* HEIHACHI *remains motionless.*

761. Wipe to low angle long shot looking up a slope to a small burial mound silhouetted against the sky. The samurai stand beside it. Villagers are grouped together in the foreground, backs to camera. The wind blows up the dust among the small gravestones of the village burial place.

762. Low angle medium long shot of the small mound with the six samurai standing on one side, and RIKICHI *and* GISAKU, *with two other farmers, on the other side. They stand with*

heads bowed. KIKUCHIYO *holds* HEIHACHI'S *sword out in front of him.*

763. Medium shot of KIKUCHIYO, *in three-quarter back view, resting on* HEIHACHI'S *sword with the burial mound on the right.* KANBEI *stands beside him with* KATSUSHIRO *and* SHICHIROJI *just behind. Suddenly* KIKUCHIYO *draws* HEIHACHI'S *sword from its scabbard; pan slightly right as he takes a couple of steps up the mound and sticks it in the top. (Production still on page 148) Pan back as he steps back again and throws down the scabbard. Tilt down as he sits down dejectedly, with his back to the others. Old* GISAKU, *who is now visible on the right, begins to kneel down.*

764. Low angle long shot looking up the hill with the samurai on one side. Continuing his movement, GISAKU *kneels down and bows his head by the mound. The villagers, who are grouped in a semicircle in the foreground, begin to kneel as well. Finally, everybody except the samurai is kneeling.*

765. Low angle medium shot of GOROBEI *and* KANBEI *silhouetted against the sky, with the sword stuck in the mound in the foreground.* KANBEI *looks at* GOROBEI *and then down at the mound. (Still on page 148)*

KANBEI : We were counting on him to cheer us when the situation became gloomy. And now he's gone!

766. Medium shot of RIKICHI *crouched down, his head resting on his clasped hands.* YOHEI *is behind him—both are seen from the side.* MANZO *stands behind them. Suddenly* RIKICHI'S *shoulders begin to tremble violently and camera pans left as he throws himself prostrate on the mound, sobbing bitterly.*

767. Low angle medium shot of KIKUCHIYO, *still seated, with* SHICHIROJI, KANBEI *and* GOROBEI *behind him. On the other side of the mound* GISAKU *is bent double on his knees, and beyond him is the weeping figure of* RIKICHI. KIKUCHIYO *looks at him angrily.*

KIKUCHIYO *furiously*: Shut up! *He stands up, camera tilting up with him.* Stop crying, fool!

768. Low angle long shot with the crowd of villagers kneeling, and now weeping as well. KIKUCHIYO *runs down the slope towards them.*

153

KIKUCHIYO *shouting*: Stop crying! Fools, idiots! *He goes off in the foreground.*

769. Medium shot tracking with KIKUCHIYO *as he runs through the village.*

770. Medium shot of KIKUCHIYO *as he runs round behind a fence, coming towards camera. Pan left as he ducks under the door of* RIKICHI'S *house, in back view, and runs through, grabbing the banner made by* HEIHACHI. *Pan back without pausing as he runs out of the house.*

771. Low angle medium shot of KIKUCHIYO *carrying the banner as he climbs the sloping thatched roof of the house, back to camera. Tilt up with him as he scrambles to the top.*

772. Medium shot of KANBEI *and* GOROBEI *in back view, standing beside the grave, with* KYUZO, KATSUSHIRO *and* SHICHIROJI *in profile beside them. In the background,* KIKUCHIYO *can be seen on the roof holding the banner. He sticks it firmly into the thatch where it flutters in the breeze, and then he sits down on the roof beside it. Suddenly* KANBEI *notices it and they all turn to look.*

773. Low angle medium shot of the banner against the sky, fluttering in the breeze. A trumpet fanfare takes over the samurai theme, faster and louder.

774. Low angle long shot up the hill towards the mound, with the villagers and the samurai all looking up at the banner, off-screen. Gradually the villagers begin to stand up, crowding forward to look at the banner.

775. Medium shot of a group of villagers looking up, holding spears.

776. Low angle medium shot of the banner.

777. Medium shot of some women, brushing away their tears and smiling as they point towards the banner. Music out.

778. Medium close-up of the banner fluttering in the breeze. Tilt down from the top over the six circles, the triangle, then the Japanese characters which mean ' Farmers '.

779. Low angle medium close-up of GISAKU, *tears in his eyes, looking towards the banner. Behind him* RIKICHI, YOHEI, MANZO *and* MOSUKE *stare towards it also.*

780. General low angle shot of the burial hill with village women in the foreground, men with spears above them, and at

*the top the samurai, silhouetted against the sky. They are all
looking up towards the banner.*

*781. Medium close-up of the banner, tilting down over the
symbols. Hold for a moment on the symbol of the farmers.*

782. Low angle medium shot of KIKUCHIYO, *arms folded, sitting
on the roof and clenching his teeth. He looks up. Suddenly he
sees something off-screen, and he unfolds his arms, staring
forward.*

*783. Low angle very long shot looking up the side of a far hill
towards the horizon. Something moves at the top; then horses
and riders appear — tiny figures silhouetted against the sky.*

784. Low angle medium shot of KIKUCHIYO. *Tilt up with him
as he stands up with a yell, pointing and waving his arms.*

KIKUCHIYO *shouting*: They've come! The bastards have finally
come!

*Pan left with him as he makes his way along the roof past the
banner, pointing, yelling and grinning happily.*

*785. Low angle shot up the burial hill (as 780). At the sound
of* KIKUCHIYO's *voice, the women begin to shriek and move off.*

786. Low angle medium shot of KIKUCHIYO *leaping up and
down beside the banner.*

*787. Low angle very long shot of the horsemen galloping over
the top of the hill. The leaders are already starting to come
down the slope.*

788. Medium shot tilting down with KIKUCHIYO *as he scrambles
down the roof.*

*789. Medium shot as he jumps down onto the ground. Camera
pans right as he starts to run, pointing towards the bandits,
off-screen.*

*790. Low angle shot of the crowd on the hillside. Shouting and
screaming, they begin to run down the hill and away in the
foreground, followed by the samurai, leaving* GISAKU *standing
alone by* HEIHACHI's *grave at the top of the slope.*

*791. Low angle very long shot of about thirty bandits galloping
down the hillside. Tilt down, over the houses, losing the horsemen, to a very high angle long shot of the crowd of villagers
rushing into the village square.*

792. Medium shot tracking right with KYUZO *who leads his
unit through the village. He runs round towards camera,*

followed by the others; then pan and track back slightly as they run off to take up their positions.

793. Medium shot of SHICHIROJI *leading his unit. Fast pan right as they run past.*

794. Medium shot panning quickly left with KANBEI *and* KATSUSHIRO, *running with their men through the village. In the background village women are running into hiding.*

795. High angle medium shot of SHICHIROJI *leading his men through the village. Pan left and crane up as they round the corner and make for the western barricade. As they reach the low inner barrier, camera tilts up over the barricade to reveal the bandits in long shot galloping towards it. (Still on page 149) Hold on them as they gallop up to the barricade. Shouting; loud hoofbeats. As they reach it, tilt down slightly to reveal* KATSUSHIRO *running towards the barricade, bending low.*

796. Low angle medium shot of KATSUSHIRO, *back to camera, running and crouching down behind the inner barrier next to* SHICHIROJI, *whose men can be seen crouching in the foreground. Behind the barricade, the bandits mill about in confusion, with a lot of shouting and neighing of horses.*

797. High angle medium shot of the bandits on horseback, milling about and jostling one another, with the top of the barricade in the foreground. Camera pans right, along the barricade, then back again to the left.

798. Medium shot of the BANDIT CHIEF *on his horse shouting orders and waving his sword.*

799. Medium close-up of SHICHIROJI, *in profile, nearest camera, with* KATSUSHIRO *beside him, peering over the low inner barrier.*

SHICHIROJI : Three guns. Don't forget, they have three guns.
KATSUSHIRO : Right!

800. High angle medium shot of the bandits with the CHIEF *in the foreground, circling round on the other side of the barricade. Pan left as some wheel their horses round and start to gallop away.*

801. High angle medium long shot, over the barricade, of a group of bandits galloping off to the left.

802. High angle long shot, with the barricade in the fore-

ground. The bandits have divided into two groups: several are
galloping off to the left, the others ride away up the hill to the
right.

803. Medium shot of KATSUSHIRO *and* SHICHIROJI *in back*
view, crouching down behind the inner wall with the barricade
beyond them. Other men of SHICHIROJI'S *unit, including*
MANZO, *are visible in the foreground. As the bandits ride off,*
KATSUSHIRO *gets up and runs off in the foreground.*

804. Medium close-up of some women in back view, only their
heads visible, looking through a window at the village square
beyond. In the background, KATSUSHIRO *runs across, camera*
panning left with him over the heads of the women, till he
reaches KANBEI *and* GOROBEI *sitting with a group of men at*
the end of the square.

805. Medium shot of KANBEI *and* GOROBEI *seated on the*
ground with the map spread out in front of them, and four
or five farmers, including RIKICHI, *behind them.* KATSUSHIRO
drops down on his knees in front of KANBEI.

KATSUSHIRO *breathlessly*: There are twenty to the north and
thirteen to the south.

KANBEI : How many guns?

KATSUSHIRO : Three in all.

KANBEI : Good. *To* GOROBEI. You go on to the south, but be care-
ful of the guns. *(Still on page 149)*

GOROBEI *nods and he gets up, picking up his bow. Pan left as*
he goes off down the street followed by RIKICHI, KATSUSHIRO
and the other men. Hold as they run off up the track.

806. High angle medium long shot, from inside, of GOROBEI
and KATSUSHIRO *leading their men into one of the outlying*
huts. Pan left past one of the wooden uprights as they run
inside towards camera.

807. Medium shot of GOROBEI, KATSUSHIRO *and some of the*
other men, backs to camera, going towards the window which
looks out over the fields. Track in after them as they press up
against the bars, bending low and looking out. One of the
bandits can be seen galloping along the edge of the fields in
very long shot. He stops, pointing, and others come to join him,
reining in their horses. They circle round, trotting about in
confusion.

157

808. Medium long shot, with the flooded fields in the fore-ground. The bandits on their horses look down uncertainly at the water.

809. Medium shot of GOROBEI, KATSUSHIRO *and* RIKICHI *looking out of the hut, back to camera (as 807). In the back-ground outside the bandits are circling round and trotting up and down, not knowing what to do.*

810. Medium long shot of the bandits with a flooded field in the foreground. (Still on page 149) A few of them ride up to the edge of the water and one dismounts. He jumps down into the water, using a stick to test the depth. In two places it is not very deep. He goes round a little further, watched by the others. Then he tests the depth again and the stick unexpectedly goes right down, water covering his hand, and he slips, sitting down ignominiously in the water.

811. Medium shot from outside the hut of GOROBEI, RIKICHI *and* KATSUSHIRO *looking out, just visible behind the bars and the rolls of matting which are hung on the wall.* GOROBEI *and* KATSUSHIRO *look at one another, grinning with delight at the bandits' obvious surprise.* GOROBEI *moves his head back slightly.*

812. Medium shot with KATSUSHIRO *in the foreground, back to camera,* GOROBEI *next to him, in three-quarter back view. Without turning round,* GOROBEI *pulls an arrow out of the quiver on his back.*

813. Medium shot of the BANDIT *up to his knees in the water, staggering as he tries to climb up the muddy bank.*

814. Medium close-up from the side of KATSUSHIRO *bending down, peering through the bamboo bars, with* GOROBEI *behind him drawing back his bow, and taking aim. He lets the arrow fly.*

815. High angle medium shot of the BANDIT *at the edge of the pool — the arrow strikes him right in the middle of the chest. He falls back into the water clutching the shaft of the arrow.*

816. Low angle medium shot of the BANDIT CHIEF, *and one of his men looking down and pulling their horses back in surprise.*

BANDIT CHIEF, *shouting and waving his sword* : To the rear ! To the rear!

817. Medium shot of KANBEI *in three-quarter back view, squatting in the middle of the deserted village square, looking at the map which is spread out in front of him.* KATSUSHIRO *appears and goes down on one knee in front of him.* KANBEI *looks up. He is holding a writing brush in one hand.*

KATSUSHIRO : Twelve of them are moving to the east now.

KANBEI : You mean thirteen.

KATSUSHIRO : One of them was shot, sir.

KANBEI *laughing appreciatively* : Good old Gorobei, eh? *He bends down to write something on the map.*

818. High angle close-up of the edge of the map with KANBEI'S *hand and arm in shot.* KANBEI *has drawn two lines of circles down the edge of the paper. He draws a cross over the first circle.*

819. Medium shot of KANBEI *and* KATSUSHIRO *kneeling on either side of the map.* KANBEI *points behind him.*

KANBEI : Now, go to the east border and make sure the bridge is cut off, and . . .

KATSUSHIRO : . . . And try to get the guns. *He runs off, and* KANBEI *grins.*

820. Low angle medium shot of a group of villagers bending over the edge of the bridge with KIKUCHIYO *standing over them in the background. They are lifting off one of the horizontal tree trunks which form the main base of the bridge. (Still on page 149)* KIKUCHIYO *helps them lift it and they stagger off, in the foreground, leaving* KIKUCHIYO *looking up towards the hills behind him.* KATSUSHIRO *comes up to him, running along one of the remaining horizontal supports.*

KATSUSHIRO : There are twelve coming! Quick — the bridge!

KIKUCHIYO *turning towards him* : Are you blind? *He looks down at what is left of the bridge and then up at* KATSUSHIRO *balancing on the log.* What do you think we've been doing?

He makes an angry gesture and KATSUSHIRO *looks down, embarrassed.* KIKUCHIYO *turns away again.*

KATSUSHIRO *nervously* : And look out for the guns.

KIKUCHIYO *turning back crossly* : I know!

KATSUSHIRO *turns back towards camera and sighs heavily. A baby can be heard crying off. He looks up, and* KIKUCHIYO

159

looks round also, as a MAN *comes into shot, balancing along the pole nearest camera, followed by his* WIFE *carrying a baby.* KIKUCHIYO *grabs the* MAN.

KIKUCHIYO : Where are you going? Are you blind?

MAN : I have to go and fetch my father.

821. Low angle medium shot of KIKUCHIYO *holding onto the* MAN's *shirt, with the latter facing him in back view. His* WIFE *stands watching, three-quarters back to camera in the foreground. In the distance is the mill house with the hills rising up behind it.*

WOMAN *nodding towards the mill* : He's over there. He always said he wanted to die there. Hearing the sound of the mill wheel.

KIKUCHIYO *turns to look at the mill.*

822. Medium shot of the mill wheel turning.

823. Medium long shot of old GISAKU *sitting inside the mill, back to camera, holding a spear. The shadow of the turning wheel can be seen beyond him and its regular knocking can be heard.*

824. Medium shot of old GISAKU *sitting back to camera, silhouetted in the sunlight.*

825. Low angle medium shot of KIKUCHIYO *with the* MAN *and* WOMAN *facing him in three-quarter back view.*

KIKUCHIYO : Stubborn old bastard. All right. Go and bring him back. *Shouting.* But hurry!

826. Medium shot of GOROBEI *leading his men through the village. Pan slightly left with* GOROBEI, *losing the others as he comes up and stands in front of* KANBEI, *who gets up.*

KANBEI *pointing left and turning towards camera* : Go to the northern border, that is where the main battle will be fought.

GOROBEI *comes forward and stands beside him.*

GOROBEI : If you knew that, why didn't you build a barricade there too?

KANBEI *steps closer to camera. Pan slightly as* GOROBEI *follows, revealing some of his men watching.*

KANBEI : Well, a good fort needs a gap, a break. The enemy must be lured into it. We couldn't keep this place only by defending it.

GOROBEI *nods, smiling, and runs off followed by his men. Camera remains on* KANBEI.

827. Low angle medium shot of KIKUCHIYO *holding up the*

160

*end of one of the bridge supports with two men behind him.
They all strain under the weight. Pan right with them as they
haul it across the stream towards the opposite bank. The
bridge is now completely dismantled and forms a barricade
on the bank.*

828. Medium shot of SHICHIROJI *in front of the barricade,
with his men lined up in front of him. Encouraged by him they
shout a fierce battle cry, raising their spears.*

829. Medium shot of KIKUCHIYO *with his men lowering the
long pole onto the river bank.* SHICHIROJI's *men can be heard
shouting, off.*

KIKUCHIYO *turning to his men* : So that's how it is, is it? Let's out-
shout them!

*He raises his hand and they all shout, raising their hands —
except for* YOHEI, *who stands opposite* KIKUCHIYO *in the foreground, giggling.* KIKUCHIYO *bellows at him to join in and then
they all shout again,* YOHEI *a second behind all the others.
Suddenly* KIKUCHIYO *looks up at something across the river
and, beckoning to his men, he dashes back across the river-bed,
camera panning left with him. Hold as he climbs up the
opposite bank where the bridge used to be and peers over the
top. Hoofbeats off. He looks back at his men, laughing
wildly.*

KIKUCHIYO : Here they come! Here they come!

Then he looks back over the bank.

*830. Long shot tracking with the bandits as they gallop across
the fields past the outlying houses. Hold as the leading* BANDIT
*turns his horse towards camera and stops at the edge of the
flooded fields. He motions to his men. Horses neigh.*

831. Medium close-up of KIKUCHIYO *peering up over the top
of the bank, grinning demoniacally. In the background his men
are looking through the barricade on the other side of the
river.* KIKUCHIYO *makes a face, and then begins to climb
up onto the bank.*

832. Medium shot of KIKUCHIYO, *back to camera in the foreground, climbing onto the bank in full view of the bandits, who
can be seen on their horses on the other side of the flooded
fields.* KIKUCHIYO *stands up and strides forward, waving his
arms. Suddenly a shot rings out, falling into the water of one*

of the flooded fields very near KIKUCHIYO. *He turns tail and dashes back towards camera, which pans left and tilts down as he jumps down the bank and crosses the river. Crane up and track back in front of* KIKUCHIYO *as he climbs up onto the top of the barricade, standing up and shouting nonsensically. (Still on page 149) Hold on medium shot of him standing on the barricade, waving his arms and waggling his backside at the bandits. He pats his bottom invitingly and another shot rings out. As it does so he leaps down to safety. Pan left and tilt down as he crouches beside* YOHEI *who is in the foreground peering between the logs. Suddenly* YOHEI *straightens up, pointing.*

833. *Long shot across the flooded fields of the outlying houses, their roofs on fire.*

834. *Medium shot of* YOHEI *and* KIKUCHIYO *standing beside the barricade, loking across. Pan slightly with* KIKUCHIYO *as he comes round behind* YOHEI *and stands slightly nearer camera to get a better view. (Still on page 149)*

835. *Medium shot of the* BANDIT CAPTAIN *on his horse, with a blazing house behind him. The horse is standing fetlock-deep in water at the edge of the flooded field.*

836. *Medium shot of* YOHEI, *with* KIKUCHIYO *standing on top of the barricade, both in back view with some of the bandits visible beyond them.* YOHEI *turns away, very upset but* KIKUCHIYO *pushes him back into position.*

837. *Medium shot of the* BANDIT CAPTAIN *on his horse, who turns to look at the flaming house behind him. Pan slightly left as he urges his horse forward, trotting along the edge of the flooded field.*

838. *Medium shot of* KIKUCHIYO *behind the barricade on the river bank, with* YOHEI *and some other men. His men are frightened and some try to run away, but he pushes them back into position, crouching behind the barricade.*

KIKUCHIYO : Hey, you. Get back to your posts. Where do you think you're going? The bastards, they've set the houses on fire!

Pan first left then right as KIKUCHIYO *runs about excitedly, watching the bandits in the distance. Another of the outlying houses bursts into flames and more bandits gallop past in long shot.*

162

839. Medium close-up of KIKUCHIYO *shouting and waving his arms.*

840. Medium shot of KANBEI *and* KATSUSHIRO, *tracking left with them as they run along the village street.*

841. High angle medium long shot of KIKUCHIYO *and his men at the barricade by the river. In very long shot the three houses blaze away.* KANBEI *and* KATSUSHIRO *appear in the foreground, backs to camera, and go up to* KIKUCHIYO. KIKUCHIYO *points at the burning houses.*

842. Medium long shot of two houses burning, the flames reflected in the flooded fields. One of the houses collapses completely into the water.

843. Medium shot of KIKUCHIYO *and* YOHEI *with* KANBEI *and* KATSUSHIRO *behind them. Furiously,* KIKUCHIYO *picks up a rock and hurls it down into the river off-screen, shouting and swearing. Suddenly* YOHEI *points.*

YOHEI : That's the grandad's house!

844. Medium long shot with YOHEI, KIKUCHIYO *and the other men leaning over the barricade. In the distance, on the other side of the flooded fields, the mill-house has been set alight.*

845. Long shot of the blazing mill.

846. Medium shot of the men at the barricade, backs to camera, staring in dismay at the mill blazing in the distance.

847. Medium close-up of KIKUCHIYO *grabbing* YOHEI *and shaking him.*

KIKUCHIYO : Hey, where's old Gisaku, where's his son? Where's the baby? *He shakes* YOHEI *free and turns towards camera.* Oh, they're all stupid! *He moves round towards camera.*

848. Medium shot of the group by the barricade with the mill blazing in the distance. KIKUCHIYO *is climbing over the barricade watched in dismay by* YOHEI, *and also* KANBEI *who has come up.* KATSUSHIRO *and the other men are staring, horror-struck, at the mill.* KANBEI *rushes to the edge of the barricade, standing back to camera and shouting down to* KIKUCHIYO *who has almost disappeared.*

KANBEI : Wait. Don't leave your post.

Circular track left with KANBEI *as he runs round behind the other men, still back to camera, and track in on him as he leans over the high bank, looking down through the bushes to the river.*

KANBEI : Come back here ! Kikuchiyo !

Track in further past KANBEI *to reveal* KIKUCHIYO *running along the river bed and going out of sight.* KANBEI *rushes along the bank after him; pan slightly left as he goes and hold as he runs through the bushes, shouting.*

KANBEI : Kikuchiyo ! Kikuchiyo !

849. Medium long shot, looking along the river to KIKUCHIYO, *back to camera, splashing along in the middle of the stream.* KANBEI *can be heard shouting off.*

850. Long shot, looking along the river, of KIKUCHIYO *coming towards camera. In the foreground the mill wheel can be seen still turning, flames licking round it. Suddenly* KIKUCHIYO *stops in his tracks, ducking down, as the sound of a child crying can be heard off. The* WOMAN *seen earlier appears at the edge of the river from behind the turning wheel. She struggles out into mid-stream carrying the baby as* KIKUCHIYO *starts to hurry forward and* KANBEI *appears, jumping down from the bank behind him.*

851. Medium shot of the WOMAN *holding her child in the middle of the stream with* KIKUCHIYO *coming up to her in three-quarter back view. The mill house blazes behind them.*

KIKUCHIYO : Where are your men folk ?

KANBEI *runs up in the foreground and stands on the other side of the* WOMAN, *also in three-quarter back view.* KIKUCHIYO *holds out his hand to her. She sways backwards and forwards with an agonised expression.*

852. Low angle medium shot of the WOMAN *holding the baby with* KIKUCHIYO *in three-quarter back view in the foreground. The mill wheel still turns in the background, now almost enveloped in flames. Without saying a word, the* WOMAN *hands the baby to him; (Still on page 149) then, throwing back her head, she staggers forward.* KANBEI *rushes up to catch her. As she falls into his arms he feels blood on his hand and looks at it.* KIKUCHIYO, *holding the child, looks at the* WOMAN's *back.*

KANBEI : She was speared. Right in the back. Yet she got as far as here. What will-power !

KANBEI *hoists the* WOMAN's *dead body onto his shoulder and* KIKUCHIYO *puts out a hand to steady him, still holding the baby in his other arm.*

KANBEI : Kikuchiyo, let's go back. *He starts to wade back down the stream towards camera.*

853. Medium shot of KANBEI *coming towards camera carrying the dead* WOMAN *over his shoulder. Behind him* KIKUCHIYO *is staring at the child in his arms, the mill blazing in the background.* KANBEI *notices that* KIKUCHIYO *is not following him and turns back, urging him on.*

KANBEI : Come on. What's the matter?

854. Medium close-up of KIKUCHIYO *holding the child, silhouetted against the flames. Tilt down with him as he sinks down onto his knees, waist-deep in the stream.*

KIKUCHIYO : This baby. It's me! The same thing happened to me! *He sobs, hugging the child tightly. (Still on page 149)*

855. Low angle medium shot of the blazing mill, with the wheel still turning, black against the flames; the baby cries off.

856. Wipe to medium shot of the mill wheel lying at an angle against the river bank, with flames still licking round some of the struts. The mill house is completely gutted. It is now night.

857. Medium shot of YOHEI *holding his spear and staring into the darkness through the barricade by the stream. He is lit from behind by the flickering light of a fire off-screen. Very slowly he pulls himself up and looks over the top of the barricade to get a better view. He looks round fearfully towards camera.*

858. High angle medium shot of KIKUCHIYO, *in the foreground, sitting by the fire surrounded by his men, who are sitting round the fire holding their spears. He looks round suddenly and they all jump, then he turns back and they all relax visibly. A short pause. Then he jumps to his feet, back to camera. The villagers all lean forward, gripping their spears.* KIKUCHIYO *looks round suspiciously, then down at the fire; then he sits down again. The men stare at him in bewilderment. A pause. Drumbeats in, very softly. He jumps up again, goes down on one knee in front of the fire, back to camera, grabs a flaming log and rushes away towards the barricade, camera tilting up slightly with him; all the other men stand up to watch him.*

859. *Medium close-up of* KIKUCHIYO *leaning over the barricade. He throws the flaming log out into the darkness.*

860. *High angle medium shot of several bandits crouching in the river. The flaming log flies past, landing on the opposite bank, and lighting them up. They stare at it in dismay.*

861. *Medium close-up of* KIKUCHIYO *leaning over the barricade and peering into the darkness. He hisses through his teeth then suddenly yells, banging on the barricade. Drumbeats louder.*

862. *Medium shot of the bandits (as 860). The brand is burning out, and* KIKUCHIYO's *voice can still be heard, off. The bandits straighten up and splash through the water away from camera. Drumbeats louder. Pan left to the barricade on the bank as the bandits begin to climb up it. Tilt up over them revealing* KIKUCHIYO, *who cuts the first* BANDIT *down as he appears at the top of the barricade. Tilt down as the* BANDIT *falls in the water, just missing two others below.*

863. *Low angle medium shot of* KIKUCHIYO *balancing on top of the barricade, looking down into the river. (Still on page 150) The men behind him get ready for action as he shouts and bangs the hilt of his sword on the top of the barricade. Behind him a man comes into shot holding a spear. He drags at* KIKUCHIYO's *sleeve to attract his attention.* KIKUCHIYO *turns round and the man points silently behind him towards the fire.* KIKUCHIYO *jumps down from the barricade and goes towards it.*

864. *Medium close-up of* YOHEI *looking terrified. He is holding onto the shaft of a spear with both hands, the end of it out of shot, with his mouth wide open.* KIKUCHIYO *comes up and stands beside him looking towards the end of the spear. Then he looks at* YOHEI *and snarls contemptuously. Pan right and track back as he walks forward beside the shaft of the spear. Hold as the track reveals one of the bandits pinioned on the end of it;* YOHEI *stands in the foreground three-quarter back to camera, still holding the spear.* KIKUCHIYO *stares down at the* BANDIT, *then grasps the spear, and puts one foot against the* BANDIT's *chest to pull it out. The man falls back dead.*

865. *Medium shot of a* BANDIT, *backing off, chased by two farmers with their spears lowered. Pan slightly as* KIKUCHIYO

and some more farmers advance on the bandits, going towards the barricade. Drumbeats louder.

866. The western barricade. Medium shot panning with one of the bandits as he crawls along by the barricade. Farmers appear from the foreground and attack him with their spears.

867. Medium shot of one of the bandits disappearing over the top of the high barricade pursued by SHICHIROJI.

868. Low angle medium shot of the BANDIT *crawling along by the barricade. He gets to his feet. The end of a spear, carried by a man just off-screen on the right, thrusts into the middle of his back and he throws back his head with a gurgle; (Still on page 150) the spear is withdrawn, and the* BANDIT *falls dead, camera tilting down slightly with him.*

869. Medium shot of SHICHIROJI *in profile, peering through the barricade, his men running up behind him. He turns to them.*

SHICHIROJI : Everybody all right? *They all nod breathlessly.*

870. The flooded fields. Medium shot of another group of farmers battling with bandits, with some of the bamboo stakes in the foreground. Some of the farmers attack from the far bank with spears, while others, including RIKICHI, *engage in hand-to-hand combat in the water. Pan slightly to include the whole battle; confused noise of shouting, the clatter of spears and splashing.*

871. High angle medium long shot of the battle in the flooded field, with a fire blazing on the bank in the background.

872. High angle medium shot of RIKICHI *fighting with two bandits in the water.*

873. Low angle medium shot panning left with KANBEI *and* KATSUSHIRO. *Samurai theme in, low, over the drumbeats. Pan continues as they run past a fire blazing in the foreground. (Still on page 150) Hold as they stop to watch the battle in the flooded fields. Music louder.*

874. High angle medium shot of RIKICHI *standing in the water, running a bandit through with his sword. The bandit is lying in the water with his head on the bank. Pan left with* RIKICHI *as he leaves the dead man and crawls up the bank towards camera, breathing heavily, his eyes wild.*

875. Low angle medium shot of KANBEI *and* KATSUSHIRO.

watching in admiration.

KANBEI : Hey, halt ! That'll do !

876. High angle medium close-up panning left with RIKICHI *as he crawls panting along the bank, dripping wet. He stops and stands up, camera tilting up with him and turns towards* KANBEI, *off-screen.*

877. Low angle medium shot of KANBEI *and* KATSUSHIRO.

KANBEI : Good job — who are you ?

878. Medium close-up of RIKICHI.

RIKICHI : I'm Rikichi.

879. Wipe to a high angle medium close-up of the circles drawn on the edge of the map. KANBEI'S *hand comes into shot and crosses off six more. (Still on page 150) Music out.*

880. Medium shot of KANBEI *crouching down over the map.* GOROBEI *is beside him in back view, and* KYUZO *is opposite, seen in profile, silhouetted against a fire. Some farmers sit watching them in the background.*

KANBEI : They attacked from three different places, yet we drove them all back. *He stands up and camera tracks after him as he walks past the fire away from the villagers, followed by* KYUZO *and* GOROBEI. *He speaks as he walks.* Next time, it will probably be here. Maybe not tonight, but they'll come.

KYUZO : It seems quiet enough.

They stop by a hut and peer into the darkness.

881. Medium shot from the side of GOROBEI, KANBEI *and* KYUZO *peering into the gloom. In the foreground some of the farmers are sitting back to camera, with a fire blazing between them and the samurai.*

882. Medium long shot looking up the avenue of trees that leads to the forest. A fire burns in the foreground and another blazes a few yards up the avenue. The trees stretch away into the darkness.

883. Medium shot (as 881). KANBEI *squats down by the fire.*

KANBEI : I know, but that's where they are, all right. I'll show you.

884. Medium long shot of the deserted village square. A fire burns in the background. KATSUSHIRO *comes towards camera carrying a stuffed suit of armour. Music in. He stops in medium shot, and stares up at something off-screen.*

885. Medium shot of SHINO, *back to camera, with* KATSUSHIRO

168

just below her, down a short slope, staring up at her. The deserted village square stretches away beyond him, with three fires burning at regular intervals along its length. SHINO *runs towards him and then stops. He takes a few steps towards her, and then, with a worried frown, runs on past her, going off in the foreground. She turns to follow him, and camera tilts up as she runs back up the slope, staring mournfully after him.*

886. High angle medium shot, with a fire blazing in the foreground, of KATSUSHIRO *running across frame carrying the stuffed armour. Pan left with him as he goes over to where* KANBEI, GOROBEI *and* KYUZO *are standing at the base of a large tree at the beginning of the avenue. Track in as* KATSUSHIRO *props up the suit of armour which is supported on a pole.* KANBEI *inspects it.*

KANBEI : Good work! Put it up there.

He points up the avenue and KATSUSHIRO *runs off with the decoy.* GOROBEI, KYUZO *and* KANBEI *turn away from camera to watch him go.*

887. Medium long shot of one of the bonfires in the avenue. Track right past it as KATSUSHIRO, *almost invisible, runs past in the background.*

888. High angle medium long shot tracking right with KATSUSHIRO *as he runs down through the trees carrying the armour. Hold as he crouches down beside a tree trunk on the far side of the track, holding the decoy out away from the track.*

889. Medium close-up of the stuffed suit of armour leaning out from behind the tree trunk. (Still on page 150) It looks quite life-like in the gloom. Suddenly a shot rings out, hitting the armour.

890. High angle medium close-up of KATSUSHIRO *crouched down holding the pole of the decoy and closing his eyes, wincing at the sound of the shot.*

891. Medium close-up (as 889). Another shot hits the decoy in the chest.

892. High angle medium close-up of KATSUSHIRO *crouching down, hanging on to the decoy which is still swaying from the force of the shot. He lowers it quickly and camera pans left as*

169

*he turns and runs swiftly off, dragging the decoy into the trees.**
893. Medium shot of GOROBEI, KANBEI *and* KYUZO *standing by the fire with the heads of some farmers in the foreground.* KATSUSHIRO *runs up dragging the decoy.* KANBEI *turns and looks at the bullet holes, then turns back and folds his arms.*

KANBEI : They'll probably attack here in the morning. We'll let them in. *He laughs and takes a few steps forward, addressing the village men in the foreground reassuringly.* But not all at once ! *Camera pans slightly right as he walks by the fire.*

894. Medium shot of KANBEI, *in back view, looking down at the farmers who are seated in front of him by the covered trenches.*

KANBEI : Just one or two. *He turns and walks away.*

895. Medium shot of KANBEI, *panning left as he walks past the fire again; he stops on the other side of it in front of the three other samurai and spreads his hands wide.*

KANBEI : Then we'll close our spearline. *He starts to walk away towards the other men sitting under the trees.*

896. Medium shot of KANBEI *from behind, looking down at another group of men sitting under the trees.*

KANBEI : The one, or two that get in will be helpless. *He turns and begins to walk towards camera, going off in the foreground as he speaks.* That way, we'll get them one by one.

897. Medium shot of KANBEI *squatting on his haunches in front of* GOROBEI, KATSUSHIRO *and* KYUZO, *with farmers' heads in the foreground.*

GOROBEI *sitting down beside* KANBEI : I'm worried about the guns. We've got to find a way to get rid of them too.

In the foreground RIKICHI *drops his spear and starts to run towards* KANBEI.

898. Medium close-up of RIKICHI, *tracking in front of him as he runs towards* KANBEI. *Hold as* KANBEI's *head comes into shot in back view in the foreground, and* RIKICHI *stares at him in close-up.*

RIKICHI : I'll go and get one. I will.

KYUZO *off* : No, you won't.

899. Medium close-up of KANBEI *facing camera with* RIKICHI *in front of him, back to camera in the foreground.* KYUZO *steps*

* End of reel 6.

170

forward, facing RIKICHI.

KYUZO : I will. *He runs off.*

Pan right, losing the others as he runs off towards the first fire at the beginning of the avenue. As he runs past the second fire, KATSUSHIRO *appears in the foreground running after him, followed by* KANBEI *who grabs him as he reaches the first fire.* KANBEI *pushes him back towards camera, out of sight of the avenue. Pan left as they come forward and* KANBEI *pushes* KATSUSHIRO *behind the tree where* RIKICHI *and* GOROBEI *are already hiding.*

900. Close-up of GOROBEI *peering round the tree trunk with* KANBEI *beside him and* RIKICHI *visible behind.* KATSUSHIRO *comes up and looks over* KANBEI's *shoulder.*

901. Long shot looking up the deserted avenue with the two fires burning. KYUZO *has disappeared into the darkness.*

902. Wipe to low angle medium shot of the first fire burnt to ashes and smoking slightly. It is dawn. The avenue is shrouded in mist and a single bird sings.

903. Medium shot of a group of farmers dozing or leaning on their spears in the covered trenches. Suddenly one of the men in the foreground starts and looks up. Others do the same, as KATSUSHIRO *comes past in back view walking away from camera up the path outside the hut. He stops and looks up towards the avenue. Then he turns and comes back dejectedly towards camera, and the men in the foreground sink back to their former positions. Soft music in. Pan left and track back as* KATSUSHIRO *walks round the hut, coming out into the clearing where* KANBEI *and* GOROBEI *are sitting on the ground. In the foreground, two farmers are sleeping, propped up on their spears.* KATSUSHIRO *sits down with the other two samurai. Then almost immediately he gets up again and looks back towards the avenue. He paces about and then stares back towards the avenue again.*

904. High angle medium shot of GOROBEI *and* KANBEI *sitting cross-legged with heads bowed.* RIKICHI *is sitting next to* GOROBEI. *He looks up as* KATSUSHIRO *comes up to them in the foreground.*

KATSUSHIRO *excitedly* : I hear something.

171

KANBEI *looking up at* KATSUSHIRO : That's enough. Now, you rest a little.

KATSUSHIRO *looking down and taking a step towards camera* : But it's true. Listen.

> KANBEI *gets to his feet and comes over and puts a hand on his shoulder. Pan slightly to frame them both in medium close-up.*

KANBEI : You must rest. You're too tired. Come and sit down. *A faint noise off, which they all hear.* Yes!

> *They both turn towards the sound, and* GOROBEI *and* RIKICHI *also stand up, looking in the same direction. Then they all rush out of shot.*
>
> 905. *High angle medium long shot looking up the mist-shrouded avenue. The three samurai and* RIKICHI *hurry forward, and stand beside the first trees of the avenue, backs to camera. The village men crowd round behind them.*
>
> 906. *Medium shot looking up the avenue through the mist.*
>
> 907. *Low angle medium close-up of* KATSUSHIRO *in profile in the foreground, with* KANBEI *next to him and* GOROBEI *just behind, staring intently.*
>
> 908. *Medium long shot looking up the avenue. A vague shape moves in the mist.*
>
> 909. *Low angle medium close-up (as 907).* KATSUSHIRO *takes a step forward; pan right with him, losing* GOROBEI.
>
> 910. *High angle medium long shot of* KYUZO *walking towards camera through the mist, trees rising up on either side of him.*
>
> 911. *Medium close-up of* KATSUSHIRO *and* KANBEI *in profile;* RIKICHI *comes and joins them.*
>
> 912. *Medium long shot, from inside a trench, of* KYUZO, *seen from the side, coming up to the waiting group at the end of the avenue. He hands a gun to* KATSUSHIRO *and then wipes his forehead with the back of his hand.*

KYUZO *jumping up onto the edge of the trench* : Killed two.

> *He jumps down into the trench, coming towards camera. The others watch him in the background. Tilt down as he sits down quietly and rests his back against the side of a hut, folds his arms round his sword and settles down to sleep. (Still on page 150) Samurai theme in, quietly.*
>
> 913. *Medium shot of* RIKICHI, KATSUSHIRO *and* MOSUKE

watching, full of admiration, with GOROBEI, KANBEI and some other farmers also watching, behind them. (Still on page 150) KANBEI reaches forward and takes the gun from KATSUSHIRO's hands and examines it. All the others crowd round to look at it except KATSUSHIRO, who takes a couple of steps forward, still staring fixedly towards KYUZO off-screen. Suddenly he steps up onto the wall of the trench, and goes off in the foreground. 914. Low angle medium shot with KYUZO in the foreground trying to sleep. KATSUSHIRO comes up behind and stands over KYUZO, looking down at him. KYUZO looks up. 915. Low angle close-up of KATSUSHIRO staring down in admiration. 916. High angle close-up of KYUZO looking up.

KYUZO : What is it?
917. Low angle close-up of KATSUSHIRO. He stares down silently. 918. High angle close-up of KYUZO.

KYUZO : What do you want? He closes his eyes. I need sleep.
919. Low angle close-up of KATSUSHIRO. He swallows nervously and licks his lips.

KATSUSHIRO : You are . . . really great.
920. High angle close-up of KYUZO, his eyes closed. He opens them and looks up again. Then he lowers his eyes again, looking rather embarrassed. 921. Low angle close-up of KATSUSHIRO, his eyes shining.

KATSUSHIRO : I've always wanted to tell you how great I think you are.
He starts to move away, still looking down, camera panning slightly left. Then he turns and dashes off. 922. High angle close-up of KYUZO looking down. He looks round after KATSUSHIRO, smiles briefly, and then, readjusting the position of his sword, prepares again for sleep. Music out.

923. Dissolve to low angle medium shot tracking left with horses' hooves as they gallop along a track, passing trees in the foreground. Loud hoofbeats. 924. Medium shot of KYUZO sitting in the trench, asleep, with sunlight on his face. (Still on page 150) Hoofbeats, hardly audible. He wakes up suddenly and looks up then grabs his

sword and dashes away from camera, leaping up onto the trench wall. He looks up the avenue for a moment, then jumps down and runs away.

925. Medium close-up of the heads of several men, in back view; they are crouching against a stone wall with their spears held upright. Over the wall Kyuzo *can be seen running round towards camera. Track back beyond the men as he comes round and ducks down by the wall on the near side of the track; on the other side, crouching down at the base of the tree, is* Gorobei *with* Rikichi *and other men behind him. They are all staring intently up the avenue.*

926. Medium long shot of horses galloping through the trees. Pan left with them. Loud hoofbeats.

927. High angle medium long shot of Gorobei *and* Kyuzo *seen over the heads of the armed villagers, all back to camera. Faint hoofbeats.*

Gorobei : We'll let one through, just one.

Kyuzo *nods his assent without taking his eyes off the track.* Gorobei *jumps up and rushes off down towards the village.*

928. Medium close-up, panning right as Gorobei *comes to the end of the village street and raises his sword. Hold as he shouts.*

Gorobei : Kanbei! We'll let one of them in!

929. Long shot looking down the road between the houses to where Kanbei *and* Katsushiro *are standing with their men lined up behind them. They both draw their swords and* Kanbei *waves his to show he has understood.*

930. Medium close-up of Gorobei *in profile. He turns away and runs back towards his men, camera panning left with him.*

931. Medium long shot over the heads of the armed men on Kyuzo's *side of the track with* Kyuzo *standing at the front, looking up the track. On the other side* Rikichi *looks back.* Gorobei *runs up and takes his place in front of* Rikichi *at the base of the tree. (Still on page 151)*

932. Close-up of Gorobei *turning his head. Re-frame slightly to include* Rikichi, *as* Gorobei *calls back to his men in a low voice.*

Gorobei : Remember, the lines must be closed quickly.

Tilt down with Gorobei *as he bends down and looks carefully round the tree trunk up the avenue.*

174

933. *Medium shot of the two units of farmers led by* GOROBEI *and* KYUZO *as they stand up and shift back, taking up their positions out of sight on either side of the track. The sound of galloping hooves gradually gets louder.*

934. *Medium close-up of* KYUZO *staring over the top of the wall with a villager holding a spear beside him. (Still on page 151) A pause. Then he slowly draws his sword. Pan left along the top of the wall, losing* KYUZO, *past the farmers staring over it, their faces showing a mixture of fear and tense anticipation. Sound of hoofbeats louder.*

935. *Low angle long shot, with one of the trench walls in the foreground, loking up the avenue as the first* BANDIT *appears, shouting a war cry as he gallops along. Others follow. Fast pan left following the* BANDIT'S *horse as it passes camera in medium shot.*

936. *Medium shot of* GOROBEI *standing up by the tree and leading his men forward with the samurai war-cry.*

937. *Low angle medium close-up of some farmers in back view, with a covered trench in front of them; the bandits can be seen between the roof supports, galloping towards camera. The farmers run across to the track as the first horseman approaches.*

938. *Low angle medium shot, from inside the trench, of* KYUZO *leading his men onto the track. Pan slightly right as* GOROBEI *and* RIKICHI *follow him.*

939. *Low angle medium shot of the* BANDIT *on his horse with the farmers' spears in the foreground. Fast pan left as he reins in his horse and it sidesteps, its eyes rolling.*

940. *Medium close-up of the horse's hooves sidestepping and kicking up dust.* KYUZO'S *legs come into shot as the horse sidesteps out of shot.*

941. *Low angle medium shot of the* BANDIT, *his head out of shot,* KYUZO *in the foreground parrying with his sword. A farmer's spear prods the horse between its front legs and it lunges sideways towards camera. (Still on page 151)* KYUZO *dodges out of the way as it does so, neighing, then falling. Tilt down with it, as the* BANDIT *falls off.* KYUZO'S *sword can be seen slashing in the foreground.*

942. *High angle medium shot with* KYUZO *in the foreground,*

175

his head and shoulders out of frame, and the BANDIT lying on the ground. He gets up, camera tilting up with him losing KYUZO.

943. Medium shot of KYUZO with the farmers behind him waving their spears. The BANDIT is in the foreground, his back against the trench wall. KYUZO raises his sword above his head. Fast pan right as he cuts the BANDIT through and he falls headlong over the wall towards camera.

944. Medium long shot looking up the track from the village square, with buildings in the background. KANBEI and KATSUSHIRO can be seen hiding on either side. A single BANDIT gallops down the track towards camera as two farmers carrying the end of a long pole run across the end of it, followed by two others carrying the other end. They hold the pole right across the track in front of the horse, blocking its way, and at the same time KANBEI and KATSUSHIRO lead their men out from cover on either side.

945. Low angle medium close-up of the horse's legs in the foreground as the BANDIT falls to the ground on the other side. The horse moves away.

946. High angle medium shot of a water-filled ditch. The BANDIT crawls along it towards camera with farmers' spears poking him from behind. (Still on page 151)

947. Medium shot of a horse galloping through the trees away from the village, followed by another. Pan slightly right as several more gallop past. As they go off, GOROBEI runs after them waving his sword, followed by KYUZO, RIKICHI and some other farmers. Suddenly a shot rings out and they all throw themselves to the ground. KYUZO waves his sword to get them to take cover, and they all retreat out of sight in the undergrowth.

948. Low angle medium shot of horsemen galloping up the path through the trees. They go off-screen and the BANDIT CAPTAIN rides into shot, waving his sword and shouting, then reining his horse in as others gallop past. Hold as he shouts at them to prepare for attack again and they go on past him. Then the BANDIT CHIEF rides up and they wheel their horses round towards the village again.

949. Medium shot tracking with one of the BANDITS as he

176

gallops down the track with sword erect.

950. Medium close-up tracking with a second BANDIT *as he gallops through the forest.*

951. Medium shot of the bandits following, galloping past trees in the foreground.

952. Low angle long shot looking up the avenue as the bandits gallop towards camera framed between the roof and walls of a trench. In the foreground, in their previous positions, are GOROBEI *and* RIKICHI, *seen over the trench wall. The first horseman gallops through. The villagers with* KYUZO *and* GOROBEI *rush through to block the way of the second horseman but he also gets through. Then they all rush forward across the track.*

953. Medium shot of KANBEI, *back to camera, with two of his men, hiding behind the corner of a house. One of the horsemen gallops forward in the background, swiftly followed by the second.* KANBEI *looks across the track.*

954. Low angle medium long shot of KATSUSHIRO *drawing his sword in his hiding place on the other side of the village square. He runs forward as the horses appear, galloping past camera. The first horse knocks* KATSUSHIRO *flying and the two horsemen gallop away.*

955. Medium shot looking up the track. The two horsemen ride towards camera, going off in the foreground. In the background KANBEI *runs forward followed by his men;* KATSUSHIRO *picks himself up and runs to join* KANBEI *with his own men. They come towards camera, yelling.*

956. Medium long shot, from the side, of the two horsemen galloping through the village square, swords raised. Camera pans left with them.

957. Medium close-up of the bars of a window in one of the houses, from outside, with several women pressed up against it, screaming, as they look through. Sound of galloping hoofs, off.

958. Medium long shot of the horsemen in the middle of the village square, seen through the barred window, with the women's heads visible in back view in the foreground. Pan slightly left as they gallop round, revealing a group of farmers bearing down on them. They wheel their horses round and gallop back again, camera panning back with them, over the women's heads.

959. *Medium long shot of the horsemen galloping through the village (as 958). Pan left as they gallop past, pursued by a band of armed villagers. Another group approaches in the background, cutting off the horsemen and surrounding them.*

960. *Medium long shot of* KIKUCHIYO *leading his unit through the village, shouting and waving his arms and leaping up and down like an ape. Camera pans left with them.*

961. *High angle long shot of* KIKUCHIYO *and his men, backs to camera, running through the village square, seen through the bars of the window over the head of one of the women. Pan right with one of the horsemen who is galloping round the other side of the village square.*

962. *Medium shot panning left with one of the horsemen. He gallops through the square, past the villagers, followed by the other horseman.*

963. *High angle medium long shot of the two horsemen wheeling round away from camera in the middle of the village square. In the background,* KANBEI *and* KATSUSHIRO *can be seen with their men, lined up across the track that leads out of the village to the avenue. They start to run forward as the two horsemen gallop towards them.*

964. *Medium shot of* KANBEI *with three of his men in the foreground, backs to camera. The horsemen gallop towards them and* KANBEI *raises his sword. (Still on page 151) Pan with the horsemen as they come level with* KANBEI, *who strikes the one nearest to him, then on again, losing* KANBEI, *as the man on the horse nearest camera starts to fall.*

965. *Medium shot tracking with the horsemen, with some of the farmers in the foreground beside a small straw fence. The* BANDIT *nearest camera falls off his horse. One of the villagers near him runs up with his spear. The other horseman and the riderless horse gallop away.*

966. *Low angle medium shot of the second horseman galloping past camera, which pans right to follow him. Hold as he gallops away up the village street followed by the other horse.*

967. *High angle medium shot of some bandits on horseback, backs to camera in the foreground, with* GOROBEI, KYUZO

and their men behind them. GOROBEI *and his band attack one of the bandits in the middle; he backs away, out of shot, just as the* BANDIT *who escaped from the village square gallops up the track towards camera.*

968. Low angle medium close-up of one of the farmers, back to camera, leaping over the wall into one of the trenches as the horseman from the village gallops past, also back to camera.

969. Low angle medium close-up of a horse's legs with villagers' legs scuffling in the dust behind it. Confused shouting, neighs, and hoofbeats, continually heard. The horse circles round, raising clouds of dust.

970. Low angle medium shot of a horse backing into shot with the villagers fighting with spears behind it. The horse circles right round.

971. Low angle medium shot of the horse in the foreground, only its legs and belly in frame, with GOROBEI *and some villagers attacking from behind. It circles round again, knocking down several men, including* GOROBEI, *and goes off as the villagers pick themselves up. Pan right with* GOROBEI *as he too gets up, waving his sword.*

972. Medium shot of the horseman galloping away from camera chased by GOROBEI *and his men.*

973. High angle medium shot of the horses galloping towards camera, pursued by the villagers, with KYUZO *in front of them, just behind the last horse. The horses gallop off in the foreground.*

974. Medium shot of the bandits retreating, riding up the path between the trees and going off in the foreground. As the last horseman goes out of shot he reveals GOROBEI *and* KYUZO *leading their band towards camera, shouting with triumph. They run into medium shot, then suddenly turn round and retreat. One of the bandits gallops into shot again in the foreground as* KYUZO, GOROBEI *and their men scatter into the trees. The horse rears up in the foreground, neighing, out of control.*

975. High angle medium close-up of KYUZO *and* GOROBEI *with* RIKICHI *just behind them and the other men crowding round in the background.*

976. Low angle medium shot of the horse bucking and kicking.

977. High angle medium close-up of KYUZO *and* GOROBEI *with the men behind them, looking up towards the horse off-screen, and backing away. (Still on page 151)*

978. Medium shot of the horse rearing, seen over the heads of some farmers.

979. Medium shot of GOROBEI *running up the track towards camera, as the horse gallops off towards the village, still bucking and kicking, watched in amazement by the farmers.* KYUZO *comes forward to join* GOROBEI.

980. Medium shot of KIKUCHIYO *standing in back view on a slight rise at the edge of the village square, leaning on his samurai sword, legs apart. The other villagers are scattered about the square in front of him, and in the background* KANBEI *stands facing him, at the end of the path leading to the avenue. Suddenly he notices something and raises his sword.* KIKUCHIYO *raises his sword in reply and shouts.* KANBEI *backs away behind a house as the horse appears, still bucking, and gallops towards camera.* KIKUCHIYO *jumps down from his vantage point, waving his sword and shouting.*

981. Medium shot, panning right with KIKUCHIYO *as he bounds across, grinning.*

982. Medium long shot of the horse galloping down the track towards KIKUCHIYO *and some farmers in the village square, with* KANBEI *behind it. The horse bucks and kicks, snorting with terror.* KIKUCHIYO *comes to a halt.*

983. Medium shot of the bucking horse at the end of the track, with the BANDIT *lolling about on its back.* KANBEI *is watching in the background.*

984. Medium close-up of KIKUCHIYO, *frowning. He circles round, camera panning left with him, watching the horseman closely all the time. (Still on page 151)*

985. Medium shot of the horse bucking, with its rider doubled up against its neck. KANBEI *stands behind it, and some of the villagers press forward, in the foreground. Pan right with the horse as it backs and sidesteps. More villagers come up in the background and they all surround it.*

986. Medium close-up of KIKUCHIYO *with* YOHEI *and another man in the background. Pan right with* KIKUCHIYO *as he leaps to the side, and hold as he jumps up and down.*

987. Low angle medium shot of the horse's rump, panning with it as it rears and backs dangerously.

988. Medium shot of KIKUCHIYO *backing away and putting an arm out to protect the men behind him. Pan with him as he waves his sword.*

989. Medium shot of the horse from the side with KIKUCHIYO'S *hand holding out the sword and waving it. Pan right with the horse and tilt down as it finally loses its balance and falls over, pulling its rider down with it.*

990. Medium close-up of KIKUCHIYO *roaring with laughter, and staring at the horse appreciatively. He jumps up and down.*

991. High angle medium long shot of the horse galloping away, leaving its rider half-stunned on the ground. As the BANDIT *slowly sits up,* KIKUCHIYO, KATSUSHIRO, KANBEI *and many of the villagers move towards him and surround him, their swords and spears all pointing towards him.* KIKUCHIYO *stands looking down at him hands on his hips, and roars at him. (Still on page 151)*

KIKUCHIYO : Now, just what do you think you're doing?

The bandit, terrified, looks round, leaps to his feet and runs away up the track pursued by all the farmers. They knock him down and spear him.

992. Low angle medium shot of SHICHIROJI, *in back view in the foreground, with* KATSUSHIRO, KANBEI *and* KIKUCHIYO *in the background, watching the farmers, off-screen. They turn towards each other grinning, and* KIKUCHIYO *raises one finger to* KANBEI. *Then they turn away and walk back into the square, camera panning left with them. Music in.*

993. Wipe to medium shot of GOROBEI, KANBEI, KATSUSHIRO, *and* KYUZO *walking towards the end of the avenue, which stretches away in the background.* KATSUSHIRO, *who is behind the others, looks towards the wall of one of the trenches.*

994. Medium shot of KATSUSHIRO *staring over the wall of the trench. On the near side of the wall lies the dead body of the bandit* KYUZO *killed first.* KYUZO, KANBEI *and* GOROBEI *are looking up towards the avenue in the background.*

995. Medium long shot of KYUZO *and* KANBEI *in back view, looking at* GOROBEI *who is facing them.* KATSUSHIRO *is still looking over the wall into the trench.* KANBEI *begins to speak as he turns to walk back towards camera.*

KANBEI : They're getting smarter. They won't try this again.

A bird sings, off. Nothing moves. They all turn towards camera and then KANBEI *turns back and looks up the avenue again.*

996. Medium long shot looking up the deserted, sunlit avenue.

997. Wipe to a high angle medium shot of a unit of farmers sitting in the trenches. Beyond them are seated KIKUCHIYO *and* RIKICHI *and beyond them, in the sunlight, sit* GOROBEI, KANBEI, KYUZO, *and* KATSUSHIRO *with other villagers behind them.* KANBEI *has the map spread out in front of him and they are holding a council of war. One of the villagers in the foreground speaks.*

VILLAGER : They've been molly-coddled. They're not so tough! *They all laugh.*

998. High angle medium shot of KANBEI *seated on the ground with* KATSUSHIRO, GOROBEI *and* KYUZO. *They are all looking towards the villagers, out of shot.* KANBEI *smiles and looks round at the others. (Still on page 152)*

KANBEI *counting on his fingers* : Four killed today, Kyuzo killed two last night.

999. High angle close-up of the edge of KANBEI's *map showing the circles and* KANBEI's *hand. He crosses out four circles in one column then camera pans with his hand as it goes to the top of the next column and crosses out two more. Music out.*

1000. Wipe to medium shot of KATSUSHIRO *kneeling beside* KIKUCHIYO, *who is lying back comfortably among the trees and shrubs on the river bank.*

KATSUSHIRO : He has the real samurai spirit. He is totally fearless. Yet, at the same time he is gentle, and modest — look how he acted after he went and got that gun. And how he went too — just as though he were going up into the hills to look for mushrooms.

1001. Medium close-up of KATSUSHIRO *sitting up, with* KIKUCHIYO *lying back in the foreground, his eyes closed.*

KIKUCHIYO *bored* : You certainly are interesting. It certainly is interesting to hear you talk. *He yawns and scratches his cheek.*

Disappointed by KIKUCHIYO's *negative response,* KATSUSHIRO *gets up and goes to lean against the barricade where the bridge used to be in the background. He stands looking out over the fields, silhouetted against the sky.* KIKUCHIYO *raises his head slightly and looks towards him then settles back again.* KATSUSHIRO *goes off and* KIKUCHIYO *looks up again, then gets up.*

1002. High angle medium shot of a group of villagers. YOHEI *stands between two men with his arms outstretched, being fitted into armour which is much too big for him.* KIKUCHIYO *appears and goes up to him.*

KIKUCHIYO : Yohei, look, you keep watch.

KIKUCHIYO *starts to go away but* YOHEI *puts out a hand to grab him.*

1003. Medium shot of YOHEI *pulling* KIKUCHIYO *back by his belt. He points fearfully.* KIKUCHIYO *shakes himself free.*

KIKUCHIYO : Oh, don't look like that. It's safe enough. You'll scare them off. *He takes hold of* YOHEI'*s breastplate. (Still on page 152)* You'll be our scarecrow.

KIKUCHIYO *goes off laughing, leaving the other men watching him fearfully, especially* YOHEI.

1004. Wipe to medium long shot of part of the forest — tangled branches and flowers. KIKUCHIYO *runs up through the undergrowth, camera panning with him as he comes nearer. Hold as he stops and looks round, then track past trees in the foreground as he runs forward again. Hold for a moment as he peers through the hanging branches. A horse neighs off. Track back as he moves forward again past camera, then tilt up as he moves away up a short slope.*

1005. Medium long shot of KIKUCHIYO *seen through leaves and branches in the foreground. Pan, then hold as he runs on up the hill framed by two branches. He halts beside a couple of horses which are tethered among the trees, and looks round carefully. Pan left past a tree trunk in the foreground, as he goes across to where more horses are tethered. Tilt down as he comes down the hill to the bottom of the tree trunk, now seen from above. Tilt up with him as he climbs the tree, using a creeper to haul himself up, then pan right as he crawls round the trunk and looks down at the horses, tethered below in the background. Suddenly something moves among the trees in the distance.*

1006. High angle general shot of the forest with a horse in the

183

foreground. Two bandits are running towards camera. Tilt down as they dash up and untie two horses. A shot rings out and one of the bandits falls dead beside his horse; the other looks round in horror.

1007. *Low angle medium close-up of* KIKUCHIYO *peering round the branch of the tree in surprise. (Still on page 152)*

1008. *Low angle medium shot of the* BANDIT *with the body of his companion in the foreground, lying in front of the horse. The* BANDIT *jumps to his feet, and camera pans left as he starts to run off.*

1009. *Low angle medium close-up of* KIKUCHIYO *peering round the tree, grinning.*

1010. *High angle medium shot of the bandit jumping onto one of the horses; two other horses in the background among the trees.*

1011. *Low angle medium close-up of* KIKUCHIYO *peering round the tree. He ducks out of sight; pan right across the tree trunk as he appears on the other side, with trees in the background.*

1012. *Medium shot of the* BANDIT *on horseback, panning left as he gallops away through the trees. Suddenly another shot rings out and he falls back. Camera pans further as the horse slows down to a trot and the* BANDIT *rolls off.*

1013. *Low angle medium close-up of* KIKUCHIYO *peering round behind the tree, his mouth open with delight. He looks round, grinning, and then ducks behind the tree again, camera panning left across the tree trunk to pick him up again peering round the other side, still grinning.*

1014. *High angle medium shot of* KIKUCHIYO, *back to camera in the foreground, leaning over the branches of the tree. Two horses are still standing tethered in the background. Something moves in the distance and* KIKUCHIYO *ducks down. A crowd of bandits appear in long shot, running towards camera.*

1015. *Low angle medium shot of the crowd of bandits with the two leaders in front. One of the bandits carries a gun. They move towards camera and stop, a horse's head visible in the foreground. On the grass at their feet lies the body of one of the dead bandits. They look down at it and then at each other. The horse circles round and trots away. The* BANDIT

CAPTAIN *comes forward and kicks the dead body. The* CHIEF
turns and looks round at his men.

BANDIT CHIEF : Remember! Every coward here will get the same
treatment.

*He looks down at the dead body at his feet and raises his foot
to kick it.*

1016. Medium close-up of the BANDIT CHIEF *as he snarls and
smashes his fist down towards the dead body. (Still on page
152) Other bandits behind him look frightened. He smashes
the dead body two or three times.*

1017. Low angle medium shot of the bandits (as 1015). The
CHIEF *slashes out with his sword at the man behind him and
the bandits back off on both sides in fear. Then the* CHIEF
turns away and strides off, followed by the CAPTAIN. *The other
bandits stare down at the dead body for a moment, before
finally turning and shuffling off after their* CHIEF. *The man
who the* CHIEF *slashed at is the last to go, and turns back to
look at the body again.*

*1018. Low angle medium shot, looking into the branches of the
tree.* KIKUCHIYO *appears, peering round and down. He disappears behind the branch; pan right and tilt down as he drops
to the ground. Music in. He looks from right to left and then
runs towards camera, which pans right as he goes up the
slope, then tilts down as he runs up to the dead body and bends
down over it.*

1019. High angle medium close-up of KIKUCHIYO *from the
side, bending over the dead body. The* BANDIT's *head, its eyes
open, is leaning back among the flowers at a grotesque angle.*
KIKUCHIYO *puts out a finger and taps the dead man's nose,
then tickles his forehead. Then he unties his own headband,
drops it on the ground, and unfastens the* BANDIT's *head gear.
Tilt up slightly as he stands up, grinning, turns towards camera
and fixes it on his head.*

*1020. Wipe to general shot of part of the forest with a steep
bank on the left. Pan right past the trees in the foreground as*
KIKUCHIYO *runs down the bank from the top. He turns towards
camera, which pans quickly right again as he bounds down
through the trees. Then he turns and runs across frame, camera
panning left with him. He stops in medium close-up, panting*

193

and snuffing the air. He is now wearing the BANDIT's *head gear and leather breastplate. He looks carefully round from side to side, then camera pans right again as he bounds off through the trees. Music out. Tilt down as he bounds down the slope, breathing loudly through his teeth, then goes out of sight.*

1021. High angle medium shot of a BANDIT *standing back to camera, waist-high in long grass, looking through the trees. He is holding a gun. The roofs of some houses are visible down the hill. He thinks he sees something and raises his gun, then changes his mind and comes back without turning round and sits down in the foreground. He is holding a slow match which he blows from time to time to keep it alight. A voice calling, off, makes him turn round and look up.* KIKUCHIYO, *dressed as a bandit, runs up in the foreground, back to camera, and sits down beside him. They both look down on the village.*

KIKUCHIYO : How is everything?

BANDIT : They're a tough bunch.

KIKUCHIYO : It'll all be over soon.

He reaches over and takes the gun and examines it.

1022. Low angle medium close-up of KIKUCHIYO *and the* BANDIT. *(Still on page 152)*

BANDIT : The whole thing is back to front. Now we're burnt out and hungrier than they are.

KIKUCHIYO *handing the gun back* : Don't complain. Your misery will be over soon enough.

BANDIT *non-committally* : Do your worst.

KIKUCHIYO *draws his sword and looks thoughtfully at the blade. The* BANDIT *glances at the sword then looks at* KIKUCHIYO. *(Still on page 152) He suddenly realises that he has never seen* KIKUCHIYO *before and screams, then runs away.* KIKUCHIYO *jumps up to follow.*

1023. High angle medium shot of KIKUCHIYO *from behind, continuing his movement as he raises his sword and dashes down the slope after the* BANDIT. *Crane up as they run down into a clearing and* KIKUCHIYO, *half-obscured by the branches of a tree, thrusts his sword into the* BANDIT's *back with a shout. Giggling, he grabs the gun and turns back towards camera. Crane down as he bounds back through the clearing; hold as* he stops, examining the gun. A shout, off, makes him turn his head, and he dashes away. Several bandits appear and dash off in pursuit.

1024. *Medium shot of* KATSUSHIRO, GOROBEI, RIKICHI, KANBEI *and* KYUZO *sitting in a half circle at the base of the tree, near the beginning of the avenue. (Still on page 152) Hearing a sound,* KANBEI *jumps to his feet. Pan left across the path, to include some of the farmers leaning over the barricade on the right, with the avenue stretching away beyond them. Shouting can be heard in the distance. Suddenly* KIKUCHIYO *appears in long shot running along the avenue towards camera.*

1025. *Long shot of* KIKUCHIYO *in the avenue, the bandits appearing behind him in pursuit. He pauses and looks back at them, then, going down on one knee, shoots at them. He falls backwards from the recoil and all the bandits fall to the ground in a heap. He rolls over on his back and then gets up, starting to run forward again, as the bandits retreat in the background.*

1026. *Close-up of* KANBEI *from the side, with* KYUZO *beside him, half-obscured, and* RIKICHI *in the background.* KANBEI *moves forward, going out of shot, and revealing* KYUZO. *They are all looking in the direction of* KIKUCHIYO. *Re-frame slightly to pick up* KANBEI *again.*

1027. *Medium long shot of* KIKUCHIYO *in the avenue, running towards camera. Pan slightly left as he comes nearer, leaping up in the air.*

1028. *Close-up of* KANBEI, *three-quarters back to camera. He turns his head as* KIKUCHIYO, *in big close-up, comes into shot in the foreground laughing, partly obscuring him from view. Pan backwards and forwards keeping* KIKUCHIYO *in close-up as he moves about triumphantly.* KANBEI *can be seen looking very stern each time he is included in the shot.*

KANBEI : You fool.

1029. *Medium close-up of* KIKUCHIYO, *puzzled, facing* KANBEI, *with* KYUZO, GOROBEI, KATSUSHIRO *and* RIKICHI *watching them in the background.*

KANBEI : Why did you leave your post?

KIKUCHIYO *grinning and raising the gun* : I don't deserve to be

195

talked to like that — look, I got the gun and the post is safe enough. *(Still on page 152)*

1030. Close-up of KANBEI, *in three-quarter front view, looking at* KIKUCHIYO.

KANBEI : Your going off like that merits no praise at all.

1031. Big close-up of KIKUCHIYO *in profile.*

1032. Medium close-up of KANBEI *and* KIKUCHIYO *with the others in the background.*

KANBEI : Listen carefully — in war, you never fight individually.

KIKUCHIYO *frowns and looks at the gun. Then he throws it down on the ground, in a fit of pique. Suddenly the sound of shouting, off, makes them all look to the left.* KANBEI *runs off, passing in front of* KIKUCHIYO, *and the others follow in the background.* KIKUCHIYO *pauses for a moment.*

1033. Close-up of KIKUCHIYO, *looking to the left, a puzzled frown on his face. Then he follows the others.*

1034. Medium shot of KANBEI *and* GOROBEI *from the side, staring forward in horror.*

1035. High angle long shot, looking down the path to the village, where villagers are fighting, gradually being driven up the path by a troop of bandits.

1036. Medium shot from the side of KYUZO, GOROBEI *and* KANBEI *with* KATSUSHIRO *and* RIKICHI *behind, just in shot.* KIKUCHIYO *appears in the foreground.* KANBEI *turns to* GOROBEI *and* KYUZO *who leans forward towards him, three-quarters back to camera.*

KANBEI : Gorobei ! Kyuzo ! You guard this entrance !

KANBEI *rushes off to the right and the others turn and go off to the left.* KATSUSHIRO *runs past* KIKUCHIYO *to follow* KANBEI. KIKUCHIYO *stands ́alone looking down towards the battle which is raging off-screen. Then he suddenly bounds away.*

1037. High angle medium shot of KYUZO *and* GOROBEI *running into shot in the foreground at the end of the avenue. They take up their positions on either side of the track, followed by the farmers, all back to camera.*

GOROBEI *turning to the farmers* : Let no one through.

Hoofbeats, off. He turns away from camera, looking up the path. Horsemen appear through the trees, galloping towards camera.

1038. *Medium shot of the bandits on their horses, reining in under the trees. The horses whinny and snort; noise of hoofbeats; dust rises around them. The* CAPTAIN *turns his horse and waves his sword at the other bandits. One of them beside him lifts a rifle and takes aim.*

1039. *High angle long shot, looking up the avenue to the bandits on their horses. The bandit fires the gun. In the foreground, the farmers led by* KYUZO *duck down behind the trench walls.*

1040. *Medium shot of the farmers ducking down behind the protective walls.*

1041. *Long shot of a* BANDIT *galloping along the avenue towards camera, waving his sword.*

1042. *Medium shot of the farmers crouching down behind the wall.* KYUZO *stands up and as the horseman gallops past he slashes at him with his sword but does not succeed in halting him. (Still on page 185) He watches briefly as the horseman disappears, then turns and runs off towards the avenue, followed by* GOROBEI *and all the farmers.*

1043. *Medium shot continuing the movement of the farmers; they appear in the foreground, backs to camera, dashing after* KYUZO *as he runs towards the rest of the bandits, who are now galloping forward, shouting.*

1044. *Medium long shot of the village square. A battle is raging between villagers and some bandits on foot who have got in from another way. The bandits run towards camera, going off in the foreground pursued by the villagers with* KATSUSHIRO *and* KIKUCHIYO. *As they do so a horse appears, galloping through the square with its rider, wounded by* KYUZO, *bent double over its neck. Pan right with the horse as it gallops towards camera.*

1045. *Long shot of the horse galloping through the village square, seen through the bars of a window in one of the houses. Pan right with it along the bars of the window, over the heads of several women in the foreground, all armed with clubs and pitchforks.*

1046. *Medium long shot of the horse galloping through the square as its rider rolls off. Pan slightly right as he lands heavily on the ground.*

1047. *Medium long shot of the crowd of women running out of the house and down a short slope towards camera, carrying picks, hoes, sickles and other weapons. Pan left as they run screaming towards the fallen* BANDIT.

1048. *Low angle medium close-up of the* BANDIT *lying on the ground. In the background, the women run screaming towards him, through clouds of dust. (Still on page 185) He starts to crawl forward; pan right with him, losing the women. He stands up, terrified, wielding his sword.*

1049. *Medium close-up of the* BANDIT *from behind, continuing his movement as he slashes out with his sword. Pan with him and tilt down as he falls to the ground again, revealing the women's legs running away. Pan continues, following him from above, as he crawls very quickly up to the verandah of a house. Tilt up slightly, to the bars of the verandah.*

1050. *Medium shot of the side of the house, continuing the pan to the left as the women rush up, screaming. The* BANDIT *looks round the entrance to the house at them, sobbing with fear. Pan slightly further as they close in on him.*

1051. *Medium close-up with the bars of the verandah in the foreground. Tilt down with the* BANDIT *who is on the other side, trying to crawl away from the women who appear in the foreground, attacking him through the bars.*

1052. *High angle medium close-up of the* BANDIT *gibbering behind the bars, with a woman's arms jabbing at him with a pitchfork. He dodges about, trying to escape the blows.*

1053. *Medium shot, tracking right with* KATSUSHIRO *and* KANBEI *as they run yelling through the village street, with* KATSUSHIRO *in the foreground, and* KANBEI *slashing at a bandit as he passes.* SHICHIROJI *passes camera as well, following them. The track continues as they battle their way through the village.*

1054. *Low angle medium shot of* KIKUCHIYO *in the foreground, battling with a* BANDIT *whose head and shoulders are in shot. Behind him* KATSUSHIRO *and some of the farmers are fighting. Track right with the battle.*

1055. *High angle medium close-up of* KIKUCHIYO, *his face distorted as he fights. Others can be seen fighting in the background. A* BANDIT *appears in the foreground, attacking him. (Still on page 185)*

1056. Medium long shot of bandits galloping through the woods towards camera. The leader carries a bow and takes aim as they ride.

1057. Medium long shot of the farmers among the trees at the end of the avenue. They scatter as the leading BANDIT *gallops towards them.*

1058. Medium shot of the BANDIT *with another behind him, galloping towards camera. The first man lets fly an arrow.*

1059. Medium close-up of KYUZO *and one of the farmers leaning over one of the barriers with the wall of a house behind them. They duck down quickly and an arrow sticks in the wall behind* KYUZO, *quivering.*

1060. High angle medium long shot of the farmers battling in the village street, among the houses. Pan slightly right as they fall on a BANDIT *who is obscured by the shadows. Two horsemen gallop past and camera pans left as the farmers run after them, disappearing and reappearing again. The pan continues across one of the houses, losing the farmers again and picking up the bandits in high angle long shot as they gallop into the village square.*

1061. Low angle medium shot of the two horsemen. Pan left as they gallop past camera, and the leading horseman draws his bow again. (Still on page 185)

1062. Medium long shot of part of the village square. The bowman gallops up, and women can be seen scattering in the foreground, and jumping over fences in the background. The bowman shoots an arrow as he gallops through.

1063. Medium shot of two women from behind. An arrow hits one of them in the back, pinning her, screaming, up against the wall of a house. (Still on page 185)

1064. Low angle medium shot of one of the bandits, his head out of shot, running away through a ditch towards the bridge barricade, followed by several others. KIKUCHIYO *appears in the foreground chasing them, followed by some of his men.*

1065. Medium shot of the bandits leaping over the barricade into the river, pursued by the villagers and KIKUCHIYO.

1066. Medium shot continuing the movement of the bandits as they leap down into the stream. Tilt up slightly as they struggle across the stream and up onto the opposite bank.

1067. Medium shot of SHICHIROJI *peering between two poles of the barricade with* KIKUCHIYO *in the middle waving his sword and shouting, and* KATSUSHIRO *and* KANBEI *standing beside him.*

1068. Medium shot of the bandits wading through the flooded fields, away from camera.

1069. Medium shot of the four samurai leaning over the barricade, watching. KIKUCHIYO *is shouting triumphantly.* KANBEI *turns away.*

1070. Low angle close-up of KANBEI *in profile. The burial mound can be seen behind him.*

KANBEI : Good god! Two more got through! *As he speaks, he starts to move away, camera panning left with him.*

1071. Medium shot of KIKUCHIYO *on the barrier, with the other three samurai running away behind him. He looks round and jumps down.*

1072. Medium long shot of KIKUCHIYO *and his men by the barrier with the dead body of a farmer lying in the ditch in the foreground, and another below the barricade. They are looking out towards the flooded fields where the bandits can just be seen running away in the distance.* KIKUCHIYO *looks down at the body at his feet and picks it up to look at the face.*

1073. Medium long shot of the village square with the two horsemen galloping round, scattering the villagers who are trying desperately to ward them off. The bowman rides towards camera.

1074. Medium shot of the bowman, panning left as he gallops across. He raises his bow high over his horse's head, aims and lets fly an arrow.

1075. Medium shot of three men throwing themselves to the ground.

1076. Medium shot of the other horseman using his spear to ward off KANBEI *who is slashing at him with his sword.* KATSUSHIRO *joins the battle.*

1077. Low angle medium long shot of the bowman galloping round towards camera in the village square, pursued by some farmers. The other horseman is also galloping round the square, *pursued by some other farmers, with* KANBEI *and* KATSUSHIRO.

1078. Medium shot of KIKUCHIYO *with his men behind him, running away from the barricade towards the second dead body, which lies in a pool of water in the foreground. (Still on page 186) He looks down at it, pulls it up to look at the face and then throws it down again and goes back to face his men.*

KIKUCHIYO *shouting* : Yohei! Where is Yohei?

1079. Medium shot of KANBEI *leading his men through the village square; pan slightly left. He stops as* KATSUSHIRO *and* SHICHIROJI *come up behind him. Sound of hoofbeats, off.*

1080. Medium long shot of KANBEI *and the others facing camera, seen through the legs of a horse in the foreground. The horse gallops away, followed by the second. The dust they raise obscures* KANBEI *and the others from view.*

1081. Medium shot panning right with the bowman as he gallops across, letting an arrow fly.

1082. Medium shot of a farmer running away. The arrow sticks in his back, and camera tilts down as he falls on his face.

1083. Low angle medium shot of one of the horses galloping past. In the background KANBEI *and the others can be seen scattering. The horse gallops away; tilt up slightly as the other horseman follows.*

1084. Medium long shot of the two horsemen galloping towards the farmers in the foreground. The first horseman pursues one of the farmers and cuts him down, then gallops off. The man falls on the ground with a terrible cry. The other horseman gallops away revealing KATSUSHIRO *and* KANBEI *running towards camera.*

1085. Medium shot of KANBEI *from the side, panning left as he runs, with two farmers in the foreground running to join him. They go off as* KATSUSHIRO *appears in the background.* KANBEI *stops, and camera holds on him as* KATSUSHIRO *runs off. More farmers appear in the background. Pan slightly right as* KANBEI *backs, and the sound of hoofbeats gets louder. The farmers in the background scatter.* KANBEI *raises his sword as the first horseman gallops past him. (Still on page 186)*

1086. Medium shot of the second BANDIT *with his spear*

lowered, charging towards camera. Pan slightly left as he approaches, revealing KANBEI'S *head in back view in the foreground. The* BANDIT *charges at* KANBEI *with his spear.* KANBEI *parries the blow with his sword.*

1087. Medium shot, from the side, of the horsemen galloping past KANBEI, *who stands three-quarters back to camera in the foreground.*

1088. Medium close-up of the BANDIT *on his horse, looking back towards* KANBEI. *Pan with him as he gallops past, following the other horseman.*

1089. Medium long shot of KIKUCHIYO *running through the village square; very fast pan left until he catches up with the horseman with the spear. The horseman gallops away but the pan continues with* KIKUCHIYO, *who runs on, joined by* KANBEI *and some of the others.*

1090. Medium close-up of the bowman aiming an arrow; very fast pan as he gallops away.

1091. Medium shot of YOHEI *running towards camera, pursued by the bowman who lets an arrow fly. Pan left with* YOHEI *as he runs past, going away from camera, with an arrow sticking out of his back. The bowman gallops on past. Hold on* YOHEI *as he sinks to his knees with a strangled cry.*

1092. Medium long shot of KIKUCHIYO *as he runs forward with other villagers behind him. Pan left with him, losing the others, as he runs towards camera, then tilt down as he goes past a post and down onto his knees beside* YOHEI, *who is lying on his face with the arrow sticking out of his back.* KIKUCHIYO *puts a hand on his shoulder.*

KIKUCHIYO *anguished* : Yohei!

He pulls the arrow out of YOHEI'S *back and tosses it away. Then he tries to lift the old farmer up, bending down and looking at him. (Still on page 186)*

YOHEI *hardly able to speak* : I did my best as look-out but you'll have to fight twice as hard now. *He falls forward, dead.*

Another arrow falls just behind them, sticking into the ground. KIKUCHIYO *looks up furiously; pan left with him as he ducks down under the fence and tilt up slightly, then hold as he runs back into the middle of the village square, turning to face the horseman who is riding up in the foreground. The horse-*

man gallops up to him, hitting out with his spear, but
KIKUCHIYO slashes and thrusts with his sword. Pan slightly
further as the horse whinnies, bucking and turning, and then
gallops away as its rider begins to fall. (Still on page 186)
1093. Low angle medium close-up of the horse's legs visible
in the foreground, galloping past, as the BANDIT falls heavily to
the ground, just behind it.
1094. Medium long shot of the BANDIT lying on the ground
with KIKUCHIYO and two of the villagers falling on him. (Still
on page 186) KIKUCHIYO goes down on one knee beside him
back to camera, and plunges his sword viciously into his back.
The other two men prod the body with their spears.
1095. Medium long shot of KIKUCHIYO and the farmers by the
dead body. The other horse gallops into shot in the foreground
and KIKUCHIYO leaps to his feet, dashing off in pursuit as it
goes off-screen, followed by KANBEI, SHICHIROJI and KATSU-
SHIRO, who appear in the foreground with a crowd of the
farmers.
1096. High angle medium close-up of the horse's back, panning
very quickly as it moves across frame. Tilt up and hold as it
gallops away up the path leading out of the village, revealing
KIKUCHIYO, KANBEI and KATSUSHIRO, chasing after it in the
foreground.
1097. Low angle medium long shot of the horse, only its legs
visible, galloping towards camera, seen between two bars of a
fence. In the background KIKUCHIYO and KANBEI can just
be seen dashing forward with others running along behind
them. Pan slightly right as the horse sidesteps in front of the
bars revealing KATSUSHIRO in the background, seen between
its legs. The horse, whinnying and sidestepping, turns and
gallops away from camera, revealing KIKUCHIYO running
forward, preparing to strike with his sword.
1098. High angle medium long shot of the BANDIT on his horse.
KIKUCHIYO runs along beside him as he gallops towards the
villagers and samurai assembled facing him in the foreground.
Pan slightly left as the horse comes forward; all the villagers
hold up their spears to bar its way, with KANBEI and SHICHIROJI
holding up their swords directly in front of it and KIKUCHIYO

and KATSUSHIRO *rushing up from behind. Pan further as the horse gallops on through; then hold as* SHICHIROJI *manages to catch hold of part of the* BANDIT's *clothing and pull him off. The farmers and samurai immediately surround the* BANDIT *with* KANBEI *in the centre slashing at the body with his sword.*

1099. Sound of a rifle shot on the cut to high angle medium close-up of the villagers, in back view, surrounding the body. KANBEI *can be seen just beyond them facing camera, with* KATSUSHIRO *behind him. They all jump back, looking anxiously in the direction of the sound. Pan right with* KANBEI *as he turns and leaves the group. Hold as another shot rings out and distant shouting can be heard. He begins to run, calling back as he does so.*

KANBEI: Shichiroji, take over! *Track right with him as he runs through the village square.*

1100. High angle medium long shot of KANBEI, KATSUSHIRO *and* KIKUCHIYO *running towards camera. Crane down and pan left as they run past.*

1101. Medium shot, looking towards the end of the avenue of trees. KANBEI, KATSUSHIRO *and* KIKUCHIYO *appear, running round one of the covered trenches, towards the avenue. There is no-one else there. Silence.*

1102. Medium shot from the side, as KANBEI *stops with* KATSUSHIRO *and* KIKUCHIYO *behind him and part of the covered trench in the foreground. They all look up the avenue.*

KANBEI: Oh! Gorobei!

Samurai theme in, played slowly by a solo horn. He runs out of shot, followed by KATSUSHIRO. KIKUCHIYO *pauses for a moment, sword in hand, looking with horror towards the avenue.*

1103. High angle medium shot of a crowd of villagers carrying GOROBEI's *body on a litter, led by* KYUZO. *They walk very slowly towards camera, looking down at* GOROBEI, *and stop as* KANBEI *and* KATSUSHIRO *join them.* KANBEI *comes over beside* KYUZO *and puts his hand on* GOROBEI's *body. (Still on page 187)*

KANBEI *sorrowfully*: Gorobei! *With anguish in his voice, he repeats the name.* Gorobei! Gorobei!

Tilt down slightly as the villagers slowly lower the body to the ground, then go down on their knees in a half circle, bowing their heads, with GOROBEI *lying on his back in the centre.*

1104. Medium shot of KIKUCHIYO *standing beside the hut, staring forward. His shoulders heave and he drops down onto his knees, bowing his head.*

1105. Wipe to a high angle medium shot of the top of a bamboo spear, lit from below, against a black night sky. Tilt down and pan slightly left to show the spear stuck upright in the top of a mound and beyond it two other burial mounds surmounted by samurai swords. KIKUCHIYO *is sitting with head bent beside them. (Still on page 187)*

1106. Medium long shot of a group of villagers sitting around a fire at the foot of the burial hill. Behind them KIKUCHIYO *can be seen sitting at the top of the hill, with the two samurai mounds at the top and three mounds with spears stuck in them below. (Still on page 187)*

1107. High angle close-up of KANBEI'S *hand; pan with it as it crosses off five more circles on the side of the map.*

1108. Medium close-up of KANBEI *kneeling down, seen from the side, with* KYUZO *and* KATSUSHIRO *sitting facing camera, just beyond him. They are looking down at the map.* KANBEI *crosses out two more circles. (Still on page 187) Music out.*

KANBEI *wearily*: There are thirteen left. But those last seven cost us a lot.

He turns to the other two, looking closely at KATSUSHIRO, *whose head suddenly nods forward, as he falls asleep.* KYUZO *looks at him also, and then he and* KANBEI *look at one another.*

1109. High angle medium shot of a crowd of villagers, backs to camera, with their spears propped up on their shoulders, most of them asleep. In the background, KYUZO *and* KANBEI *sit beside a blazing fire, looking towards them. Between them,* KATSUSHIRO *is sitting with his head bowed, fast asleep.*

1110. Medium shot, from the side, of SHICHIROJI, *sitting crosslegged, leaning on his spear. Villagers can be seen behind him, propped up against the inner barricades, most of them asleep. A fire burning in the background lights up the large barricade.*

1111. Medium shot of KYUZO, KANBEI *and* KATSUSHIRO.
KANBEI *turns to* KATSUSHIRO, *whose head is bowed.*
KANBEI : Katsushiro! *He does not wake.* Katsushiro!
KATSUSHIRO *suddenly wakes up and lifts his head, looking towards* KANBEI.
1112. Wipe to medium long shot of KATSUSHIRO, *panning right as he runs down and away from camera, towards the barricade.*
1113. Medium close-up of KATSUSHIRO, *with* SHICHIROJI *in the foreground, back to camera, only his head and shoulders in frame.*
KATSUSHIRO : Kanbei says you are to try and get some sleep now. Two sentries will keep watch. Also, the men can visit their families, one by one.
1114. High angle medium close-up of SHICHIROJI *facing camera with* KATSUSHIRO *back to camera in the foreground.*
SHICHIROJI : So tomorrow is the big fight, then?
1115. Reverse angle medium close-up of KATSUSHIRO *with* SHICHIROJI *in the foreground.*
KATSUSHIRO : I think so. Please spread the word. *He dashes away.*
1116. High angle medium long shot looking towards the barricade as KATSUSHIRO *runs back towards camera.*
SHICHIROJI *begins to stand up*
1117. Medium close-up from the side, continuing SHICHIROJI's *movement, as he pulls himself up on his spear. Tilt up with him and pan slightly left as he turns to face his men. He walks towards a group of them sitting around by the inner barricades, and stands looking down at them.*
SHICHIROJI : Well, you heard the order. *He turns back towards camera.* I'll keep the watch. *Pan right with him as he turns and walks over to* MANZO. You Manzo, you run home now and see your daughter. *He grins.* I mean your son. *He chuckles.*
MANZO *does not move at this remark about* SHINO, *but stands and looks embarrassed. (Still on page 187)*
1118. Medium long shot in the village, looking towards a large bonfire in the distance, surrounded by people. Another bonfire burns in the foreground. KATSUSHIRO *walks wearily towards camera. Suddenly* SHINO *runs across his path and disappears behind the flames of the bonfire for a moment. Quiet music in.*

KATSUSHIRO *stops and looks after her.*

1119. Medium shot of KATSUSHIRO, *back to camera, looking towards* SHINO, *who stands looking back at him on the other side of the bonfire. She is no longer dressed as a boy but wears a flower-patterned kimono. They stand staring at one another for a moment and then* KATSUSHIRO *begins to walk slowly towards her.*

1120. Low angle medium shot of SHINO *standing facing camera with the flames of the bonfire flaring up in the foreground. (Still on page 188) She turns and runs towards a hut behind her, then looks back.*

1121. Reverse angle medium shot of KATSUSHIRO, *with the fire blazing in the foreground. He takes a few steps forward. (Still on page 188)*

1122. Medium shot of SHINO *standing beside the door of the hut. Still staring towards* KATSUSHIRO, *she backs towards it.*

1123. Low angle medium shot of KATSUSHIRO. *He walks towards camera.*

1124. Medium close-up of SHINO. *She backs a couple of steps again, still staring towards* KATSUSHIRO *out of shot.*

1125. Low angle medium close-up of KATSUSHIRO. *He moves forward.*

1126. Medium close-up of SHINO. *She turns and goes to stand on the threshold of the hut, and looks back again. Then she backs through the entrance, disappearing in the darkness.*

1127. Medium shot of KATSUSHIRO *from behind, with the fire blazing in the foreground. He walks slowly away from camera towards the entrance of the hut, pauses, and then ducks down and goes in.* SHINO *can just be seen darting forward to pull the door to.*

1128. Medium shot of KATSUSHIRO *and* SHINO *inside the hut. Through the entrance the fire can be seen blazing outside in the background. Continuing her movement,* SHINO *grabs* KATSUSHIRO's *hand and pulls the door closed with her free hand. Music out. They stare at each other.*

SHINO *desperately sobbing*: We're going to die, aren't we? All of us, going to die tomorrow, aren't we?

KATSUSHIRO: Maybe not.

207

SHINO *pulling him towards her*: But we probably will, won't we, won't we?

She flings her arms round his shoulders; pan right as they fall against the wall of the hut, clinging to each other. Then still clasped together they begin to fall towards camera.
1129. High angle medium close-up continuing their movement as they fall onto the straw matting on the ground. They lie together, breathing heavily, SHINO still sobbing slightly, locked in a passionate embrace. The firelight through the bamboo walls covers them with a flickering, striped pattern.
1130. Medium shot of village women all lying asleep on the floor of a hut. MANZO comes in through the door in the background and looks round.

MANZO *whispering*: Shino! *He steps over one of the sleeping bodies, looking round, and calls louder.* Where are you, Shino?
He lifts the head of one of the women lying just beside him. But it is not SHINO. He continues to pick his way among the sleeping bodies, calling SHINO's name. Fade out. *

1131. Fade in on a low angle medium long shot of the samurai banner, fluttering on the top of the roof, against the sky. It is pouring with rain.
1132. Medium long shot of KATSUSHIRO, KYUZO and KANBEI standing looking up towards the avenue. In the foreground, the villagers are crouching down beside the trench walls, with their spears at the ready. Suddenly the three samurai draw their swords at exactly the same time. Then KANBEI turns towards the villagers. (Still on page 189)

KANBEI: There are only thirteen left so we're going to let them all in at once. *Gesturing with his sword.* As soon as they pass us we'll follow and trap them inside. *Pointing.* This is the final battle. It will decide the outcome. *He turns back and looks up the avenue again.*
1133. Medium shot through the entrance of a hut with villagers in back view in the foreground, looking out. Outside, SHICHIROJI walks up and stands looking up the street. He turns and takes a few steps towards his men, who crouch down in the foreground.

SHICHIROJI: Hey! *Suddenly he runs off.*

* End of reel 7.

Pan left past the wall of the hut and track back slightly to reveal SHICHIROJI *just visible on the other side of the bamboo fence, shouting at some other men on the other side of the village street. The men look rather dejected. Track back with* SHICHIROJI, *then hold, as he walks into medium shot and turns back towards them, still haranguing them. He stands three-quarters back to camera, leaning on his spear.*

SHICHIROJI : Look up, now! What you need to win this battle is real fighting spirit!

1134. Medium long shot of SHICHIROJI *standing back to camera in the middle of the village street. His men are huddled on either side of the street getting what shelter they can from the pouring rain. Suddenly some weapons are thrown across frame in the foreground and land on the ground, just out of sight.* SHICHIROJI *turns towards camera at the noise. Then two swords appear and a hand sticks them in the ground as* SHICHIROJI *turns and begins to run up a short slope. Pan slightly right to reveal* KIKUCHIYO *sticking swords into a slightly raised bank in front of him as* SHICHIROJI *comes up. (Still on page 189)*

SHICHIROJI : Kikuchiyo! What are you doing?

KIKUCHIYO : When you kill — you kill.

KIKUCHIYO *draws his own sword and they both turn away from camera, and begin to walk back along the street. Pan back slightly left, as they go and take up their positions, backs to camera, looking up the track between the houses.*

1135. Medium long shot of KATSUSHIRO, KYUZO *and* KANBEI *seen from the side near the end of the avenue, looking up it. In the foreground, their band of men are crouching down behind the stone walls. Faint sound of hoofbeats through the rain. Suddenly* KANBEI *moves across and takes up his position behind a tall tree-trunk, with* KATSUSHIRO *behind him.* KYUZO *ducks down and the men in the foreground shuffle backwards leaving a wide path for the bandits to come through.*

1136. High angle long shot, looking down through the trees to the track in the forest. A horseman gallops down it followed by others. Pan slightly left with them.

1137. Medium close-up of KANBEI, *sword at the ready, with* KATSUSHIRO *and* RIKICHI *behind him. Sound of hoofbeats and the rain falling.*

1138. Medium long shot of one of the bandits galloping through the forest. Pan slightly left as he rides off, followed by all the others, splashing across a small stream.

1139. High angle medium shot of KIKUCHIYO. *Hearing the sound of distant hoofbeats he crouches down at the ready. His five extra swords are stuck in the earth in the foreground. In the background, the other men crouch down beside the houses.* KIKUCHIYO *begins to run forward.*

1140. Medium long shot, looking down towards the track, as KIKUCHIYO *runs away from camera, with* SHICHIROJI *behind him. They stop for a moment and then* KIKUCHIYO *raises his sword and yells. Their men begin to run out from their hiding place.*

1141. Medium long shot, looking up the avenue, as the bandits ride into view through the relentless rain. In the foreground KYUZO *is bending low, peering over one of the stone walls. The first bandits gallop past unimpeded. Pan slightly left, as more follow. Pan continues past one of the uprights of a hut; the horses' legs can be seen galloping past. On the other side of the path,* KANBEI, *his head obscured, can be seen crouching down at the ready beside the tree trunk.*

1142. Medium close-up of KANBEI, *with* KATSUSHIRO, RIKICHI *and another man behind him.* KANBEI *looks towards the retreating horsemen; very fast pan left as he runs off after them. Hold as he goes off, swiftly followed by* KATSUSHIRO *and all the other villagers.*

1143. High angle medium long shot of KIKUCHIYO *and* SHICHIROJI *with their band of villagers retreating from the end of the avenue as the hoofbeats sound louder. (Still on page 189)*

1144. Medium shot of the first two bandits galloping round past the houses, camera panning with them.

1145. Medium close-up of KIKUCHIYO *from the side, panning very quickly to the right as he charges forward yelling. One of the bandits flashes past him and* KIKUCHIYO *slashes out at him so fast that his movement is just a blur in the rain.*

1146. Medium shot of KIKUCHIYO *waving his sword by the side of the path. Tilt down as he loses his balance and falls back-*

210

wards down a bank as more bandits gallop by in the background. He gets swiftly to his feet again.

1147. Low angle medium shot from behind of two of the villagers, splashing through the mud. A horse's legs come into shot in the foreground, obscuring them from view.

1148. Low angle medium shot of SHICHIROJI *charging towards a fence in the foreground with his spear held out in front of him. A horse passes between him and the fence, obscuring him from view. It gallops away very fast, revealing* SHICHIROJI *again, momentarily. Another horse comes into shot, jumping over the fence from the foreground; tilt down with its rider as he falls to the ground.*

1149. High angle medium close-up of KIKUCHIYO *crouching down on the ground, wielding his sword. Very fast pan as he slashes out at two horses which gallop past in quick succession, their legs moving across frame in the foreground. The horses go off revealing* KIKUCHIYO *down on his knees in a rain-filled ditch.*

1150. Medium close-up of a horse's legs galloping past camera. Its rider falls off, and lands heavily in a shower of mud as the horse disappears.

1151. High angle medium shot of KIKUCHIYO *getting to his feet, now covered with mud, and brandishing his sword. Another horse gallops across in the foreground and* KIKUCHIYO *lashes out at the rider from behind.*

1152. Low angle medium shot of the BANDIT *landing in the mud as a horse's legs gallop by, in soft focus. Another horse passes, and yet another* BANDIT *lands on the ground. Villagers can be seen rushing up to the first* BANDIT *behind him as he tries to get to his knees.*

1153. High angle medium shot, panning swiftly with another horseman as he gallops round behind KIKUCHIYO, *who slashes out at him.*

1154. High angle medium shot of the horse in the foreground with its rider falling off. Some villagers rush forward in the background. The rider lands with a splash in the mud as another BANDIT *gallops by. Tilt up slightly as he rolls over and over.*

1155. Medium shot of KIKUCHIYO *down on his knees in the*

mud. A BANDIT *gallops by and breaks the blade of* KIKUCHIYO'S *sword in half, leaving only a short length of metal near the hilt. Another horseman gallops by as* KIKUCHIYO *furiously tosses the useless sword away.*

1156. *High angle medium long shot of* KIKUCHIYO *continuing his movement as he throws the sword away and runs splashing through the mud. (Still on page 189) The battle continues in the background with farmers fighting with fallen bandits and horsemen galloping around.* KIKUCHIYO *runs towards his supply of swords stuck in the mound of earth.*

1157. *High angle medium shot of* KIKUCHIYO *grabbing another sword from the mound. (Still on page 189) Pan slightly left as he leaps round beside* SHICHIROJI *who is standing just behind him. At that moment* KANBEI *and* KATSUSHIRO *come running down the path towards camera leading their men. They exchange hasty words and then part company,* SHICHIROJI *running off after* KATSUSHIRO *and* KANBEI *turning to run towards camera, with* KIKUCHIYO *in the foreground.* KANBEI *comes up onto the mound and, sticking his sword in the ground, leans down and picks up a bow and arrow from the supply of arms that* KIKUCHIYO *has gathered there.*

1158. *Low angle medium shot of the bandits galloping into shot at the foot of the burial mound. Pan slightly right as they wheel their horses round and gallop back to attack again.*

1159. *Medium shot of the bandits, tracking sideways with them as they gallop through the village square, past some posts and a fence in the foreground.*

1160. *Medium shot from the side of* KIKUCHIYO *with some of his men, moving back as they watch the approaching bandits off-screen. Very fast pan left, losing* KIKUCHIYO *and his men, to medium close-up of* KANBEI. *He holds his bow high above his head, drawing the arrow back.*

1161. *Medium close-up of one of the bandit chiefs galloping along, camera panning with him; hold as he reins in his horse, waving his sword, and then gallops back the way he came.*

1162. *Medium close-up from the side of* KANBEI *calmly aiming the arrow. (Still on page 189) He lets it fly.*

1163. *Low angle medium close-up of the horses' hoofs galloping through the mud. As they pass, one of the bandits lands face* down in the mud with an arrow in his back.

1164. High angle medium shot of four of the bandits galloping across the screen, camera panning left with them; (Still on page 189) hold as they wheel their horses round and pan right as they gallop back in the other direction.

1165. Low angle medium shot of a horse's legs throwing up mud as it gallops past, followed by another.

1166. Medium shot of KANBEI, *back to camera, preparing to loose another arrow.* KYUZO *and some of the villagers duck down towards him, ready for the attack.* KANBEI *lets his arrow fly. (Still on page 189)*

1167. Low angle medium shot of horses' legs galloping by through the mud. As a second horse passes another BANDIT *lands on his back on the ground with an arrow through his chest.*

1168. Medium shot, panning with one of the bandit leaders and some other bandits as they gallop across to the low mound in the middle of the square, where KANBEI *is standing with the other villagers.* KANBEI *slashes out at the two leading horsemen with his sword. Pan back as they wheel their horses round and the villagers close in round them with their spears.*

1169. Low angle medium shot of a horse's legs galloping towards camera and going off in the foreground. Other horses pass by and some villagers can be seen in the background.

1170. Low angle medium shot of KIKUCHIYO, *legs apart, preparing for the attack. A horse gallops past behind him and another in the foreground. He strikes out and falls over in the mud as the horses gallop away. Hold on* KIKUCHIYO *as he gets to his feet. He chases after them as* KYUZO *appears with some of his men.*

1171. High angle medium shot of one of the bandit leaders on his horse with two other bandits behind him; (Still on page 190) pan left with him then hold as he stops at the edge of one of the flooded fields and wheels round towards camera. The other bandits do the same. Pan with them as they gallop off, then hold for a moment as the last BANDIT *comes past on his horse and slips off onto the muddy ground, looking behind him as he does so. Very fast pan left as he runs through the mud, back towards the flooded field.*

1172. Low angle medium close-up of the BANDIT's *feet running through the mud. Tilt up as he reaches the barricade and starts to climb up. At that moment* KATSUSHIRO *and* RIKICHI *appear in back view in the foreground. Tilt up further as the bandit climbs the barricade but* KATSUSHIRO *reaches him in time and thrusts his sword into his back. Track back slightly and tilt down as* KATSUSHIRO *backs off and the bandit falls back into the mud.* KATSUSHIRO, *his head out of frame, watches in the foreground as the bandit writhes in agony for a moment and then finally lies still.* KATSUSHIRO *drops down onto his knees, exhausted. (Still on page 190)*

1173. Medium close-up from the side of SHICHIROJI *inside one of the houses with his spear held out in front of him, prodding at something on the right.* MANZO *appears in the foreground for a second, helping* SHICHIROJI *prod with his spear.*

1174. Medium shot, panning slightly with a BANDIT *who is cowering in the corner of the house, partly obscured by a pillar in the foreground. He is being prodded constantly by* SHICHIROJI *and* MANZO. *Tilt down slightly as he staggers forward against the flimsy wall of the hut, breaking it as he falls.*

1175. Medium close-up of SHICHIROJI *and* MANZO *in the foreground, lunging forward with their spears. Pan right with* SHICHIROJI *as he steps forward for the* coup de grâce.

1176. Medium shot, outside the hut. Tilt down and pan to the right as the BANDIT *falls through the wall of the hut, bringing a piece of it down with him, with* SHICHIROJI's *spear sticking out of his back. He writhes and gurgles and then rolls over, dead.*

1177. Medium shot of the entrance to the hut as some of the farmers come out, carrying their spears, followed by SHICHI-ROJI *and* MANZO. SHICHIROJI *pauses for a moment at the door of the hut and calls.*

SHICHIROJI : Katsushiro! Rikichi!

1178. Medium shot of KATSUSHIRO *and* RIKICHI *crouched in front of the corpse with the barricade in the background.*

SHICHIROJI *off, shouting* : Katsushiro!

KATSUSHIRO *looks up towards camera.*

1179. Medium shot of SHICHIROJI *outside the hut with* MANZO *and the other men running off behind him.*

SHICHIROJI *shouting towards* KATSUSHIRO : Katsushiro, go to the eastern section!

1180. Medium shot of KATSUSHIRO *and* RIKICHI *by the barricade.* KATSUSHIRO *gets to his feet and goes off in the foreground, followed by* RIKICHI *and another man who was previously out of shot.*

1181. Medium shot of SHICHIROJI *with his men following him and the barricade in the background; they run off in the foreground. Then* KATSUSHIRO *appears, jumping over one of the inner walls. He runs off after* SHICHIROJI *with* RIKICHI *and the other man behind him. They are all splashing through the mud which is now ankle-deep.*

1182. Medium close-up of several women, backs to camera, staring into the village square through the barred windows of a hut. Pan left over their heads as SHICHIROJI *and his unit run past in the rain outside. The women crane their necks to watch, then suddenly one of them turns towards camera and screams. (Still on page 190) They all turn, backing against the window, shrieking hysterically; pan slightly right as they jostle each other.*

1183. Medium close-up of the BANDIT CHIEF, *carrying a gun, as he runs towards camera followed by another* BANDIT. *He ducks down through the entrance of the hut, camera panning with him in close-up, three-quarter back view. Tilt up slightly as, followed by his henchman, he walks threateningly towards the women, who cower against the back wall of the hut. (Still on page 190)*

BANDIT CHIEF : You'll be quiet or you'll die.

Pan with the BANDIT CHIEF *as he turns away from the women, leaving his henchman on guard, and walks over to one of the barred windows. Track in slightly to show him in back view as he stares through the bars into the village square. Horsemen gallop past in the background.*

1184. Medium long shot of three horsemen galloping towards camera and wheeling their horses round. In the background four other riderless horses can be seen cantering towards them, followed by a crowd of villagers.

1185. Medium shot of three of the riderless horses, galloping towards camera, pursued by KIKUCHIYO. *Track back slightly as the horses go off with* KIKUCHIYO *bounding through the mud after them.*

1186. *Medium long shot of the three horsemen, backs to camera, in the middle of the village square, with the three riderless horses galloping towards them and the crowd of villagers led by* KIKUCHIYO *chasing after.*

1187. *High angle medium shot of* KIKUCHIYO *with the horses' heads in the foreground. Very fast pan as he runs across the square driving them forward. They go off in the foreground and a mounted* BANDIT *appears, obscuring* KIKUCHIYO *from view. The horse goes half out of shot, revealing* KIKUCHIYO *slashing at its rider with his sword.*

1188. *Big close-up of one of the horse's hoofs splashing in the mud, with the village square visible in the background. The horse disappears as, with a terrible cry, its rider falls on his back in a shower of mud. (Still on page 190) Short, very fast pan with the body as it is dragged through the mud, still attached to the saddle by one foot.*

1189. *High angle medium shot of the horse's legs, tracking very fast as it gallops along dragging the* BANDIT *through the mud. Hold as it moves away from camera following another horse, and some villagers in the foreground run forward to attack.*

1190. *High angle medium shot of villagers running away from camera, pursuing a horseman and the loose animal dragging its rider through the mud. (Still on page 190) Pan slightly and tilt up as the horses gallop away round the corner, followed by the villagers.*

1191. *Medium shot of the* BANDIT CAPTAIN *on his horse, circling round and round, with* KIKUCHIYO *beside him, attacking with his sword. When the horse circles, it reveals* KYUZO *and* KANBEI *attacking on the other side. Villagers' spears can be seen on either side of the frame as they surround the horse.*

1192. *Medium long shot of the* BANDIT CAPTAIN *on his horse with the villagers and the samurai half surrounding it. There is a large pool of water in the foreground. The horse circles round and round as the* BANDIT CAPTAIN *tries to ward off the blows.*

1193. High angle medium close-up of the horse's legs, panning very fast with it as it circles round and round in the mud. The villagers' legs can be made out dodging about in the background.

1194. Low angle medium close-up of KIKUCHIYO *with the horse's rump in the foreground and* SHICHIROJI *just behind him. Pan left with* KIKUCHIYO *as he circles round, roaring and attacking with his sword. The whole scene is partly obscured by the rain and mud.*

1195. Low angle medium shot of two of the villagers attacking with their spears with the horse's rump in the foreground. The horse backs across the frame, obscuring them from view.

1196. Medium shot of the BANDIT CAPTAIN *on his horse with* KANBEI *visible in the background and some villagers just in frame on the right. Pan slightly with the horse as it backs.*

1197. Low angle medium close-up of the horse's hooves in the mud. Camera pans swiftly left as it backs.

1198. Medium shot of the BANDIT CAPTAIN *on his horse as the animal rears up, with* KYUZO *in front of him and the villagers and other samurai surrounding him. They slash at him with their swords and spears but he manages to break through.*

1199. Low angle medium close-up of KYUZO *and* KIKUCHIYO *with the horse behind them, only its legs in shot. Very fast pan with the horse, losing the two samurai, as it circles round, coming nearer to camera.*

1200. High angle medium close-up of the BANDIT CAPTAIN, *back to camera on his horse, with the villagers in the background and* KYUZO *beside him on the ground attacking with his sword.* KYUZO *finally makes contact and the* CAPTAIN *starts to fall backwards.*

1201. High angle medium shot of the large pool of water. The horse stumbles into shot on the right, going down onto its knees in the pool, and the CAPTAIN *tumbles headlong into the water in the foreground. The horse struggles to get to its feet.*

1202. Medium shot with KYUZO *in the foreground and* KANBEI *next to him.* RIKICHI *stands beside* KANBEI, *with* SHICHIROJI *behind him, his spear erect, and* KIKUCHIYO *just visible beyond. (Still on page 190) Camera pans slightly left as they come up and stand by the edge of the pool and* KANBEI *looks down towards the* BANDIT CAPTAIN *who is out of shot.*

KANBEI : Kyuzo, well done!

Everyone shouts with delight. Then a different shout makes them turn and run back across the mud-filled square, camera panning right as they move away from it. KYUZO *is the last to go. As they cross the square a shot rings out and camera holds as* KYUZO *falls to the ground. The others all freeze and turn to look back at him in horror.*

1203. Medium shot of KIKUCHIYO *and* KATSUSHIRO *with some of the villagers, staring towards* KYUZO *off-screen.*

1204. Medium shot of KYUZO *on his knees in the mud with* KANBEI *behind him and the villagers all watching. He clutches his stomach and tries to get to his feet. Camera pans left as he staggers through a muddy puddle almost on his knees. He grasps his sword, stands and then flings it away from him as he topples on his face.* KATSUSHIRO *screams.*

1205. Medium shot of KATSUSHIRO *and* KIKUCHIYO *rushing towards* KYUZO *who lies in the foreground. Camera tilts down as* KATSUSHIRO *falls on his knees with a strangled cry and tries to lift* KYUZO's *body. He sobs bitterly as* KANBEI *and several of the villagers rush and pick up the mud-stained body. (Still on page 190)* KANBEI *pulls the weeping* KATSU-SHIRO *away as three of the villagers carry the body off, camera panning right with them, picking up* SHICHIROJI *as he urges them out of the line of fire.*

1206. Medium long shot of KIKUCHIYO *in the middle of the square with* KATSUSHIRO *and* KANBEI. KATSUSHIRO *lurches forward in a fury to where the shot came from, camera panning with him, losing* KANBEI. KIKUCHIYO *runs with him and forces him out of the way, pushing him down into the mud. Camera pans further with* KIKUCHIYO *as he rushes up to the terrace in front of the house where the shot came from.*

1207. Medium long shot of KANBEI *and* SHICHIROJI *splashing through the village square which the rain has turned into a quagmire,* KATSUSHIRO *still lying face down in the middle.*

KANBEI *shouts desperately* : Kikuchiyo, Kikuchiyo!

1208. Medium shot from the side of KIKUCHIYO *coming to*

218

the door of the hut. He is about to wrench it open when another shot rings out and he falls backwards, camera tilting down with him. (Still on page 191)

1209. Medium shot of KANBEI, *horror-struck. He starts forward.*

1210. High angle medium shot of KIKUCHIYO *outside the hut. He tries to sit up, clutching his stomach. With a tremendous effort he gets to his feet and lurches towards the door of the hut. Camera pans right along the outside wall to one of the windows. Through it the women can be seen cowering against the further wall as* KIKUCHIYO *staggers in. The* BANDIT CHIEF *can also just be made out standing inside.*

1211. Medium shot looking towards the entrance of the hut. The BANDIT CHIEF'S *henchman backs out, still looking in at the scene.*

1212. Medium long shot looking in through the barred window. Camera pans with KIKUCHIYO *as, clutching his stomach, he gradually walks towards the* BANDIT CHIEF *with a terrible look on his face. The latter backs away, while the women watch fearfully, crouched in the background. Camera pans further along the outer wall as* KIKUCHIYO *drives the* CHIEF *through to the outer part of the building at the back. The* BANDIT CHIEF *goes out of shot for a moment, then the pan continues as* KIKUCHIYO, *still clutching his stomach, gradually closes in on him. The* CHIEF *is still carrying the gun and staring at* KIKUCHIYO, *amazed that he is still alive. They come out of the house at the back. With a final effort,* KIKU-CHIYO *lunges forward and runs the* BANDIT CHIEF *through. (Still on page 191) Camera tilts down and holds as they both fall to the ground, at the edge of a small bridge.*

1213. Medium close-up of the BANDIT CHIEF *and* KIKU-CHIYO *lying on the bridge. The* CHIEF *rolls over, and camera tilts down as his body falls lifeless into the stream.*

1214. Medium shot of KIKUCHIYO, *lying spreadeagled on the bridge. (Still on page 191)*

1215. Medium long shot of KANBEI, KATSUSHIRO *and* SHI-CHIROJI *running between the fences towards camera followed by a crowd of villagers. Camera cranes down as they do so to reveal* KIKUCHIYO *lying on the bridge in the foreground.*

*The three samurai splash through the stream. Camera tilts
down further as they stand in the stream beside the bridge
looking up at* KIKUCHIYO's *body.* KANBEI *and* SHICHIROJI *both
call his name.* KIKUCHIYO *does not move. Suddenly a horse
neighs and all three turn away again. Camera cranes up again
losing* KIKUCHIYO, *as they run back to join the villagers in the
square. Three riderless horses gallop past; hold as they are
followed by several more. Suddenly* KATSUSHIRO *runs forward.
1216. Medium shot from behind of* KATSUSHIRO *running
backwards and forwards in front of* KANBEI, SHICHIROJI *and
the villagers, shouting hysterically. Camera pans to and fro
with him.*

KATSUSHIRO *screaming hysterically* : The bandits, the bandits!

Hold as KANBEI *grabs his arm and looks at him sternly.*

KANBEI : All dead!

With a terrible cry KATSUSHIRO *sinks to his knees in front of*
KANBEI, *camera tilting down with him. He begins to sob
bitterly.*

1217. High angle medium long shot of SHICHIROJI *and* KANBEI
*standing backs to camera in the middle of the village square
with* KATSUSHIRO *on his knees beside them. Crowds of villagers, also in back view, are standing on either side. They
all begin to drop down on their knees. A horse whinnies some-
where, off, and* KATSUSHIRO *continues to sob.*

1218. Medium shot of KATSUSHIRO *on his knees, sobbing,*
KANBEI *in the centre and* SHICHIROJI *standing beside him. The
villagers can be seen kneeling in the background.* KANBEI
leans on his sword and SHICHIROJI *on his spear. (Still on page
191) They look at each other, breathless and exhausted.*

KANBEI *to* SHICHIROJI *in a low voice* : Again — we've survived.

*1219. Low angle medium long shot of the flag flying on top
of the thatched roof. (Still on page 191) A horse neighs off
as the wind blows flurries of rain across the thatch. Fade out.*

*1220. Fade in on high angle medium long shot of a group of
village men standing knee-deep in one of the flooded fields
playing drums and flutes. They are swaying about in time
with the music. Among them is* RIKICHI *playing a drum which
he has hanging round his neck. (Still on page 192)*

1221. *High angle long shot across the paddy fields, a line of women in the foreground planting rice. (Still on page 192) Behind them the band play, backs to camera, and in the background more women and men of the village are also planting rice. Some children run along one of the raised banks between two fields while the planters bend and straighten in time with the music.*

1222. *High angle medium shot of two women in the paddy field. Camera tracks back to show four of them in line, planting rice shoots and stepping back exactly in time to the music.*

1223. *High angle medium shot of* RIKICHI *and another man playing their drums, with the paddy field stretching out behind them. They are swaying and chanting a song.*

1224. *Long shot of two women and a man in the paddy fields.*

1225. *High angle medium shot of* MANZO *playing the flute with another man banging a hand drum, the flooded field behind them.*

1226. *Medium long shot of women planting, men raking the fields and two children hurrying across one of the raised banks carrying bags of rice shoots.*

1227. *Medium shot of* MANZO, *back to camera, and another of the musicians, swaying backwards and forwards as they play. Two women face camera, planting in the foreground, and there is an area of planted rice between them and the two men. Camera tracks sideways over the paddy fields showing the work progressing happily.*

1228. *Medium shot from behind of* KANBEI *and* SHICHIROJI *standing on the bridge over the stream, with* KATSUSHIRO *nearest camera, watching the villagers planting rice in the distance. (Still on page 192) The hills rise up behind them and the music and chanting can be faintly heard.*

1229. *Medium close-up of* KANBEI *with* SHICHIROJI *and* KATSUSHIRO *behind him, all looking towards the fields with the houses of the village in the background.*

1230. *High angle medium close-up of* RIKICHI *chanting and playing the drum with* MANZO *just beyond him playing the flute.* RIKICHI *looks happy and he slaps his thigh and smiles as he shouts out the rhythmic chant.*

1231. *Medium close-up of* KANBEI *with* SHICHIROJI *and*

221

KATSUSHIRO *behind him.* KANBEI *looks down rather sadly and turns away.*

1232. Medium shot of KANBEI *turning towards camera with* SHICHIROJI *in three-quarter back view beside him, and* KATSUSHIRO *in the foreground, back to camera.* KANBEI *walks away and the others turn to watch him go.*

1233. Medium shot of SHICHIROJI *looking over his shoulder in the direction of the paddy fields with* KATSUSHIRO *standing beside him.* KANBEI *is walking away along the path. Camera pans slightly as the other two turn to follow him.*

1234. Medium long shot of KANBEI *from the side walking along and looking up towards the burial hill where, silhouetted against the sky, are the graves of the four dead samurai with their swords standing upright in them.* KANBEI *stops as* SHICHIROJI *and* KATSUSHIRO *join him and they all stand backs to camera looking up towards the graves. (Still on page 192) Then they look towards the paddy fields.* SHICHIROJI *and* KANBEI *turn back to the graves again, but something catches* KATSUSHIRO'S *eye and he steps onto the path, looking at something off-screen. A line of women trot past behind him carrying yokes with panniers full of rice shoots hanging from them.* KATSUSHIRO *turns to watch them as do* KANBEI *and* SHICHIROJI. *The last girl in the line stops in front of* KATSUSHIRO. *It is* SHINO.

1235. Close-up of SHINO *wearing a hat and scarf, with the yoke on her shoulder. She stares up towards* KATSUSHIRO, *off-screen.*

1236. Low angle close-up of KATSUSHIRO *with one of the samurai graves behind him, silhouetted against the sky. He stares searchingly towards* SHINO *and takes a few steps forward.*

1237. Close-up of SHINO *looking towards him rather fearfully. She lowers her head and goes off.*

1238. Close-up of KATSUSHIRO *frowning. The top of* SHINO'S *hat can be seen passing behind him; he turns to watch her go, then moves out of shot.*

1239. Medium long shot of KANBEI *and* SHICHIROJI *standing at the foot of the burial hill with* KATSUSHIRO *walking away, back to camera. The two older samurai watch him go.* SHI-

CHIROJI *turns to look at* KANBEI *then back in the direction of* KATSUSHIRO.

1240. Medium close-up of KATSUSHIRO *with* KANBEI *and* SHICHIROJI *standing on the path in the background.* KATSUSHIRO *frowns, staring at something out of shot.*

1241. Low angle medium shot, of SHINO *from behind, camera tilting down slightly as she bends to pick up a bundle of rice shoots. Beyond her a line of other women can be seen planting.* SHINO *turns and looks over her shoulder and then makes her way through the waterlogged paddy fields to take her place among the women.*

1242. Medium close-up of KATSUSHIRO *watching her, with* KANBEI *and* SHICHIROJI *behind him.*

1243. Medium close-up of KANBEI *with* SHICHIROJI *beside him nearest camera. They look towards the paddy field and then turn their heads slightly to look in the direction of* KATSUSHIRO.

1244. Medium shot of KATSUSHIRO, *back to camera, standing on the bridge. The paddy fields stretch away beyond him and the line of women planting rice can just be seen. The chants and music continue as the women sway, bending and planting in time with the music.*

1245. High angle medium close-up of RIKICHI *joyfully shouting his chant.*

1246. Low angle close-up of SHINO *bending down, her face half obscured by the rim of her hat. She raises a muddy hand to wipe her brow and straightens up, camera tilting up with her. Camera tilts down again as she begins planting again and joins in the song, but looking rather sad. (Still on page 192)*

1247. Medium close-up of KATSUSHIRO *with* KANBEI *and* SHICHIROJI *in the background. (Still on page 192)*

1248. Medium shot of KANBEI *and* SHICHIROJI *looking towards* KATSUSHIRO *off-screen.* SHICHIROJI *looks round at* KANBEI, *then stares back towards the fields.* KANBEI *lowers his head and looks at the ground. He takes a few steps towards camera and then stops, looking back towards the paddy fields. Then he turns and walks back to stand beside* SHICHIROJI *again.*

KANBEI : We've lost again.

SHICHIROJI *is surprised. He looks questioningly at* KANBEI.

KANBEI : No, the farmers are the winners. *He looks down.* Not us. KANBEI *turns away from camera and looks up;* SHICHIROJI *does likewise; (Still on page 192) the camera tilts up the side of the burial hill, losing the two samurai and holding on the four samurai burial mounds silhouetted against the sky. (Still on page 192) The samurai theme comes in over the planting music as the wind blows up the dust among the mounds. As the theme continues, the picture fades out and the words THE END come up on the black screen; as they fade out again the music comes to a climax and ends.*

SEVEN SAMURAI

Akira Kurosawa's brilliant new film is a long episodic reconstruction of an incident in 16th century Japan. A peasant village is harried by brigands; in despair the villagers decide to hire professional soldiers to defend them; after recruiting difficulties, seven are collected; they organise the village's defence and succeed in wiping out the bandits completely. This basically simple plot Kurosawa elaborates in two ways. He introduces a profusion of incidents and subplots—the youngest samurai falling in love with a village girl disguised by her mistrustful father as a boy, the attempts of a wandering humorous braggart to be accepted by the others as a samurai; and he gives to each of the many characters an intensely differentiated individual personality—the mature, kindiy, selfless leader, the unassuming but obsessive professional swordsman, the traditional braggadocio.

In *The Seven Samurai* (Films de France), and in the light it throws back on *Rashomon*, Kurosawa's method and personality emerge clearly. He is, above everything else, an exact psychological observer, a keen analyst of behaviour—in a fundamentally detached way. His handling of the young lovers is typical of this. He notes and traces with precision and truth their first, half-terrified awareness of each other sexually, the growth of mutual attraction, the boy's *gauche* admiration, the girl's aching and almost frantic abandonment; what he fails to do is to convey any feeling for, or identification with, the individuals themselves. He strives for this, he uses other images to heighten their scenes—the flower-covered hillside, the sun filtering through the tops of trees (an echo of its more successful use as an orgasm metaphor in *Rashomon*), the dappled light swarming like insects over them as they lie together in a bamboo hut—but somehow these remain perfunctory, a little cold, lacking in real poetry.

In this it is not unrewarding to compare Kurosawa with Ford—by whom, report has it, he claims to have been influenced. There are many superficial resemblances—the reliance on traditional values, the use of folk ceremonies and rituals, the comic horseplay—to Ford in particular and to the Western in general. The fast, vivid handling of the action sequences, the staccato cutting, the variety of angles, the shooting up through horses rearing in the mud, are all reminiscent of recent films in this genre. But the difference is more revealing. The funeral of the first samurai, killed in a preliminary skirmish, is exactly the sort of scene to which Ford responds, with all his reverence and honour for times past and the community of beliefs and feeling which they embodied. Kurosawa uses the scene in two ways, first as a further observation of the character of the "crazy samurai"—who, in a defiant attempt to satisfy his own feelings of frustration and impotence, raises the flag the dead man had sewn—and secondly, as an effective incident for heightening the narrative tension: the bandits launch their first onslaught during the funeral. One of the love scenes is used in a similar way, and in both cases one feels an ultimate shying-away from any direct, committed emotion—except anger.

Of course, to say Kurosawa is not Ford is critically meaningless; the comparison has value only in so far as it is a way of gauging the film's intentions, and its realisation of them. What made *Rashomon* so unique and impressive was that everything, the subject, the formal structure, the playing, even perhaps the period, allowed for this exterior approach to behaviour. In *The Seven Samurai* Kurosawa is striving for something different, a re-creation, a bringing to life of the past and the people whose story he is telling. Here, for all the surface conviction of period, the perceptive observation, the raging vitality and the magnificent visual style, the film doesn't quite succeed. All the elements are there except the depth and the generosity of life. One feels that each incident is too carefully worked into the texture as a whole. The Donskoi of the *Gorki* trilogy is a much simpler and, in many ways, more ordinary personality; but he achieved, almost without realising it, what Kurosawa labours for. Life itself seems to have taken over from Donskoi, carrying him along on its great stream, but Kurosawa has engineered a stunning aqueduct along which it must flow. Only in his handling of the "crazy samurai" does it occasionally overflow. Toshiro Mifune, gibing at the samurai, waving in mocking triumph, a fish caught in a stream, and—another Falstaff— bullying his hopeless recruits, brings to his portrayal a reckless and at moments out-of-hand gusto. It is a splendid performance, losing no opportunity, and it only fails to integrate a gratuitously introduced class motivation—he is really a peasant wanting to be a samurai. (The fault here lies with the script rather than the performer.) This is perhaps a momentary and rather glib contemporary analogy out of keeping with the rest.

These ultimate reservations should not, however, prevent us from recognising the film's astonishing qualities. Incident after incident is created with biting precision for the whole 2½ hour length (the exported version, incidentally, is an hour shorter than the original)—the villagers shunning the samurai on their arrival only to tumble towards them in panic as the alarm is sounded, the capture of a thief, and, brilliantly suspended in slow motion, his death, a brief and wonderful sketch of a farmer's wife abducted by the brigands stirring, guilty but sated, in her sleep. On a different level, Kurosawa is a virtuoso exponent of every technique of suspense, surprise, excitement, and in this he gives nothing to his Western masters. Only in his handling of the series of battles is there a hint of monotony. He knows exactly when to hold a silence; how to punch home an extraordinary fact with maximum effect; and his use of the camera is devastating—dazzling close-ups as the village deputation, overawed and desperate in their quest for samurai, scan the crowded street, or wild tracking shots as the drunken Mifune stumbles after his assailant. Visually the film makes a tremendous impression. Kurosawa can combine formal grace with dramatic accuracy, and many scenes create a startling pictorial impact. The raid on the bandits' hideout, when their slaughtered bodies are hurled, naked and haphazard, into the muddied pools outside their burning hut, is not unworthy of the Goya of *Los Desastres*. The final effect indeed, of *The Seven Samurai* is not unlike that of "Salammbo," a triumph of rage and artifice; and one's final acknowledgement is not of the intrinsic fascination of the material but the wrested skill of the artificer.

TONY RICHARDSON.